AF905076

Internally Displaced Persons and International Refugee Law

Internally Displaced Persons and International Refugee Law

BRÍD NÍ GHRÁINNE

OXFORD
UNIVERSITY PRESS

OXFORD
UNIVERSITY PRESS

Great Clarendon Street, Oxford, OX2 6DP,
United Kingdom

Oxford University Press is a department of the University of Oxford.
It furthers the University's objective of excellence in research, scholarship,
and education by publishing worldwide. Oxford is a registered trade mark of
Oxford University Press in the UK and in certain other countries

© Ní Ghráinne 2022

The moral rights of the author have been asserted

First Edition published in 2022

Impression: 1

All rights reserved. No part of this publication may be reproduced, stored in
a retrieval system, or transmitted, in any form or by any means, without the
prior permission in writing of Oxford University Press, or as expressly permitted
by law, by licence or under terms agreed with the appropriate reprographics
rights organization. Enquiries concerning reproduction outside the scope of the
above should be sent to the Rights Department, Oxford University Press, at the
address above

You must not circulate this work in any other form
and you must impose this same condition on any acquirer

Public sector information reproduced under Open Government Licence v3.0
(http://www.nationalarchives.gov.uk/doc/open-government-licence/open-government-licence.htm)

Published in the United States of America by Oxford University Press
198 Madison Avenue, New York, NY 10016, United States of America

British Library Cataloguing in Publication Data

Data available

Library of Congress Control Number: 2021951440

ISBN 978–0–19–886844–6

DOI: 10.1093/oso/9780198868446.001.0001

Printed and bound by
CPI Group (UK) Ltd, Croydon, CR0 4YY

Links to third party websites are provided by Oxford in good faith and
for information only. Oxford disclaims any responsibility for the materials
contained in any third party website referenced in this work.

Dedicated to Clodagh Higgins

Foreword

Over the past few years, Dr Ní Ghráinne has taken her thesis, which I had the pleasure of supervising, and refined and relocated its central argument. Although much has been and continues to be written about internally displaced persons (IDPs), until this book appeared, there was nothing that provided a comparable inquiry into the relationship of IDP protection to international refugee law. The question is whether measures on behalf of the internally displaced can stand as an alternative to asylum; or, as Dr Ní Ghráinne puts it, does IDP protection complement, conflict with, or undermine international refugee law?

To a large extent, these are very much twenty-first century issues never contemplated by the drafters of the 1951 Convention. They proceeded on the assumption that persecution, more likely than not, was the product of a monolithic State enjoying a monopoly on the use of force. Moreover, the idea of an 'internal flight alternative' was no more likely than that IDPs should be entitled to international protection, while the activities of international organisations on behalf of IDPs, if they should occur, could never stand in the way of recognition of refugee status. But the 1951 Convention has moved on, and as the scope of international protection has expanded in the jurisprudence of States (for example, with regard to membership of a particular social group or a fear of being persecuted by non-State actors), so the relationship of international refugee law and the newly emergent doctrine of IDP protection has entered the scene, with potentially worrying results.

The primary responsibility for the protection of and assistance to IDPs rests with the territorial State, given its sovereignty and the principle of non-intervention, as successive General Assembly resolutions have maintained. In practice, however, internal displacement is often the result of civil conflict, in situations where the authority of the central government is itself disputed, and its capacity or willingness to provide protection is equally in doubt. Indeed, the Guiding Principles on Internal Displacement, promulgated in 1998, sought to fill this gap with a doctrine of protection, although it seems clear that one motive behind the development of IDP protection was the desire to curb the outflow of refugees. All well and good, perhaps, if considered from a purely pragmatic perspective, but as Dr Ní Ghráinne shows, there is a risk that IDP protection may be used by States as a reason to deny refugee status to those who, having crossed an international frontier, seek recognition and asylum.

The novel idea of an 'internal protection alternative' (IPA) means that one who is returned under that 'rule' is effectively returned to become an IDP: Does international law permit such a solution, and by what standard is the efficacy of internal protection to be judged?

Dr Ní Ghráinne considers these pressing issues and critically examines the role of UNHCR as a potential 'actor of protection' on behalf of IDPs, reminding us nonetheless, as both the UNHCR Executive Committee and the UN General Assembly have done repeatedly, that its activities must not undermine the institution of asylum, including the right to seek and to enjoy in other countries protection from persecution. She rightly concludes that UNHCR's *primary* mandate is refugees, and that it is not legally capable or competent to provide IDPs with such a level of non-temporary protection as would justify denial of refugee status. Here, she also considers and rejects analogous arguments that States might raise by way of interpretation of Article 1D of the 1951 Convention.

Current efforts to curb the movement of refugees, and so to limit the application of international obligations, particularly *non-refoulement*, are cause for concern at many levels. The basic premises of international refugee law remain the objective of securing protection, ensuring human rights, and promoting durable solutions; in this context, denial of refugee status depends on whether they receive effective protection in their own country, such that there is no risk of persecution. With these goals in mind, this book aims to provide the detailed material for rebutting arguments that may prejudice the refugee, and for 'ensuring that the development of an IDP protection framework is not used as a substitute for asylum.'

All who are concerned by the challenges to international refugee law that arise today from both internal and external displacement will find in this work the means necessary to resist further efforts to limit refugee protection. At the same time, they will likely be inspired to think further about Dr Ní Ghráinne's proposals for a new global treaty and a specialised agency for IDP protection. As she says, the debate regarding the relationship between IDP protection and international refugee law has only just begun...

Guy S. Goodwin-Gill
Honorary Professor
Kaldor Centre for International Refugee Law
Faculty of Law & Justice
University of New South Wales, Sydney
Emeritus Fellow
All Souls College, Oxford
December 2021

Acknowledgements

This book grew out of the doctoral thesis I defended at the University of Oxford in 2014 and has been 10 years in the making. Its completion has depended on a great deal of support and guidance from many people along the way.

First and foremost, I would like to thank my supervisor, Professor Guy S Goodwin-Gill for his exceptional mentorship, detailed and constructive feedback, and constant support both during my time at Oxford and well beyond graduation. I owe an intellectual debt to my undergraduate and LLM lecturers who started me on the path of studying international law, particularly to Dr Ciara Smyth and Professor Freya Baetens.

I am also thankful to my examiners, Professors Cathryn Costello and Chaloka Beyani, the reviewers of this manuscript, and all my friends and colleagues who have provided me with feedback on this project: Professor Dapo Akande, Veronika Bílková, Adam Blisa, Professor David Cantor, Federica Cristiani, Professor Matthew Gibney, Rotem Giladi, Damian Gonzalez-Salzburg, Ben Hudson, Miles Jackson, Regina Jefferies, Ondřej Kadlec, Yin Harn Lee, Jan Lhotský, Sandra Meredith, Madalina Moraru, Aoife Ní Chearbhaill, Mairéad Ní Ghráinne, Tereza Papoušková, Jan Petrov, Jessica Schultz, Matthew Scott, Andrew Shacknove, Marina Sharpe, Katarína Šipulová, Samuel Spáč, Mirjam Streng, Nino Tsereteli, Marína Urbániková, and Karen Walsh. I am grateful to be part of networks and institutions which helped me refine the ideas in this book, notably at the Wednesday morning Public International Law seminars at All Souls College, Oxford University; Judicial Studies Institute, Masaryk University; Refugee Law Initiative, University of London; Institute of International Relations, Prague; and the Migration Research Workshops at the University of Ottawa, organised by David Hughes. I was very fortunate to have the constant support and mentorship of my colleagues in Maynooth and Masaryk universities while writing this book, particularly from Michael Doherty and David Kosař. I am also thankful to Oxford University Press, particularly to Jack McNichol, Rebecca Lewis, and Merel Alstein for their guidance in turning this project into a book.

This book would not be written without the generosity of numerous institutions. I would like to thank the Faculty of Law, University of Oxford, for funding this project by means of the Graduate Assistance Fund, the Freshfields

Bruckhaus Deringer Scholarship, and the Peter Birks Scholarship. I am grateful to the National University of Ireland for awarding me the Travelling Studentship in Law, and to St Antony's College and the Law Faculty at the University of Oxford for funding my attendance at conferences where I had the opportunity to present and receive feedback on my work. Thank you to Maynooth University for providing me with invaluable financial support during the final stages of writing. I am especially grateful for the opportunity to work with two exceptional research assistants—Jaya Duignan and Jobitha Prince—whose support was crucial for the completion of this manuscript.

On a more personal note, I am immensely grateful to my family and friends who have supported me throughout the years. Clodagh Higgins always managed to make me laugh, even during stressful times. Aisling McMahon has been a wonderful colleague, friend, and fellow student over the last fifteen years. Děkuji to my parents in law, Dana Smekalová and Roman Smekal, for their encouragement and for generously providing me with a beautiful and inspiring place to write the final chapters of this book. I am deeply grateful to my parents Philomena Uí Ghráinne and Seán Ó Gráinne for their support and relentless encouragement of my education and career. Finally, I owe the greatest debt to my husband, Hubert, for his infinite support, love, and encouragement.

Contents

Table of Cases

AFRICAN COMMISSION ON HUMAN AND PEOPLE'S RIGHTS

AFRICAN COURT OF HUMAN AND PEOPLES' RIGHTS

COMMITTEE AGAINST TORTURE

COURT OF JUSTICE OF THE EUROPEAN UNION

EUROPEAN COURT OF HUMAN RIGHTS

INTER-AMERICAN COMMISSION ON HUMAN RIGHTS

INTER-AMERICAN COURT OF HUMAN RIGHTS

INTERNATIONAL COURT OF JUSTICE

INTERNATIONAL CRIMINAL COURT

INTERNATIONAL CRIMINAL TRIBUNAL FOR RWANDA

INTERNATIONAL CRIMINAL TRIBUNAL FOR THE FORMER YUGOSLAVIA

UNITED NATIONS COMMITTEE AGAINST TORTURE

UNITED NATIONS HUMAN RIGHTS COMMITTEE

NATIONAL CASES

Australia

Canada

Colombia

United States (US)

Table of Legislation

EUROPEAN UNION

Directives

Table of International Instruments

UNITED NATIONS

UN Security Council Resolutions

1
Introduction

1.1 Overview

This book represents the first detailed study on the relationship between the protection of internally displaced persons (IDPs) and international refugee law. IDPs are persons who have been forced or obliged to leave their places of habitual residence as a result of armed conflict, violence, human rights violations, or natural or human-made disasters, but who have not crossed an international border.[1] IDPs often have similar wants, fears, and needs as refugees.[2] However, unlike refugees, IDPs do not have a legal status under international law and there is no specific global (as opposed to regional) treaty that deals specifically with IDP protection.

Recent decades have nonetheless seen a gradual development of legal and institutional protection of IDPs at international level, such as the Guiding Principles on Internal Displacement and regional IDP treaties,[3] the appointment of a UN Special Rapporteur on the Human Rights of IDPs,[4] the extension of the mandate of the United Nations High Commissioner for Refugees (UNHCR) to include IDPs,[5] the creation of the UN Secretary-General's

[1] UNCHR, 'Report of the Representative of the Secretary-General, Mr. Francis M. Deng, submitted pursuant to Commission resolution 1197/39. Addendum: Guiding Principles on Internal Displacement' (11 February 1998) UN Doc E/CN.4/1998/53/Add (hereafter 'Guiding Principles').

[2] A refugee is a person who 'owing to well-founded fear of being persecuted for reasons of race, religion, nationality, membership of a particular social group or political opinion, is out- side the country of his nationality and is unable or, owing to such fear, is unwilling to avail himself of the protection of that country'. Convention Relating to the Status of Refugees (adopted 28 July 1951, entered into force 22 April 1954) 189 UNTS 137 (Refugee Convention) art 1A.

[3] Guiding Principles (n 1); Pact on Security, Stability and Development in the Great Lakes Region (adopted 16 December 2006, entered into force 21 June 2008) 46 ILM 175; African Union Convention for the Protection and Assistance of Internally Displaced Persons in Africa 52 ILM 400 (adopted 22 October 2009, entered into force 6 December 2012).

[4] OHCHR, 'Special Rapporteur on the Human Rights of Internally Displaced Persons' <https://www.ohchr.org/en/issues/idpersons/pages/idpersonsindex.aspx> accessed 16 January 2019.

[5] Guy S Goodwin-Gill, 'UNHCR and Internal Displacement: Stepping into a Legal and Political Minefield' in US Committee for Refugees, *World Refugee Survey* (2000) 26; UNHCR, 'Operational Review of UNHCR's Engagement in Situations of Internal Displacement: Final Report' (2018) 13 International Journal of Refugee Law 373.

Internally Displaced Persons and International Refugee Law. Bríd Ní Ghráinne, Oxford University Press. © Ní Ghráinne 2022.
DOI: 10.1093/oso/9780198868446.003.0001

High-Level Panel on Internal Displacement,[6] and the creation of 'safe zones' within countries of origin.[7] Although these measures are generally welcome, some have expressed fears that that such activities are in reality about circumventing refugee flows and 'may be (mis)interpreted as obviating the need for international protection and asylum'.[8] Indeed, some states have explicitly stated that IDP protection measures are an alternative for asylum.[9]

This book asks whether such interpretation is legally correct, and explores whether the IDP protection framework complements, conflicts with, or undermines international refugee law. In addressing this overarching question, the book examines a number of key sub-questions pertaining to the relationship between IDPs and refugees, namely: (i) what is the legal and normative relationship between IDPs and refugees? (ii) to what extent is an individual's risk of internal displacement in their country of origin relevant to the qualification and cessation of refugee status? (iii) to what extent is the availability of IDP protection measures an alternative to asylum?

In answering these questions, the book argues that the IDP protection framework does not—at least in a legal sense—undermine refugee law. This is because an individual is not a refugee where there is protection from persecution in their home state, and the standard required to constitute such protection is high. Simply put, the protection available in the country of origin must constitute effective protection from persecution and there must be no risk of *refoulement*. IDP protection measures are generally weak and thus would not satisfy this high standard. However, should the protection available to IDPs meet this standard, it is appropriate that refugee status is not applicable as the

[6] United Nations, 'Terms of Reference: High Level Panel on Internal Displacement' <https://www.un.org/internal-displacement-panel/sites/www.un.org.internal-displacement-panel/files/tor_of_the_panel.pdf> accessed 7 July 2021.

[7] For example safe zones / safe havens / buffer zones to protect IDPs were established in Sri Lanka (1990), Bosnia (1992), and Rwanda (1994). See H Yamashita, *Humanitarian Space and International Politics: The Creation of Safe Areas* (Routledge 2004).

[8] UNHCR, 'Internally Displaced Persons – The Role of the High Commissioner for Refugees' (20 June 2000) UN Doc EC/50/SC/INF.2, 140. See also the address of the former High Commissioner for Refugees, Sadako Ogata, who stressed that 'any attempt to develop protection standards for the internally displaced should take care not to undermine the existing obligations of refugee law, particularly that of asylum and non-refoulement'. S Ogata, Norwegian Government Roundtable Discussion on United Nations Human Rights Protection for Internally Displaced Persons (Norwegian Refugee Council, Nyon, Switzerland, February 1993), 84.

[9] For example Turkey, USA. See Katy Long, 'No Entry! A Review of UNHCR's Response to Border Closures in Situations of Mass Refugee Influx' (UNHCR Policy Development and Evaluation Service, June 2010); 'Erdogan, Trump, Consider Creating Security Zone in Syria', *Euractiv* (15 June 2009) <https://www.euractiv.com/section/global-europe/news/erdogan-trump-consider-creating-security-zone-in-syria/> accessed 1 February 2019.

protection available to IDPs directly addresses the root causes of refugeehood and is an 'antidote'[10] to the persecution feared.

It is important to note that the arguments set out in this work are based on rigorous legal analysis, drawing primarily on the rules of treaty interpretation as enshrined in the Vienna Convention on the Law of Treaties.[11] However, the central claim of this book—that the IDP protection framework does not undermine refugee law—depends on states adopting the same correct legal understanding as this book. The IDP protection framework would therefore undermine refugee law when states wrongly invoke the IDP protection framework as a reason for denying refugee status. Moreover, outside of the legal context, IDP protection might undermine refugee protection in other ways such as by providing a justification for containment practices. The latter issue is outside the scope of this work but is nonetheless an important avenue for future research.

1.2 The Book's Significance

There were roughly 26.4 million refugees in the world at the end of 2020, as well as a further 4.1 million asylum-seekers.[12] International refugee law has appropriately been the subject of countless treatises.[13] The worldwide IDP population is significantly larger—numbering 55 million—and yet IDPs have been remarkably understudied.[14] Although the 20th Anniversary of the Guiding Principles on Internal Displacement generated some renewed interest in IDP

[10] James C Hathaway and Michelle Foster, *The Law of Refugee Status* (OUP 2014) 334 (hereafter Hathaway and Foster, *The Law of Refugee Status*).

[11] Vienna Convention on the Law of Treaties (adopted 23 May 1969, entered into forced 27 January 1980) 1155 UNTS 331.

[12] UNHCR, *Global Trends: Forced Displacement in 2020* (2021) (hereafter UNHCR, *Global Trends 2020*).

[13] Guy S Goodwin-Gill and Jane McAdam, *The Refugee in International Law* (3rd edn, OUP 2011); Hathaway and Foster, *The Law of Refugee Status* (n 10); Marina Sharpe, *The Regional Law of Refugee Protection in Africa* (OUP 2018); Andreas Zimmermann (ed), *The 1951 Convention Relating to the Status of the Refugees and its 1967 Protocol: A Commentary* (OUP 2011); Cathryn Costello, *The Human Rights of Migrants and Refugees in European Law* (OUP 2015); Violeta Moreno-Lax, *Accessing Asylum in Europe* (OUP 2017); Bruce Burson and David J Cantor, *Human Rights and the Refugee Definition* (Brill 2016); Jessica Schultz, *The Internal Protection Alternative in Refugee Law* (Brill 2018); Ruvi Ziegler, *Voting Rights of Refugees* (CUP 2017); Jane McAdam, *Complementary Protection in International Refugee Law* (CUP 2007); Meltem Ineli-Cigur, *Temporary Protection in Law and Practice* (Brill 2017); Madalina Moraru, Galina Cornelisse, and Philippe De Bruycker (eds), *Law and Judicial Dialogue on the Return of Irregular Migrants from the European Union* (Hart 2020); Cathryn Costello, Michelle Foster, and Jane McAdam (eds), *The Oxford Handbook of International Refugee Law* (OUP 2021).

[14] Internal Displacement Monitoring Centre, *Global Report on Internal Displacement 2021* (2021).

issues,[15] there has been a particular paucity of IDP literature over the last 10 years, particularly when compared to refugees.[16]

The two main book-length works focusing on IDP protection in international law are *The International Protection of Internally Displaced Persons* by Catherine Phuong and *The Internally Displaced Person in International Law* by Romola Adeola.[17] Both are extremely important contributions to our understanding of the IDP legal framework. However, the former book was published in 2005 and therefore does not reflect recent significant developments in the IDP protection framework. Although the latter book gives a more up-to-date overview of the legal protection of IDPs, it does not examine the IDP–refugee relationship but nonetheless calls for building 'normative connections between various frameworks relevant to the furtherance of IDP protection'.[18] This call reflects the fact that IDPs and refugees have almost always been studied separately. There is very little published to date on the relationship between IDPs and refugees, most of which is in the form of briefing documents by the UNHCR that are now at least 14 years old.[19] There *are no book-length studies of the relationship between IDPs and refugees* and hence this work fills a major gap in the literature.

A detailed analysis of the relationship between IDPs and refugees is long overdue. The Guiding Principles on Internal Displacement are now 23 years of age, there are now two regional treaties on IDP protection in the African continent,[20] the international coordination of IDP protection was overhauled

[15] 'Special Issue: Twenty Years of the Guiding Principles on Internal Displacement' (2018) 59 Forced Migration Review (hereafter 'Special Issue: Twenty Years of the Guiding Principles'); 'Special Issue on the 20th Anniversary of the Guiding Principles on Internal Displacement' (2018) 13(2) International Journal of Refugee Law (hereafter 'Special Issue on the 20th Anniversary of the Guiding Principle').

[16] Ala Al-Mahaidi, Léa Gross, and David J Cantor, *Revitalising IDP Research: A 'State of the Art' Review* (Refugee Law Initiative, University of London, 2018).

[17] Catherine Phuong, *The International Protection of Internally Displaced Persons* (CUP 2005); Romola Adeola, *The Internally Displaced Person in International Law* (Edward Elgar Publishing 2020) 150 (hereafter Adeola, *The Internally Displaced Person in International Law*). See also DJ Cantor, *Returns of Internally Displaced Persons during Armed Conflict: International Law and its Application of Colombia* (Brill 2018), which also focuses on IDPs but in a narrower context than the other two works (specifically on returns in Colombia).

[18] Adeola, *The Internally Displaced Person in International Law* (n 17) 150.

[19] UNHCR, 'The Protection of Internally Displaced Persons and the Role of UNHCR' (21 February 2007); UNHCR, 'Internally Displaced Persons: the Role of the United Nations High Commissioner for Refugees' (6 March 2000); UNHCR Policy Development and Evaluations Service and Division of Operational Services, 'UNHCR's Expanded Role in Support of the Inter-Agency Response to Internal Displacement Situations' (November 2006) UN Doc PDES/2006/06. See also James C Hathaway, 'Forced Migration Studies: Couldn't we Agree Just to "Date"?' (2007) 20 Journal of Refugee Studies 349; Michael Barutciski, 'Tensions between the Refugee Concept and the IDP Debate' (1998) 3 Forced Migration Review 11.

[20] Pact on Security, Stability and Development in the Great Lakes Region (adopted 16 December 2006, entered into force 21 June 2008) 46 ILM 175; African Union Convention for the Protection and Assistance of Internally Displaced Persons in Africa 52 ILM 400 (adopted 22 October 2009, entered into force 6 December 2012); Miriam Bradley, 'Unintended Consequences of Adjacency

in 2005,[21] at least 27 states now have laws and policies on the protection of IDPs,[22] and there is a growing body of international and domestic case law on the rights of IDPs.[23] All of these developments justify a fresh analysis of the IDP protection landscape and how it relates to international refugee law.

Moreover, we are now witnessing the highest level of displacement on record,[24] which has led to significant state hostility towards refugees,[25] and a focus on in-country protection to reduce refugee numbers. For example, states are increasingly invoking the doctrine of the 'internal protection alternative' (IPA), which purports to provide a basis to reject claims for refugee status where there is a part of the refugee's county of origin where he/she can relocate and receive protection from persecution.[26] In applying this concept, states have explicitly cited IDP protection measures (such as the availability of safe zones) as a basis for refusing refugee status.[27] In addition, the urgent need for an analysis on the IDP–refugee relationship is underscored by the fact that Iran, Russia, Turkey, and the USA have all considered establishing a 'safe zone' in Syria to reduce the need for IDPs to leave and seek asylum, with Turkey eventually following through with this plan in 2019.[28]

More generally, the relationship between refugee and IDP protection has garnered renewed interest in light of the controversial failure of states to address IDPs in the Global Compacts on Refugees and Migrants,[29] the recent 20-year

Claims: The Function and Dysfunction of Analogies between Refugee Protection and IDP Protection in the Work of UNHCR' (2019) 25 Global Governance: A Review of Multilateralism and International Organizations 620.

[21] UNHCR, 'Cluster Approach' <https://emergency.unhcr.org/entry/61190/cluster-approach-iasc> accessed 1 May 2019.

[22] David J Cantor, 'The IDP in International Law'? Developments, Debates, Prospects' (2018) 30 International Journal of Refugee Law 191, 191.

[23] See jurisprudence in chapter 3.

[24] UNHCR, *Global Trends 2020* (n 12). These figures are likely to be a significant underestimate. See chapter 2.

[25] Harold H Koh, *The Trump Administration and International Law* (OUP 2018); Shaun Walker, 'No Entry: Hungary's Crackdown on Helping Refugees' *The Guardian* (4 June 2018) <https://www.theguardian.com/world/2018/jun/04/no-entry-hungarys-crackdown-on-helping-refugees> accessed 13 July 2021; Bríd Ní Ghráinne, 'Left to Die at Sea: State Responsibility for the May 2015 Thai, Indonesian and Malaysian Pushback Operations' (2017) 10 Irish Yearbook of International Law 109.

[26] The IPA is not applicable to some regional instruments. See chapter 4.

[27] Katy Long, 'In Search of Sanctuary: Border Closures, "Safe Zones" and Refugee Protection' (2013) 26 Journal of Refugee Studies 458.

[28] BBC News, 'Syria War: Turkey Ready to Create "Safe Zone" for Kurds – Erdogan' *BBC News* (15 January 2019) <https://www.bbc.co.uk/news/world-middle-east-46877308> accessed 8 July 2021; L Rosen, 'US, Russia Hold Secret Talks over South Syria Safe Zone' *Al Monitor* (1 June 2017); A Bendix, 'Safe Zones in Syria', *The Atlantic* (4 May 2017).

[29] General Assembly, 'Global Compact on Refugees' (13 September 2019) UN Doc A/73/12 (Part II); General Assembly, 'Global Compact for Safe, Orderly and Regular Migration' (13 July 2019) UN Doc A/CONF.231/3. IDPs are mentioned in passing in the Global Compact on Refugees ([12], [39]) and their relative omission has generated significant controversy. See IDMC, 'Internal Displacement and the Global Compact on Refugees: Are Today's Returning Refugees Tomorrow's IDPs?', November

anniversary of the Guiding Principles on Internal Displacement,[30] high-profile events such as the war in Syria, which has generated a large number of IDPs and refugees,[31] and the Covid-19 pandemic, which has created new challenges for the protection of forced migrants.[32] Put simply, this book is important because it helps us understand the legal and normative relationship between IDPs and refugees, it illustrates the relevance of a real risk of internal displacement to the qualification and cessation of refugee status, and it challenges the practice of invoking IDP protection efforts as an alternative to asylum.

1.3 Structure of the Book

The book contains seven chapters. Chapter 1—the present chapter—provides an overview of the book's scope, significance, key claims, and structure. Chapter 2 sets out in detail the precise nature of the relationship between IDPs and refugees, and hence forms the book's conceptual backdrop. It introduces the concepts of IDP and refugee, respectively, and gives a brief overview of the current figures and demographics of both categories of forced migrants. It then sets out the similarities and differences between IDPs and refugees, explores whether these two categories of forced migrants should be merged, and sets out areas where the protection of IDPs and refugees might complement and conflict with each other. It advocates for continuing separate legal treatment of refugees and IDPs because the Refugee Convention clearly applies only to those who are, inter alia, outside their country of nationality.[33] Nonetheless, it argues that the normative and legal relationship between IDPs and refugees merits detailed analysis because of: (i) the similarity between the plight of IDPs and refugees in terms of needs and reasons for displacement; (ii) the fact that

2017, <https://www.unhcr.org/events/conferences/5a12a6467/internal-displacement-global-compact-refugees-todays-returning-refugees.html> accessed 1 May 2019; OHCHR, 'The Rapporteur Calls upon States to include IDPs in the Global Compact on Safe, Regular and Orderly Migration, in line with the New York Declaration on Refugees and Migrants' (12 March 2018) <https://www.ohchr.org/_layouts/15/WopiFrame.aspx?sourcedoc=/Documents/Issues/IDPs/OpenLetterInclusion12March2018.pdf&action=default&DefaultItemOpen=1> accessed 1 May 2019.

[30] Special Issue: Twenty Years of the Guiding Principles (n 15); Special Issue on the 20th Anniversary of the Guiding Principles (n 15).

[31] BBC News, 'Syria's War' <https://www.bbc.com/news/world-middle-east-17258397> accessed 1 May 2019.

[32] Bríd Ní Ghráinne, 'Covid-19, Border Closures and International Law' (Reflection Paper, Institute of International Relations Prague, 4 May 2020) <https://www.dokumenty-iir.cz/Publikace/Reflections/reflection_Br%C3%ADd%20N%C3%AD_04_2020_covid-19_DEF.pdf> accessed 8 July 2021.

[33] Refugee Convention, art 1A.

many IDPs go on to cross a border and become refugees; and (iii) the fact that UNHCR is involved in both IDP and refugee protection. The legal analysis that will follow in the remaining chapters will be set against this conceptual background.

Chapter 3 will first provide essential background knowledge on the development of the legal and institutional protection of IDPs. It identifies three key stages in this respect, which correspond with the chapter's structure: (i) the era of 'preventive protection' in the 1990s and early 2000s; (ii) the development of a distinct IDP legal framework from the 1990s onwards; (iii) the parallel development of an IDP institutional framework from 1990s onwards. The chapter's key arguments will be that the IDP legal and institutional framework is significantly weaker than that of refugees, that many of the developments in IDP protection were motivated, at least in part, by a desire to curb refugee flows, and that the issue of refugee protection continues to dominate the international agenda, to the detriment of IDP protection.

The analysis in chapters 1–3 lays the foundation for addressing the work's core question; namely, the extent to which IDP protection conflicts with or complements international refugee law. The remaining substantive chapters will therefore examine specific aspects of international refugee law and how they interact with the IDP protection framework.

Chapter 4 will focus on the IPA concept, which is based on the idea that if there is a safe place within an individual's state of nationality or habitual residence where they can relocate, they are not a refugee. Specifically, the chapter will examine whether and to what extent a real risk of becoming an IDP on return and/or the availability of IDP protection measures on return is relevant to the IPA inquiry. It will explain the relationship between the refugee definition and the IPA and set out the applicable criteria in the IPA inquiry. By analysing relevant case law from domestic and international courts, the chapter will then illustrate that the IDP label does not carry significant weight when determining whether a location qualifies as an IPA. Even though return to a situation of internal displacement might give rise to human rights violations, the fact that an individual will become an IDP on return does not rule a place out of being a valid IPA. This is the case even where that individual might have to live in an IDP camp or in a critical shelter arrangement, such as an unfinished or abandoned makeshift shelter, tent, mosque, church, or squat in a government building. The chapter will also illustrate how its analysis of the IDP–IPA relationship is also relevant to the cessation of refugee status. It will conclude by arguing that it is even more unlikely that the cessation clauses will be found to apply where there is a situation of internal displacement.

Chapter 5 will focus on whether UNHCR's activities on behalf of IDPs could undermine international refugee law. Although there are many different organizations and institutions involved in IDP protection, the focus on UNHCR is justified because its primary mandate focuses on refugees. Moreover, it is one of the major global players in IDP protection, evidenced by the fact that by the end of 2020, UNHCR was providing protection and assistance to IDPs in 34 states, including in Colombia (8.3 million IDPs), Syria (6.7 million IDPs), DRC (5.2 million IDPs), Yemen (4 million IDPs), and Somalia (3 million IDPs).[34] Specifically, the chapter will examine whether the in-country protection the UNHCR offers to IDPs might be interpreted as 'protection of that country' under the Refugee Convention and may thus be used by states to deny refugee status. It will argue that a textual interpretation of the Refugee Convention supports the contention that 'protection of that country' may in principle include contracted-out mechanisms of protection provided by international organizations such as the UNHCR that are genuinely accessible and for which the state remains fully accountable.[35] However, the UNHCR is not capable in law of satisfying this high standard required to constitute 'protection of that country'. Where the UNHCR provides in-country protection, the obligation of a state to protect its nationals is not, as a matter of international law, transferred to the UNHCR and the UNHCR is not endowed with the powers and attributes of the state. In addition, the UNHCR is not in control of the state or a substantial part of the territory of the state. Moreover, the UNHCR is not capable, in fact, of providing such protection. The UNHCR does not have the capacity or legal authority to offer 'effective' protection from persecution, which would likely require a legal system for the detection, prosecution, and punishment of persecutory acts. Furthermore, the UNHCR's protection efforts are of a transient nature, designed to capacitate states in finding a long-term solution to the IDP problem.

Chapter 6 is the book's final substantive chapter. It will focus on Article 1D of the Refuge Convention, which provides that the Refugee Convention shall not apply to persons who receive protection or assistance from organs or agencies other than the UNHCR. Article 1D is drafted in vague terms and it has been accepted that, in theory, this provision could be applied to any group of refugees that satisfy its conditions, including those who have previously been IDPs within their country of origin.[36] Thus, this chapter asks a pertinent question

[34] UNHCR, *Global Trends 2020* (n 12).

[35] James C Hathaway and Hugo Storey, 'What is the Meaning of State Protection in Refugee Law? A Debate' (2016) 28 International Journal of Refugee Law 486, 486 (Hathaway's position).

[36] Mutaz M Qafisheh and Valtentina Azarov 'Article 1D 1951 Convention' in Andreas Zimmermann (ed), *The 1951 Convention relating to the Status of Refugees and its 1967 Protocol: A Commentary*

that has not yet been answered in the literature—would an IDP who received protection from UN agencies other than the UNHCR trigger the application of Article 1D of the Refugee Convention? This question is important because if it is answered affirmatively, it would mean that the availability of IDP protection in countries of nationality or habitual residence can be lawfully invoked by host countries as grounds to deny refugee status. This chapter answers this question in the negative, arguing that the drafting history of the Refugee Convention, as well as an examination of the logistical and practical context of IDP protection, illustrates that Article 1D is only applicable to Palestinian refugees receiving protection from the United Nations Relief and Works Agency.

The final chapter will draw together the arguments made in the substantive chapters to illustrate that the development of the IDP protection framework does not, as a matter of law, undermine refugee protection. The availability of protection within a country of origin cannot be a substitute for granting refugee status unless it constitutes effective protection from persecution and there is no danger of *refoulement*. The book concludes by identifying current and future challenges in the relationship between IDPs and refugees, by illustrating the overall impact and importance of the findings of the research, and by setting out questions for future research.

Having set out the book's scope, significance, key claims, and structure; our analysis now turns to the book's conceptual background, which will be addressed in chapter 2.

(OUP 2011) 542; UNHCR Policy Development and Evaluation Service and Division of Operational Services, 'UNHCR's Expanded Role in Support of the Inter-Agency Response to Internal Displacement Situations' (November 2006) UN Doc PDES/2006/06, 9; Erika Feller, 'UNHCR's Role in IDP Protection: Opportunities and Challenges' [2006] Forced Migration Review 11 https://www.fmreview.org/brookings/feller

2

The Relationship between Internally Displaced Persons and Refugees

2.1 Introduction

IDPs and refugees have traditionally been treated as separate categories of forced migrants, both in terms of their legal and institutional protection. Yet there are many similarities between IDPs and refugees and there are many areas in which IDP protection can complement, conflict with, and undermine refugee protection (and vice versa). The aim of this chapter is to set out in more detail the precise nature of the relationship between these two categories of forced migrants. Sections 2.2 and 2.3 will explain the concepts of IDP and refugee, respectively, and will give a brief overview of the current figures and demographics of both categories of forced migrants. Section 2.4 will examine IDPs and refugees together. It will set out the similarities and differences between IDPs and refugees, explore whether these two categories of forced migrants should be merged, and set out areas where the protection of IDPs and refugees might complement and conflict with each other. The main argument of this chapter is that, because of the close relationship between IDP and refugee protection, an analysis of how the protection of these two categories of forced migrants interact with each other is long overdue. Hence, this chapter provides the conceptual basis for the analysis that follows in the remainder of the book.

2.2 Internally Displaced Persons

IDPs outnumber refugees by almost two to one, totalling 55 million at the end of 2020.[1] The most cited description of IDPs was originally set out in the United Nations Guiding Principles on Internal Displacement,[2] a soft law document

[1] Internal Displacement Monitoring Centre, *Internal Displacement Index 2020 Report* (2020) 6.
[2] UNCHR, 'Report of the Representative of the Secretary-General, Mr. Francis M. Deng, submitted pursuant to Commission resolution 1197/39. Addendum: Guiding Principles on Internal Displacement' (11 February 1998) UN Doc E/CN.4/1998/53/Add.2 (hereafter Guiding Principles).

Internally Displaced Persons and International Refugee Law. Bríd Ní Ghráinne, Oxford University Press. © Ní Ghráinne 2022.
DOI: 10.1093/oso/9780198868446.003.0002

which has been described as a 'standard'[3] and an 'important tool'[4] in IDP protection. The introduction to the Guiding Principles describes IDPs as:

> Persons or groups of persons who have been forced or obliged to flee or to leave their homes or places of habitual residence, in particular as a result of or in order to avoid the effects of armed conflict, situations of generalised violence, violations of human rights or natural or human made disasters, and who have not crossed an internationally recognised state border.[5]

It is important to emphasize that this is a 'descriptive identification',[6] rather than a legal definition of IDPs. The choice of a descriptive, rather than legal identification was probably driven by two factors. First, as is set out in more detail in chapter 3, the drafters of the Guiding Principles did not set out to create new legal rights, nor did they have the authority to do so. There was no appetite from states at the time for any legally binding document on the rights of IDPs. Thus, in the words of the drafters, the aim of Principle 1 was 'not to create a new legal category to which rights and obligations would be attached, but to improve the legal protection of the internally displaced'.[7]

Second, it would probably be near impossible to develop a legally binding definition of an IDPs. The drafting of the Guiding Principles in the late 1990s coincided with the NATO bombing of Kosovo, which left states particularly cynical towards any purported effort of the international community to reform human rights domestically. Thus, there was a reluctance to develop any legally binding instrument at that time. In particular, it would be a huge challenge to develop criteria that would be amenable to states but at the same time broad enough to capture the complexity of the phenomenon of internal displacement. It is therefore not surprising that the drafters opted for a descriptive overview rather than a legal definition. Further analysis on the significance of the choice of a non-legal description is included in section 2.4 below, and chapter 3 will show how this description later inspired legal definitions of IDPs in both domestic legislation and regional treaties.

The above description is therefore very broad and a number of elements in this description merit particular attention. First, the reference to 'persons' does

[3] UNGA Res 58/177 (12 March 2004) UN Doc A/RES/58/177.
[4] ibid.
[5] Guiding Principles (n 2).
[6] Annotations, [3].
[7] Catherine Phuong, *The International Protection of Internally Displaced Persons* (CUP 2004) 57; Romola Adeola, *The Internally Displaced Person in International Law* (Edward Elgar Publishing 2020) 5 (hereafter Adeola, *The Internally Displaced Person in International Law*).

not mean that IDPs, by definition, never flee or leave their homes or places of habitual residence on an individual basis. In the words of Adeola, 'what is imperative to underscore in the description is not so much the plurality, rather it is whether a person fits the description'.[8] In fact, the decision to use the term 'persons' was precisely with the aim of avoiding the impression of quantification.[9] Moreover, the fact that Principle 1 refers to 'persons or groups of persons' suggests that the first use of 'persons' refers to individual persons. Hence although most situations of internal displacement concern large population movements,[10] it is possible that there can be individualized cases of internal displacement.

Second, an IDP may be (a) forced to flee, (b) obliged to flee, (c) forced to leave, or (d) obliged to leave their homes or places of habitual residence. The use of four terms ('forced', 'obliged', 'flee', and 'leave') casts a very wide net regarding the circumstances under which the IDP has departed from their home or place of habitual residence. 'Forced' may involve an element of compulsion, such as physical or authoritative in nature. 'Obliged' implies a sense of duty or legal onus. 'Flee' contemplates the act of movement that is quick and either due to danger or fear, whereas 'leave' implies a broader variety of reasons for movement.[11] Taken together, these terms provide further support that the IDP description is very broad indeed.

Third, the IDP description is backward-looking, in that it refers to '*have been* forced or obliged' to leave their homes or places of habitual residence (emphasis added). The emphasis is thus on events that have occurred in the past, as opposed to future risk of harm. The backward-looking nature of the IDP description is analysed further in section 2.3 of this chapter.

Fourth, the drafters did not limit the description of IDPs to those who have departed their 'home', which might imply some sense of ownership of the property from which they have departed. The description also includes those who have departed their places of 'habitual residence'. This term encompasses 'residence of some standing or duration'.[12] The relevant consideration is an individual's connection with a place, which would include tenants and even squatters who are illegally present in the property.[13] Arguably, it would

[8] Adeola, *The Internally Displaced Person in International Law* (n 7) 8; Phil Orchard, *Protecting the Internally Displaced, Rhetoric and Reality* (Routledge 2019) 54 (hereafter Orchard, *Protecting the Internally Displaced*).

[9] Adeola, *The Internally Displaced Person in International Law* (n 7) 8.

[10] ibid 8.

[11] ibid 8.

[12] ibid 12; Atle Grahl-Madsen, *The Status of Refugees in International Law* (AW Sijthoff 1966) (hereafter Grahl-Madsen, *The Status of Refugees in International Law*).

[13] Adeola, *The Internally Displaced Person in International Law* (n 7) 12.

also include people who were homeless provided they had a place of 'habitual residence'.

Fifth, the description sets out four circumstances under which an IDP may have fled or left their home or place of habitual residence: armed conflict, generalized violence, human rights violations, and natural or human-made disasters. The most commonly accepted definition of an *armed conflict* was set out by the International Criminal Tribunal for the Former Yugoslavia (ICTY), which established that 'an armed conflict exists whenever there is a resort to armed force between states or protracted armed violence between governmental authorities and organised armed groups or between such groups within a state'.[14] This threshold is quite high. Hostilities must reach a magnitude that requires confrontation and the parties to the conflict are usually states and/or organized armed groups which must exert a public power (eg capable of planning and carrying out sustained and concerted military operations and imposing discipline in the name of a de facto authority), and are responsible and identifiable (eg has a minimum of organization and structure, and a chain of command).[15] Internal disturbances and tensions such as riots and isolated and sporadic acts of violence would therefore not qualify as armed conflict.[16] Yet we know that these circumstances (riots, isolated and sporadic acts of violence) can cause individuals to flee and leave their homes and places of habitual residence.[17] Hence the Guiding Principles also include *situations of generalized violence* as one of the reasons for which displacement may occur. 'Generalised violence' includes various forms of indiscriminate violence that may be perpetrated either by state or non-state authorities, casting the net even wider than those fleeing 'armed conflict' regarding who might fall within the description of an IDP.[18]

[14] ICTY, *The Prosecutor v Duško Tadic, Decision on the Defence Motion for Interlocutory Appeal on Jurisdiction*, ICTY-94-1-A (2 October 1995) [70].

[15] The ICTY has summarized a non-exhaustive and non-cumulative list of indicative factors based upon its case law to determine whether an armed conflict exists: the number, duration and intensity of individual confrontations; the type of weapons and other military equipment used; the number and calibre of munitions fired; the number of persons and type of forces partaking in the fighting; the number of casualties; the extent of material destruction; and the number of civilians fleeing combat zones. The involvement of the UN Security Council may also indicate the intensity of a conflict. For discussion see Sandesh Sivakumaran, 'Non-International Armed Conflicts and Internal Tensions and Disturbances' in *The Law of Non-International Armed Conflict* (OUP 2012).

[16] ibid.

[17] David J Cantor, 'Gang Violence as a Cause of Forced Migration in the Northern Triangle of Central America' in David J Cantor and Nicolás Rodríguez Serna (eds), *The New Refugees: Crime and Forced Displacement in Latin America* (University of London 2016); David J Cantor, 'As Deadly as Armed Conflict? Gang Violence and Forced Displacement in the Northern Triangle of Central America' (2016) 23(34) Agenda Internacional 77.

[18] Adeola, *The Internally Displaced Person in International Law* (n 7) 8.

The IDP description also includes *violations of human rights* as a reason for which IDPs may have departed their homes or places of habitual residence. This inclusion reflects the fact that not all harms resulting in displacement are in the context of violent or armed conflict situations. Violations of human rights may arise from the rich catalogue of national, regional, or international instruments in existence,[19] and may encompass a range of practices leading to an individual feeling forced or compelled to depart their home or place of habitual residence. For example, a forcible eviction might give rise to a violation of the right to home, private life, and correspondence as per Article 8 of the European Convention of Human Rights and the right to property under Article 1 of Protocol 1 of the European Convention of Human Rights.[20] Hence an individual in that situation might fall within the description of an IDP.[21] Finally, Principle 1 also makes reference to *natural or human-made disasters*. Natural disasters could include earthquakes, droughts, hurricanes, and torrential floods.[22] Human-made disasters could include nuclear explosions, oil spillages, and mining accidents. The line between a natural and man-made disaster is not always clear-cut, as many 'natural' disasters are caused—at least in part—by human activities. One important example would be displacement due to climate change.[23] However regardless of whether a disaster is characterized as 'natural' or 'man-made', an individual displaced within a state by any type of disaster would be likely to fall within the IDP description.

Although the Guiding Principles set out four reasons for which IDPs may have fled their homes or places of habitual residence, it is imperative to note that 'the listed examples are non-exhaustive'.[24] This is indicated by the words 'in particular'. Hence an individual might be described as an IDP where they

[19] Rhona KM Smith, *International Human Rights Law* (9th edn, OUP 2020); Dinah Shelton (ed), *The Oxford Handbook of International Human Rights Law* (OUP 2013).

[20] European Convention for the Protection of Human Rights and Fundamental Freedoms (adopted 4 November 1950, entered into force 3 September 195) ETS 5; Protocol 1 to the European Convention on Human Rights and Fundamental Freedoms (adopted 20 March 1952, entered into force 18 May 1954) ETS 9.

[21] *Loizidou v Turkey* App no 15318/89 (ECtHR, 18 December 1996).

[22] Thekli Anastasiou, 'Public International Law's Applicability to Migration as Adaptation: Fit for Purpose?' in Simon Behrman and Avidan Kent (eds), *Climate Refugees: Beyond the Legal Impasse?* (Routledge Taylor and Francis 2018) 173; Adeola, *The Internally Displaced Person in International Law* (n 7) 18; Matthew Scott, 'Natural Disasters, Climate Change and Non-Refoulement: What Scope for Resisting Expulsion under Articles 3 and 8 of the European Convention on Human Rights?' (2014) 26 International Journal of Refugee Law 404.

[23] Matthew Scott, 'Finding Agency in Adversity: Applying the Refugee Convention in the Context of Disasters and Climate Change' (2016) 35(4) Refugee Survey Quarterly 26; Adeola, *The Internally Displaced Person in International Law* (n 7) 18.

[24] Walter Kälin, 'Guiding Principles on Internal Displacement Annotations' (2008) 38 Studies in Transnational Legal Policy 4 (hereafter Kälin, 'Guiding Principles'); Orchard, *Protecting the Internally Displaced* (n 8) 17.

depart their homes or places of habitual residence for reasons other than those listed above, such as in the context of climate change or development projects.[25] Displacement stemming from this latter situation is actually envisaged by the Guiding Principles, as Principle 6(2)(c) recognizes large-scale development projects as a root cause of internal displacement.[26]

The final—yet arguably the most important—aspect of the IDP description that merits analysis is that an IDP is someone who, inter alia, has 'not crossed an internationally recognised state border'. Kälin (one of the drafters of the Guiding Principles) has noted that this term should be 'understood in a broad sense'.[27] There is no mention in the description of an IDP of any limitation in terms of nationality, hence an individual can be an IDP in a country other than their own if they have become displaced within that country. As such, the IDP description also seems to include a refugee who subsequently becomes displaced within their host country, such as a Syrian refugee who is internally displaced in Turkey.

It is also important to note that the border crossed must be one that is 'internationally recognised'. Arguably this term was included to exclude state borders which are still contested, such as Kosovo's border with Serbia. However, given that recognition of a state is merely declaratory—and not a constitutive—of statehood,[28] and given that a purported state's borders might be recognized by some states and contested or unrecognized by others, the inclusion of the term 'internationally recognised' does little to clarify the situation of an individual who crosses a border which is recognized by at least one state but contested by at least one other. It is unclear, for example, whether someone who was displaced from Pristina and ended up in Belgrade would satisfy this geographical element of the IDP description. Further analysis about the significance of the border crossing to the concept of both refugee and IDP is in section 2.4 below.

The above considerations serve to emphasize that—unlike the refugee definition—the description of IDPs is intentionally broad.[29] The fact that it is a descriptive, rather than a legal term lends even more support to the contention

[25] Matthew Scott and Albert Salamanca, 'A Human Rights-Based Approach to Internal Displacement in the Context of Disasters and Climate Change' (2020) 39(4) Refugee Survey Quarterly 564.

[26] Adeola, *The Internally Displaced Person in International Law* (n 7) 12; Irge Satiroglu and Narae Choi (eds), *Development-Induced Displacement and Resettlement: New Perspectives on Persisting Problems* (Routledge 2015).

[27] Kälin, 'Guiding Principles' (n 24) 3.

[28] Convention on the Rights and Duties of States adopted by the Seventh International Conference of American States (adopted 26 December 1933, entered into force 26 December 1934) 165 UNTS 19 art 1; James R Crawford, *The Creation of States in International Law* (OUP 2007).

[29] Orchard, *Protecting the Internally Displaced* (n 8) 54.

that it is intended to be interpreted broadly, because falling within the description of an IDP does not entitle one to specific rights under international law. At the same time, certain aspects of the definition are vague, such as the requirement of not crossing an 'internationally recognised state border', as mentioned above. Moreover, it is unclear whether children of IDPs should automatically be described as IDPs, and neither the IDP description nor the Guiding Principles more generally give any indication of when displacement ends or whether there is any minimum distance that an individual needs to move to fall within the IDP description.[30] These factors make it very difficult to ascertain who fits the IDP description and to accurately assess how many IDPs are in the world today. Nonetheless, numerous organizations such as the UN High Commissioner for Refugees (UNHCR), the Internal Displacement Monitoring Centre (IDMC), and the International Organisation for Migration (IOM) have engaged in significant data collection so that we have some rough understanding of the scale and causes of internal displacement today. The following section will give a brief overview of these figures.

2.2.1 Internal Displacement in 2020

As aforementioned, some elements of the IDP description are vague and thus statistics on IDPs should be treated with caution. Additional problems with gathering data on internal displacement include the facts that some IDPs do not want to be counted because they do not trust the officials charged with registering them, that the methods used to gather data can be problematic (eg IDP deaths are sometimes not counted when comparing IDP data from year to year), that linguistic and cultural barriers hamper data collection, that states and other actors have powerful incentives to suppress and manipulate data to construct a preferred narrative, and that IDPs move often, making them difficult to count.[31] The IDMC has also noted that it is difficult to compile accurate

[30] The Framework for Durable Solutions, adopted by the Inter-Agency Standing Committee, provides a definition, a description of the process, and criteria for when displacement ends. Inter-Agency Standing Committee, 'IASC Framework On Durable Solutions For Internally Displaced Persons' (The Brookings Institution University of Bern 2010) <https://www.unhcr.org/50f94cd49.pdf> accessed 13 July 2021.

[31] Bríd Ní Ghráinne and Ben Hudson, 'The International Organisation for Migration's Engagement with the Guiding Principles on Internal Displacement' in Cathryn Costello, Megan Bradley, and Angela Sherwood (eds), *IOM Unbound? Obligations and Accountability of the International Organization for Migration in an Era of Expansion* (CUP forthcoming 2022) (hereafter Ní Ghráinne and Hudson, 'The International Organisation for Migration's Engagement with the Guiding Principles on Internal Displacement'); Gabriel Cardona-Fox, 'The Politics of IDP Data' (2020) 39(4) Refugee Survey Quarterly 620 (hereafter Cardona-Fox, 'IDP Data'); Martina Caterina and Andrés Lizcano Rodríguez,

data on the sex and age of IDPs due to lack of information and the fact that age groups are not standardized amongst local data collectors.[32] The year 2020 brought even more challenges to IDP data collection in the form of the Covid-19 pandemic, when movement restrictions obstructed data collection and fear of infection discouraged people from seeking emergency shelter. Considering all these factors, the most recent figures on IDPs are likely to be a significant underestimate.[33] The following overview of IDP figures should therefore be read with these caveats in mind.

When Francis Deng was appointed as the first Representative of the Secretary-General on Internally Displaced Persons in 1992, the global IDP population numbered 25 million people.[34] That figure has more than doubled since. According to the IDMC, the number of IDPs in the world reached a record 55 million in 2020.[35] The countries with the highest number of IDPs at the end of 2020 were Syria (6.6 million), Democratic Republic of Congo (5.3 million), Colombia (4.9 million), Yemen (3.6 million), and Afghanistan (3.8 million).[36] Around 40.5 million new displacements were recorded in 2020, the highest number in a decade. States with at least one million new IDPs included China (5.1 million), Philippines (4.5 million), Bangladesh (4.6 million), India (3.9 million), Democratic Republic of Congo (2.5 million), Ethiopia (2.36 million), Syria (1.8 million), United States (1.7 million), Vietnam (1.3 million), and Somalia (1.29 million).[37] Countries with at least 500,000 new IDPs included Honduras (937,000), Pakistan (829,000), South Sudan (714,000), Mozambique (617,000), Cuba (639,000), and Burkina Faso (515,000).[38]

Most IDPs live in urban areas in developing countries,[39] and the largest demographic of IDPs is individuals in the broad age bracket of 25–64 years

'The Question of Data in Internal Displacement Law- and Policy-Making' 39(4) Refugee Survey Quarterly 634 (hereafter Caterina and Rodríguez, 'The Question of Data'); WHO (Regional Office for Europe), 'Collection and Integration of Data on Refugee and Migrant Health in the WHO European Region: Technical guidance' (2020).

[32] Internal Displacement Monitoring Centre, *Global Report on Internal Displacement 2021* (2021) 18 (hereafter IDMC, *GRID 2021*).

[33] ibid 8.

[34] Elizabeth Ferris, 'Order from Chaos: Unpacking the Numbers on Global Refugees' (*Brookings*, 20 June 2017) <https://www.brookings.edu/blog/order-from-chaos/2017/06/20/unpacking-the-numbers-on-global-refugees/> accessed 13 July 2021.

[35] IDMC, *GRID 2021* (n 32) 3. This is different from the figure cited by UNHCR, which reports that there were 48.6 million conflict-affected IDPs in the world at the end of 2020.

[36] ibid.

[37] ibid.

[38] ibid.

[39] ibid; UNHCR, *Global Trends: Forced Displacement in 2020* (2021) (hereafter UNHCR, *Global Trends*)

(22 million).[40] UNHCR estimates that women and girls constituted on average 52 percent of all IDPs in 2020,[41] and just under half of all IDPs were children.[42] In several countries, the proportion of IDP children was significantly higher than 52 percent: Somalia (61%); Afghanistan (58%); Chad, Cameroon, and Niger (all 55%); and Yemen (54%).[43] Many IDPs also live in protracted displacement, which refers to IDPs who are prevented from taking or are unable to take steps for significant periods of time to progressively reduce their vulnerability, impoverishment, and marginalization and find a durable solution.[44] In addition, IDPs can live in a variety of different circumstances. For example, an IDP who can live with relatives and has access to employment will probably be significantly better off than an IDP who is forced to live in destitution in an IDP camp.[45] As the following paragraphs will illustrate, the causes of global displacement in 2020 have varied greatly.

Disasters were responsible for more than three-quarters of new displacements in 2020.[46] The countries with the highest number of disaster-induced IDPs at the end of 2020 were Afghanistan (1.1 million), India (929,000), Pakistan (806,000), Ethiopia (633,000), and Sudan (454,000).[47] The IDMC notes that there is a 'major knowledge gap' on the issue of disaster-induced displacement, and that that their figures are likely to be a 'significant underestimate'.[48] Weather-related disasters, such as storms, floods, droughts, extreme temperatures, landslides, cyclones, hurricanes, typhoons, and wildfires were the cause of 98 percent of new disaster displacements in 2020.[49] Additional causes of disaster displacement included geophysical disasters, such as earthquakes and volcano eruptions.[50] Examples of high-profile disaster-induced displacement include the bushfires in Australia, which resulted in 65,000 newly displaced IDPs,[51] and the monsoon in Nepal, which was responsible for 48,000 newly displaced IDPs.[52]

[40] IDMC, *GRID 2021* (n 32).
[41] UNHCR, *Global Trends* (n 39) 28.
[42] This data is taken from the 14 countries for which age and sex disaggregation was available according to UNHCR statistics. ibid.
[43] ibid.
[44] Walter Kälin and Hannah Entwisle Chapuisat, 'Breaking The Impasse: Reducing Protracted Internal Displacement As A Collective Outcome' (*OCHA Policy and Studies Series* 2017).
[45] For further discussion, see chapter 4.
[46] IDMC, *GRID 2021* (n 32) 11.
[47] ibid 8.
[48] ibid 15.
[49] ibid.
[50] ibid 12.
[51] ibid 46.
[52] ibid 56.

Conflict was the second most significant driver of displacement in 2020. At the end of the year, 48 million people were living in conflict-induced internal displacement in 59 countries.[53] At the time of writing, Syria (6.5 million),[54] Democratic Republic of the Congo (5.2 million),[55] and Colombia (4.9 million)[56] are the countries with the most conflict-induced IDPs, making up more than 30 percent of the total worldwide IDP population.[57] The majority of displacement caused by violence and conflict occurred in Sub-Saharan Africa, which accounts for 69.4 percent of the global total of conflict-induced displacement, followed by the Middle East and North Africa, which accounts for 21.2 percent.[58] The main causes of conflict-induced displacement in 2020 were armed conflict, as well as criminal, political, and communal violence.[59] Examples include the violent protests that took place in Côte d'Ivoire in the run-up to their October elections, which led to the displacement of 15,000 people,[60] and the clashes between Azerbaijan and Armenia in connection with the Nagorno-Karabakh conflict, resulting in 84,000 newly displaced IDPs.[61] Escalating violence and the expansion of extremist groups in Mozambique, Ethiopia, and Burkina Faso fuelled some of the world's fastest growing displacement crises while persistent conflict continued to force people to flee in Syria, Democratic Republic of the Congo, and Afghanistan.[62]

These two factors—conflict and disaster—are the most common drivers of internal displacement. This is reflected by the fact that the two latest and most detailed annual reports on IDP figures (by the IDMC and UNHCR, respectively) focused exclusively on IDPs in conflict and disaster situations.[63] However, it is important to (re)emphasize that the concept of an IDP is not limited to those who fled conflict and disasters. This is supported by the non-exhaustive list of displacement drivers as set out in the Guiding Principles on Internal Displacement. As such, many IDPs are displaced by factors other than conflict and disaster, such as human rights violations and/or displacement

[53] ibid.
[54] IDMC, 'Syria' (*IDMC*, 31 December 2020) <https://www.internal-displacement.org/countries/syria> accessed 5 July 2021.
[55] IDMC, 'Democratic Republic of the Congo' (*IDMC*, 31 December 2020) <https://www.internal-displacement.org/countries/democratic-republic-of-the-congo> accessed 5 July 2021.
[56] IDMC, 'Colombia' (*IDMC*, 31 December 2020) <https://www.internal-displacement.org/countries/colombia> accessed 5 July 2021.
[57] IDMC, *GRID 2021* (n 32) 14.
[58] ibid 20.
[59] ibid 11.
[60] ibid 26.
[61] ibid 70.
[62] ibid.
[63] ibid; UNHCR, *Global Trends* (n 39).

projects.[64] Many IDPs are also displaced because of environmental reasons that do not include disaster, such as slow-onset climate change.[65] Covid-19 also had a profound effect on displacement figures in 2020, influencing displacement patterns through the fear of infection,[66] and exacerbating pre-existing issues, such as food insecurity, which leads to displacement.[67] It is also important to note that an individual's displacement is often not attributable to one single cause and often does not occur just once in an individual's lifetime. IDPs often flee for a variety of reasons and are often displaced multiple times. For example, Somalia's recent drought drove people to flee from rural to urban areas, where there is a more significant risk of eviction and attacks, leading to secondary displacement.[68]

Having set out the concept of IDP and explained the scope of the IDP problem today, the following section will provide a similarly structured overview of the refugee concept.

2.3 Refugees

Article 1A(2) of the 1951 Convention relating to the Status of Refugees ('Refugee Convention') provides that the term 'refugee' shall apply to any person who:

> owing to well-founded fear of being persecuted for reasons of race, religion, nationality, membership of a particular social group or political opinion, is outside the country of his nationality and is unable or, owing to such fear, is unwilling to avail himself of the protection of that country[69]

[64] Robert Muggah, 'A Tale of Two Solitudes: Comparing Conflict and Development-induced Internal Displacement and Involuntary Resettlement' (2003) 41(5) International Migration 5–31; Bjorn Pettersson, 'Development-induced Displacement: Internal Affair or International Human Rights Issue?' (2002) 12 Forced Migration Review 16–19; Nadine Walicki, 'Expert Roundtable on Displacement Caused by Development: Event Summary' (*IDMC*, 2017) <www.internal-displacement.org/publications/expert-roundtable-on-displacement-caused-by-development> accessed 7 July 2021; Michèle Morel, *The Right not to be Displaced in International Law* (Intersentia 2014) (hereafter Morel, *The Right not to be Displaced*).

[65] Romola Adeola and Frans Viljoen, 'Climate Change, Development Projects and Internal Displacement In Africa' (2018) 62(3) Journal of African Law 335; IOM, 'Internal Displacement in the context of the slow-onset adverse effects of climate change: submission by the International Organisation for Migration to the Special Rapporteur on the human rights of Internally Displaced Persons' (2020).

[66] IDMC, *GRID 2021* (n 32) 28.

[67] ibid 63.

[68] ibid.

[69] Convention Relating to the Status of Refugees (adopted 28 July 1951, entered into force 22 April 1954) 189 UNTS 137 (Refugee Convention) art 1A(2) (hereafter Refugee Convention 1951).

The 1967 Refugee Protocol extended the application of the Refugee Convention to the situation of 'new refugees', namely persons who, while meeting the Refugee Convention definition, had become refugees as a result of events that took place after 1 January 1951 without any geographic limitation.[70] The Refugee Convention has 146 States Parties, and some of its provisions are customary international law, meaning they bind even those states which are not a party to the Refugee Convention.[71] In addition, regional refugee systems exist—such as in Europe, America, and Africa—which may extend but cannot narrow the rights in the Refugee Convention.[72] Although each of these regional systems has specific legally binding instruments introducing specific procedures and rights, the text of the Refugee Convention remains the common globally binding instrument connecting all regional legal orders. The refugee definition in the 1951 Refugee Convention is therefore the global standard as to who qualifies as a refugee.

This definition is made up of a number of cumulative criteria, all of which must be satisfied for an individual to qualify as a refugee. These criteria have been analysed in detail elsewhere,[73] hence this section will be concise in its analysis. First, the individual must have a 'well-founded fear of being persecuted'. There is no definition of what constitutes persecution in the Refugee Convention and it is generally accepted that the drafters intentionally declined to define 'being persecuted' because they recognized the impossibility of exhaustively listing all the forms of maltreatment that might entitle persons to refugee status.[74] However, many scholarly authorities propose a human rights interpretation of the term 'persecution',[75] and this approach is generally

[70] Protocol Relating to the Status of Refugees (adopted 31 January 1967, entered into force 4 October 1967) 606 UNTS 267 (Protocol).

[71] Guy S Goodwin-Gill and Jane McAdam, *The Refugee in International Law* (3rd edn, OUP 2007) (hereafter Goodwin-Gill and McAdam, *The Refugee in International Law*).

[72] Council Directive 2011/95/EU of the European Parliament and of the Council of 13 December 2011 on standards for the qualification of third-country nationals or stateless persons as beneficiaries of international protection, for a uniform status for refugees or for persons eligible for subsidiary protection, and for the content of the protection granted (recast) [2011] OJ L337/9 (hereafter Qualification Directive); Convention Governing the Specific Aspects of Refugee Problems in Africa (adopted 10 September 1969, entered into force 20 June 1974) 1001 UNTS 45; Colloquium on the International Protection of Refugees in Central America, Mexico and Panama, 'Cartagena Declaration on Refugees' (19–22 November 1984) (Cartagena Declaration); Joined Cases C-175–179/08 *Aydin Salahadin Abdulla and Others* ECLI:EU:C:2010:105.

[73] Goodwin-Gill and McAdam, *The Refugee in International Law* (n 71); James C Hathaway and Michelle Foster, *The Law of Refugee Status* (2nd edn, CUP 2014) (hereafter Hathaway and Foster, *The Law of Refugee Status*).

[74] Hathaway and Foster, *The Law of Refugee Status* (n 73); Hugo Storey, 'What Constitutes Persecution? Towards a Working Definition' (2014) 26 International Journal of Refugee Law 272 (hereafter Storey, 'What Constitutes Persecution? Towards a Working Definition').

[75] Andreas Zimmermann, *The 1951 Convention Relating to the Status of Refugees and its 1967 Protocol: a Commentary* (OUP 2010); Goodwin-Gill and McAdam, *The Refugee in International Law* (n 71); Hathaway and Foster, *The Law of Refugee Status* (n 73); Eric Fripp, 'International Humanitarian

accepted in state practice.[76] Yet not all human rights violations will necessarily constitute persecution. Assessment will turn on factors including (i) the nature of the freedom threatened; (ii) the nature and severity of the restriction;[77] and (iii) the likelihood of the restriction eventuating in the individual case.[78] In addition, persecution is not confined to acts by state authorities. Acts by non-state actors may constitute persecution if the state is unwilling or unable to provide protection from those acts.[79] Finally, it should be noted that the requirement of a 'well-founded fear of being persecuted' is a forward-looking test, which focuses on the likelihood of future persecution.[80] Persecution need not actually have occurred in the past, although past persecution may be evidence that a risk of future persecution exists.[81]

Second, the persecution must be 'for reasons of race, religion, nationality, membership of a particular social group or political opinion'. The term 'membership of a particular social group' merits some attention, as the meaning of this term is perhaps more unclear than that of the other terms. 'Membership of a particular social group' is not defined by the Refugee Convention, but domestic court decisions and scholarly authorities have developed indicators of what might constitute membership of a particular social group, such as voluntary association with the social group, involuntary linkages (eg family, shared past experiences, innate characteristics), and the perception of others.[82]

Law and the Interpretation of Persecution in Article 1A(2) CSR51' (2014) 26 International Journal of Refugee Law 382; Jaakko Kuosmanen, 'What's So Special About Persecution?' (2014) 17 Ethical Theory and Moral Practice 129; Nicholas R Bednar and Margaret Penland, 'Asylum's Interpretative Impasse: Interpreting Persecution and Particular Social Group Using International Human Rights Law' (2017) 26 Minnesota Journal of International Law 145; Michelle Foster, 'Economic Migrant or Person in Need of Protection? Socio-Economic Rights and Persecution in International Refugee Law' in Bruce Burson and David James Cantor (eds), *Human Rights and the Refugee Definition,* (Brill Nijhoff 2016) 229; Linda J Kirk, 'Island Nation: The Impact of International Human Rights Law on Australian Refugee Law' in Bruce Burson and David James Cantor (eds), *Human Rights and the Refugee Definition* (Brill Nijhoff 2016) 49; Jason M Pobjoy, *The Child in International Refugee Law* (CUP 2017).

[76] For example, the EU's Qualification Directive has explicitly adopted the human rights approach by defining 'an act of persecution' as an act that is 'sufficiently serious by its nature or repetition as to constitute a severe violation of basic human rights, in particular the rights from which derogation cannot be made' or an 'accumulation of various measures, including violations of human rights'. See Qualification Directive (n 72) art 9(1)(a), (b).

[77] For example, the EU Qualification Directive notes that the violation(s) must be 'sufficiently serious by its nature or repetition' art 9(1)(a).

[78] Goodwin-Gill and McAdam, *The Refugee in International Law* (n 71) 90–131.

[79] *Horvath (AP) v Secretary of State for the Home Department* [2001] 1 AC 489; Pia Zambelli, 'Knowing Persecution When We See It: Non-State Actors and the Measure of State Protection' (2020) 32 International Journal of Refugee Law 28.

[80] Storey, 'What Constitutes Persecution? Towards a Working Definition' (n 74).

[81] Goodwin-Gill and McAdam, *The Refugee in International Law* (n 71). See also chapter 4, section 4.1.

[82] ibid; *Canada (Attorney General) v Ward* [1993] 2 SCR 689; *Islam (AP) v Secretary of State for the Home Department; R v Immigration Appeal Tribunal and Another Ex Parte Shah* (AP) (Conjoined Appeals) [1999] UKHL 20, [1999] Imm AR 283, [1999] 2 AC 629; *Cheung v Canada* [1993] 2 FC 314.

Examples of particular social groups for the purposes of the refugee definition might include women, members of the LGBTQIA community, and individuals living with HIV/AIDS.[83] The requirement that persecution must be linked with one of the Refugee Convention reasons has meant that the Refugee Convention will not generally apply to those who fear other forms of generalized harm, such as those fleeing from natural disasters, civil war, or economic crises. However, removal of individuals at real risk of these types of harms may give rise to violations of other international law rules.[84]

Finally—and perhaps most importantly for the purposes of this book—a refugee is 'outside the country of his nationality and is unable or, owing to such fear, is unwilling to avail himself of the protection of that country'. It is therefore not possible to be a refugee inside one's own country, even if all the other criteria of the Refugee Convention are satisfied. In such a situation, an individual will probably fall within the description of an IDP, which was explained above in section 2.2.

2.3.1 Refugees in 2020

Many of the above difficulties in relation to IDP data collection also apply to refugee data collection, such as refugees' distrust of authorities, problematic methodologies applied by researchers (eg not counting refugee deaths when comparing figures from year to year), the fact that states and other actors have powerful incentives to suppress and manipulate data to construct a preferred narrative, and/or the fact that refugees move often, making them difficult to count.[85] As such, as in the case of IDP figures, the figures we have for refugees are also likely to be underestimated.

According to the UNHCR's most recent *Global Trends* report,[86] there were approximately 26.4 million refugees in the world at the end of 2020, as well as a further 4.1 million asylum-seekers.[87] Sixty-eight percent of refugees and

[83] Goodwin-Gill and McAdam, *The Refugee in International Law* (n 71); Tawseef Khan, 'Sexual Orientation and Refugee Law: How Do Legal Sanctions Criminalizing Homosexuality Engage the Definition of Persecution?' in Satvinder Singh Juss (ed), *Research Handbook on International Refugee Law* (Edward Elgar 2019) 310.

[84] Bríd Ní Ghráinne, 'Complementary Protection and Encampment' (2021) 21 Human Rights Law Review 54 (hereafter Ní Ghráinne, 'Complementary Protection'); Jane McAdam, *Complementary Protection in International Refugee Law* (OUP 2007).

[85] Ní Ghráinne and Hudson, 'The International Organisation for Migration's Engagement with the Guiding Principles on Internal Displacement' (n 31); Cardona-Fox, 'IDP Data' (n 31); Caterina and Rodríguez, 'The Question of Data' (n 31).

[86] UNHCR, *Global Trends* (n 39).

[87] ibid 12. An asylum-seeker is someone whose refugee claim is yet to be processed. See UNHCR, 'Asylum-Seekers' (*UNHCR*) <https://www.unhcr.org/en-ie/asylum-seekers.html> accessed 8 July 2021.

Venezuelans displaced abroad originated from just five countries:[88] Syria (6.7 million); Venezuela (4.0 million);[89] Afghanistan (2.6 million); South Sudan (2.2 million); and Myanmar (1.1 million).[90] Other major refugee-generating countries included the Democratic Republic of Congo (0.8 million), Somalia (0.8 million), Sudan (0.8 million), Central African Republic (0.6 million), and Eritrea (0.5 million).

The top five countries that hosted the largest number of refugees in 2020 were: Turkey (hosting 3.7 million, the majority of which were Syrian); Colombia (hosting 1.7 million including Venezuelans displaced abroad); Pakistan (1.4 million); Uganda (1.4 million); and Germany (1.2 million).[91] These top five refugee hosting countries remained unchanged from 2019.[92] Although the full impact of the Covid-19 pandemic on global displacement is not yet clear, UNHCR has reported that arrivals of new refugees and asylum-seekers were sharply down in most regions in 2020—about 1.5 million fewer people than would have been expected in non-Covid-19 circumstances.[93] Measures implemented by governments to curb the spread of Covid-19, such as restricting freedom of movement and closing borders, made it much harder for people to flee their countries and claim asylum abroad.[94]

In terms of demographics, refugees are usually hosted in neighbouring countries (73%).[95] The vast majority of the world's refugees are hosted in developing countries (76%) and live in cities (78%).[96] Although children accounted for 30 percent of the world's population at the end of 2020, 41 percent of people displaced across borders were children,[97] and 47 percent of all refugees are estimated to be women and girls.[98] UNHCR estimates that some 15.7 million

[88] Venezuelans displaced abroad 'refers to persons of Venezuelan origin who are likely to be in need of international protection under the criteria contained in the Cartagena Declaration, but who have not applied for asylum in the country in which they are present'. See UNHCR, 'Persons who are Forcibly Displaced, Stateless, and Others of Concern to UNHCR' (*UNHCR*) <https://www.unhcr.org/refugee-statistics/methodology/definition/> accessed 8 July 2021.

[89] This is the number of Venezuelan refugees and Venezuelans displaced abroad.

[90] UNHCR, *Global Trends* (n 39) 3.

[91] ibid 2.

[92] ibid 19.

[93] ibid.

[94] Bríd Ní Ghráinne, 'Covid-19, Border Closures and International Law' (Reflection Paper, Institute of International Relations Prague, 4 May 2020) <https://www.dokumenty-iir.cz/Publikace/Reflections/reflection_Br%C3%ADd%20N%C3%AD_04_2020_covid-19_DEF.pdf> accessed 8 July 2021 (hereafter Ní Ghráinne, 'Covid-19, Border Closures and International Law').

[95] UNHCR, *Global Trends* (n 39).

[96] UNHCR, 'What is a Refugee Camp?' (*UNHCR*) <https://www.unrefugees.org/refugee-facts/camps/> accessed 8 July 2021.

[97] UNHCR notes that demographic data by age and sex is available for 79% of refugees.

[98] UNHCR, *Global Trends* (n 39) 16.

refugees (more than half the global population) were in a protracted situation at the end of 2020, similar to 2019.[99]

Refugees flee their countries for a variety of reasons, but most of all due to conflict. For example, the ongoing situation in Syria led it to become the main country of origin for refugees in 2020,[100] and the continued persecution of the Rohingya people in Myanmar has led 1.1 million people to flee the country under the threat of violence.[101] The situation in Venezuela also continued to worsen, with over 4.8 million Venezuelans becoming displaced abroad in 2020 because of violence,[102] developing into 'one of the largest displacement crisis in the world'.[103] Ongoing armed conflict in the Nagorno-Karabakh region, a disputed territory at the centre of the clash between Azerbaijan and Armenia, resulted in mass displacement, causing 90,000 people to flee to Armenia, where they remain in a 'refugee-like' situation.[104]

In Africa, Sudan received an influx of 54,000 refugees from Ethiopia, who were escaping violence between the Tigray People's Liberation Front (TPLF) and Prime Minister Abiy Ahmed's government,[105] as well as large numbers of refugees from the Central African Republic. Many refugees also fled South Sudan to the Democratic Republic of Congo following the overthrow of former President Omar al-Bashir.[106] Tensions in the Sahel region, as a result of the marginalization of communities, led to the increasing displacement of residents of Mali, Niger, and Burkina Faso,[107] with the UNHCR noting that the situation in the Sahel region is 'complex and volatile'.[108]

Although most refugees flee conflict situations—which is reflected by the fact that the UNHCR's figures focus exclusively on such contexts—the causes of flight for refugees vary widely. Individuals might be targeted for their religious beliefs, such as Christians in the Central African Republic or Hindus in Pakistan.[109] Refugees might also flee persecution based on their political

[99] UNHCR defines a protracted refugee situation as 'a situation in which 25,000 or more refugees from the same nationality have been in exile for at least five consecutive years in a given host country'. It is important to bear in mind that this definition does not refer to circumstances of individual refugees, but rather is a reflection of refugee situations as a whole. ibid.

[100] ibid 17.

[101] ibid 18.

[102] ibid 14.

[103] UNHCR, 'Venezuela Situation' (*UNHCR*) <https://www.unhcr.org/en-ie/venezuela-emergency.html> accessed 21 June 2021.

[104] UNHCR, *Global Trends* (n 39) 14.

[105] ibid 14.

[106] ibid 14.

[107] IDMC, *GRID 2021* (n 32) 29.

[108] UNHCR, *Global Trends* (n 39) 14.

[109] Ewelina U Ochab, 'The Religious War In The Central African Republic Continues' *Forbes* (9 May 2018) <https://www.forbes.com/sites/ewelinaochab/2018/05/09/the-religious-war-in-central-african-republic-continues/?sh=1280e1f73c0d>; Maria Abi-Habib and Zia ur-Rehman, 'Poor and Desperate,

beliefs. High-profile examples include Gloria Estefan (who fled the Castro regime in Cuba), Alexander Ginsburg (who fled the Kremlin during the Cold War), and the Dalai Lama (Tibet's leader-in-exile).[110] Many refugees are targeted because of their sexual orientation, such as gay people in Chechnya.[111] Other grounds for fleeing include targeting on the basis of: sex and gender; gender identity; congenital conditions, such as albinism; disabilities; acts which transgress moral codes, such as adultery; contravening social norms, such as parents refusing to have their child undergo female genital mutilation (FGM) or women refusing to take a subordinate role to their husbands; and conditions and serious illnesses, such as HIV/AIDS.[112]

In sum, the global displaced population is at a record high, numbering 82.4 million.[113] However, as set out in this book's introductory chapter, there has not yet been a detailed examination of the relationship between the two largest categories of forced migrations: IDPs and refugees.[114] Such an examination is long overdue because we do not understand to what extent the protection of IDPs complements, conflicts with, or undermines international refugee law. The next section explains in more detail the similarities, differences, and overlaps between these two categories of forced migrants and will further justify why the relationship between these two categories needs further attention.

2.4 Examining Internally Displaced Persons and Refugees Together

IDPs and refugees are similar in the sense that their movement is involuntary and/or coerced and often both categories of persons may have fled their places of habitual residence for similar reasons. In fact, the very same person might have been an IDP and a refugee at different times of their life, because many

Pakistani Hindus Accept Islam To Get By' *The New York Times* (Delhi, 4 August 2020) <https://www.nytimes.com/2020/08/04/world/asia/pakistan-hindu-conversion.html> accessed 8 July 2021.

[110] International Rescue Committee, 'Famous Refugees: Stand with Refugees' (*International Rescue Committee*, 9 January 2017) <https://www.rescue.org/article/famous-refugees> accessed 8 July 2021.

[111] Masha Gessen, 'Fleeing Anti-Gay Persecution In Chechnya, Three Young Women Are Now Stuck In Place' *The New Yorker* (New York, 1 October 2018) <https://www.newyorker.com/news/our-columnists/fleeing-anti-gay-persecution-in-chechnya-three-young-women-are-now-stuck-in-place> accessed 8 July 2021.

[112] European Asylum Support Office, 'EASO Guidance on Membership of a Particular Social Group' (EASO Practical Guides Series, Publication Office of the European Union, March 2020) <https://easo.europa.eu/sites/default/files/EASO-Guidance-on%20MPSG-EN.pdf> accessed 8 July 2021.

[113] UNHCR, *Global Trends* (n 39).

[114] Largest in terms of numbers.

IDPs go on to cross a border and qualify as refugees and many refugees become IDPs in their host countries.[115] This is reflected by the fact that many countries (eg Syria, Afghanistan, South Sudan, Myanmar, and Somalia) have significant IDP populations and generate huge numbers of refugees.

In addition, both IDPs and refugees might have experienced violence or trauma, which can have long-lasting effects. Both IDPs and refugees find themselves away from their homes, often in a place that is unfamiliar to them. Both IDPs and refugees often face a breakdown of social norms: they are often separated from family members and lose social networks, and new tensions may arise within IDP or refugee families. As aforementioned, most of the world's IDPs and refugees are located in developing countries and live in urban areas. IDPs and refugees often also live in rural areas, sometimes in camps and sometimes in host communities. They can experience tension and/or discrimination in their new environment.[116]

The global IDP and refugee population is made up of people of every age and gender and every form of diversity. IDPs and refugees often face the same practical problems such as lack of documentation (which may be necessary to enjoy certain rights or access services), adequate shelter, food, water, sanitation, and healthcare. IDPs and refugees are often also impoverished. They may have fled in a hurry, bringing very little with them. They may have lost their property back home and have also lost their livelihood. Even when their assets remain, they often cannot recover them. Because of poverty, exacerbated by displacement, both IDPs and refugees may be more vulnerable to exploitation and gender-based violence, and they often have inadequate access to justice. Being an IDP or refugee also compounds existing vulnerabilities, such as for people with disabilities, elderly people, and children. It can also exacerbate pre-existing risks of violence, discrimination, or marginalization. Often displacement can last years, decades, or a lifetime, and imagining a future, planning one's life trajectory, and acting in the present become difficult.[117] Both IDPs and refugees face significant uncertainty about the future and are often unsure about when their situation of displacement will come to an end, if at all.[118]

[115] David James Cantor and Jacob Ochieng Apollo, 'Internal Displacement, Internal Migration, and Refugee Flows: Connecting the Dots' (2021) 39(4) Refugee Survey Quarterly 647.

[116] Module 2, 'Internal Displacement: Overview and Key Concepts' (Council of Europe, Human Rights Education for Legal Professionals) <http://help.elearning.ext.coe.int/course/view.php?id=2467#section-0> accessed 8 July 2021 (hereafter 'Internal Displacement: Overview and Key Concepts').

[117] Ní Ghráinne, 'Complementary Protection' (n 84) 59; Simon Turner, 'What Is a Refugee Camp? Explorations of the Limits and Effects of the Camp' (2015) 29(2) Journal of Refugee Studies 139; Simon Turner, 'Suspended Spaces: Contesting Sovereignties in a Refugee Camp' in Thomas Blom Hansen and Finn Stepputat (eds), *Sovereign Bodies: Citizens, Migrants and States in the Post-Colonial World* (2005) 312.

[118] 'Internal Displacement: Overview and Key Concepts' (n 116).

Nonetheless, there remain substantial differences between the two categories of forced migrants. The first, most fundamental distinction, as set out above, is that the refugee has crossed an international frontier while the IDP remains within their country of origin. The crossing of a border represents the breaking of the bond between the refugee and their country of origin and thus puts the refugee within the protective reach of the international community.[119] International refugee protection has thus been described as 'surrogate' to national protection, in the sense that refugee protection is only applicable where protection is not available from the state of nationality.[120] The responsibility for IDP protection on the other hand stems from the notion of sovereignty as responsibility. The responsibility to protect IDPs primarily lies with their governments even though these may, but by no means necessarily will, be the very actors that have caused the displacement in the first place.

Second, internal displacement is not explicitly prohibited by international law,[121] although there are a number of rights which imply that internal displacement is contrary to international law.[122] In fact, there are a number of situations in which internal displacement may be compatible with international law, such as where asylum-seekers are returned to an 'Internal Protection Alternative' in their countries of origin,[123] during armed conflict for the purposes of the

[119] Grahl-Madsen, *The Status of Refugees in International Law* (n 12) 79; Andrew Shacknove, 'Who is a Refugee?' (1985) 95(2) Ethics 274, 275.

[120] *R v Secretary of State for the Home Department, Immigration Appeals Tribunal, Ex parte Anthonypillai Francis Robinson* [1998] QB 929 [16]; James Hathaway, *The Law of Refugee Status* (Butterworths 1991) 135 (hereafter Hathaway, '*Law of Refugee Status*'); *Randhawa v Minister for Immigration, Local Government and Ethnic Affairs* [1994] 52 FCR 437, 124 ALR 265, 441; Emma Haddad, *The Refugee in International Society: Between Sovereigns* (CUP 2008).

[121] Some regional conventions prohibit internal displacement. See African Union Convention for the Protection and Assistance of Internally Displaced Persons in Africa (adopted 23 October 2009, entered into force 6 December 2012) (Kampala Convention), art 3; Protocol on the Protection and Assistance to Internally Displaced Persons (adopted 30 November 2006, entered into force 21 June 2008), art 3. For further discussion, see chapter 3; Romola Adeola and Francis Viljoen, 'The Right Not to Be Arbitrarily Displaced in Africa' (2017) 25 African Journal of International and Comparative Law 459.

[122] For further analysis, see chapter 3; Morel, *The Right not to be Displaced* (n 64); Kerrin Geoffrey Buck, 'Displacement and Dispossession: Redefining Forced Displacement and Identifying When Forced Displacement Becomes Pillage under International Humanitarian Law' (2017) 2 Journal of International Humanitarian Action 5; Bree Akesson, Andrew R Basso, and Myriam Denov, 'The Right to Home: Domicide as a Violation of Child and Family Rights in the Context of Political Violence' (2016) 30 Children and Society 369.

[123] The Internal Protection Alternative is based on the premise that if there is a safe place within an individual's state of nationality or habitual residence where they can relocate, they are not a refugee. See chapter 4; Bríd Ní Ghráinne, 'Safe Zones and the Internal Protection Alternative' (2020) 69(2) International and Comparative Law Quarterly 335 (hereafter Ní Ghráinne, 'Safe Zones'); Bríd Ní Ghráinne, 'Internal Protection Alternative' in Cathryn Costello, Michelle Foster, and Jane McAdam (eds), *Oxford Handbook on International Refugee Law* (OUP 2021); Bríd Ní Ghráinne, 'The Internal Protection Alternative Inquiry and Human Rights Considerations—Irrelevant or Indispensable?' (2015) 27(1) International Journal of Refugee Law 29; Jessica Schultz, *The Internal Protection Alternative in Refugee Law* (Brill Nijhoff 2018).

protection of civilians or for the purposes of military necessity,[124] in the context of disasters to protect the 'safety and health of those affected',[125] or where displacement is necessary for the purposes of development projects justified by 'compelling and overriding public interest'.[126] In contrast, the element of persecution in the creation of a refugee situation rationally entails a breach of international law. Although there is no definition of persecution in the Refugee Convention, there is widespread acceptance that persecution entails a systemic violation of human rights and is thus,[127] ipso facto, contrary to international law.[128]

Third, as set out above, the IDP description is far broader than the refugee definition. In order to satisfy the refugee definition, an applicant must show, inter alia, that they have fled their country of nationality owing to a well-founded fear of persecution based on race, religion, nationality, membership of a particular social group, or political opinion.[129] This list of persecutory grounds is exhaustive. However, there is no need to show an element of persecution in order to be described as an IDP. Moreover, as aforementioned, the list of reasons for which an IDP has fled or left their home or place of habitual residence is not exhaustive.[130] An individual who is forcibly displaced within their country's borders because of natural or man-made disasters or as a result of development projects would fall within the IDP definition, but an individual who had left their country for the same reasons would probably not qualify as a refugee. It is noteworthy that although conflict and violence is a major driver of both refugee flows and internal displacement, disaster was the biggest cause of internal displacement in 2020.

Fourth, the demographic of IDPs and refugees differs in some respects. Refugees have crossed a border, hence they may—at least at the time of displacement—be better off financially than IDPs who remain within their countries. In addition, more than half of IDPs are women and girls, whereas more than half of refugees are men and boys.

[124] Guiding Principles (n 2) principle 6(2)(b).

[125] ibid principle 6(2)(d).

[126] Peter Penz, 'Development, Displacement, and Ethics' (2002) 12 Forced Migration Review 4; ibid principle 6(2)(c).

[127] UNHCR, 'Guidelines on International Protection No. 1: Gender-Related Persecution within the Context of Art. 1(a)(2) of the 1951 Convention and/or its 1967 Protocol Relating to the Status of Refugees (2002)' (7 May 2002) UN Doc HCR/GIP/02/01 [13]; Hathaway, *Law of Refugee Status* (n 120) 104–05.

[128] For further analysis of the meaning of persecution, see chapter 4.

[129] Refugee Convention 1951 (n 69); Christopher D Boom, 'Beyond Persecution: A Moral Defence of Expanding Refugee Status' (2018) 30 International Journal of Refugee Law 512.

[130] Guiding Principles (n 2) principle 1.

Fifth, as previously mentioned, refugee status determination is often described as forward-looking.[131] The issue is not whether the claimant had good reason to fear persecution in the past, but whether, at the time the claim is being assessed, the claimant has a 'well-founded fear' of future persecution. Evidence of past persecution may nonetheless support the likelihood of exposure to future persecution. The description of an IDP, on the other hand, is solely based on past events. The Guiding Principles refer to 'persons or groups of persons who *have been* forced or obliged to flee or to leave their homes or places of habitual residence' (emphasis added).[132] This further supports the contention that the description of an IDP is broader than the refugee definition. It is easier to show that past events have actually taken place than it is to convince an adjudicator that certain events or treatment will probably come to pass, as the future is always inherently uncertain.

Sixth, the definition of refugee is legal in nature whereas the definition of IDP is descriptive in nature. This means that the refugee has a legal status under international law and is entitled to the range of rights set out in the Refugee Convention, which encompasses a duty of non-discrimination vis-à-vis citizens or other residents of the asylum country and refugees regarding a list of rights.[133] These include general provisions, administrative measures, rights relating to juridical status, and rights relating to employment. In this sense, refugee law is distinct from the protection offered to IDPs as it deals with questions relating to immigration, an area in which states are very cautious about guarding their sovereignty. Being categorized as an IDP does not, ipso facto, entitle a person to any additional rights under international law.[134] Refugee status also brings a person within the protection mandate of the UN Refugee Agency, the United Nations High Commissioner for Refugees.[135] IDPs, on the other hand, have no specific international agency to protect them although in recent years the UNHCR—as well as other institutions—have become involved

[131] Adreienne Anderson and others, 'Imminence in Refugee and Human Rights Law: A Misplaced Notion for International Protection' (2019) 68 International and Comparative Law Quarterly 111; Goodwin-Gill and McAdam, *The Refugee in International Law* (n 71).

[132] Guiding Principles (n 2) Introduction.

[133] James Hathaway and Michelle Foster, 'Internal Protection/ Relocation/ Flight Alternative as an Aspect of Refugee Status Determination' (Global Consultation on International Protection, Expert Rountable Discussion organised by the UNHCR, 2001) 44.

[134] However, there are certain regional and non-binding instruments which grant rights to IDPs. See discussion in Chapter 3.

[135] UNGA, 'Statute of the Office of the United Nations High Commissioner for Refugees' (14 December 1950) UN Doc A/RES/428(V), [6] (hereafter UNGA, 'Statute of the Office of the United Nations High Commissioner for Refugees'); Miriam Bradley, 'Unintended Consequences of Adjacency Claims: The Function and Dysfunction of Analogies between Refugee Protection and IDP Protection in the Work of UNHCR' (2019) 25 Global Governance: A Review of Multilateralism and International Organizations 620 (hereafter Bradley, 'Unintended Consequences of Adjacency Claims').

in IDP protection activities under the cluster approach. More details about the international protection regime applicable to IDPs is in chapter 3.

Seventh, it is possible for a person to be excluded from the benefits of the Refugee Convention where there are serious reasons for believing that the person has committed certain acts or crimes.[136] No such exclusionary criteria are provided in the Guiding Principles on Internal Displacement, although the Guiding Principles are 'without prejudice to individual criminal responsibility under international law, in particular relating to genocide, crimes against humanity, and war crimes'.[137] The purpose of this paragraph is that persons who are suspected of having committed these serious offences 'cannot avoid prosecution and punishment under international law simply on account of their being internally displaced, or by otherwise invoking the Guiding Principles'.[138]

Eighth, while it is clear when refugee status begins and ends,[139] the same cannot be said for a situation of internal displacement. Refugee status accrues when an international frontier is crossed, provided that all other elements of the refugee definition are satisfied. However, it is unclear when a person becomes internally displaced (and indeed whether a person is internally displaced at all), as there is no consensus about when a movement is voluntary or involuntary, nor is it clear whether the element of coercion should be assessed in objective or subjective terms. Moreover, as outlined in section 2.3 of this chapter and in chapter 4, refugee status ceases with the application of Article 1C of the Refugee Convention. However, when a person ceases to become an IDP is unclear, as often displaced persons will never return to their original place of residence, notwithstanding the fact that it is safe to do so. Principle 28 of the Guiding Principles nonetheless gives some guidance on when it may be considered that a 'durable solution' has been found to a situation of internal displacement. This principle is analysed in more detail in chapter 3.

Finally, and relatedly, the terminology and substance of application relating to durable solutions for IDPs and refugees differ in various respects. For refugees, this could entail residence or naturalization in the host country,[140] whereas the IDP will generally remain within the country of origin and either return to their community of origin, integrate in the place of displacement, or settle in another part of the country.[141] In addition, the return of a refugee

[136] Refugee Convention 1951 (n 69) art 1F.
[137] Guiding Principles (n 2) principle 1.
[138] Kälin, 'Guiding Principles' (n 24) 14.
[139] Refugee Convention (n 69) art 1A, art 1C.
[140] Katy Long, 'Rethinking "Durable Solutions"' in Elena Fiddian-Qasmiyeh and others (eds), *The Oxford Handbook of Refugee and Forced Migration Studies* (OUP 2014) 475.
[141] Gloria Nguya and Nadia Siddiqui, 'Triple Nexus Implementation and Implications for Durable Solutions for Internal Displacement: On Paper and in Practice' (2020) 39(4) Refugee

entails a cross-border movement, which is not the case for IDPs. Furthermore, resettlement for a refugee entails movement to a third country, whereas for an IDP it entails movement to another part of the country.

2.4.1 The Nexus between Refugeehood and Internal Displacement

Given the similarities and differences between IDPs and refugees set out in the previous section, the question arises as to what extent a real risk of internal displacement in the country of nationality or habitual residence is relevant to qualification as a refugee. An individual who was outside their country and claimed refugee status on the grounds that they were at risk of becoming an IDP in their country would probably not be successful in their claim for two main reasons.

First, although internal displacement is not, in itself, a human rights violation, a situation of internal displacement might entail the violation of various provisions of human rights law.[142] As set out in section 2.3, there is a general consensus that human rights law informs the meaning of the term 'persecution', therefore a risk of internal displacement might be relevant to the inquiry as to whether a risk of persecution exists. For example, in the 2015 case of *X (Re)*, the Refugee Appeal Division of the Immigration and Refugee Board of Canada paid close attention to the fact that women living in IDP camps in Haiti were at increased risk of sexual violence.[143] The fact that the woman in question was not likely to end up in such a camp was one of the factors which the Refugee Appeal Division relied on in finding that she did not have a well-founded fear of persecution. This case is therefore authority for the fact that a risk of internal displacement is relevant to the persecution analysis, even though persecution was not found to be present in this particular case.

In fact, it is quite unlikely that a situation of internal displacement, in itself, will give rise to 'persecution' in the sense of the refugee definition. As outlined above in section 2.3, the threshold for establishing persecution is very

Survey Quarterly 466; Ala Al-Mahaidi, 'Financing Opportunities for Durable Solutions to Internal Displacement: Building on Current Thinking and Practice' (2020) 39(4) Refugee Survey Quarterly 481; Anne Davies and Alice Jenner, 'A Tale of Two Cities—IDPs Plan for their Durable Solutions in Darfur' (2020) 39(4) Refugee Survey Quarterly 507; Ben Hudson, 'Challenges in the Law of IDP Returns' (Thesis, University of Bristol, 2019).

142 See chapter 3.
143 [2015] CanLII 60522 (CA IRB)

high, involving 'serious harm'[144] and/or the 'sustained or systematic violation of basic human rights demonstrative of a failure of state protection'.[145] Thus not only would the claimant need to establish that there is a real risk of exposure to circumstances that would constitute a human rights violation(s), but they would also need to establish that the alleged violations are 'sustained or systematic'. For example, the Australian Refugee Review Tribunal found that although an applicant had to 'move around in IDP camps' this did not amount to 'serious harm' such as to constitute persecution.[146]

Second, even if an individual could establish that the circumstances to which they would be exposed as an IDP constituted persecution, it would be difficult to establish a nexus between internal displacement and one of the discriminatory grounds in the Refugee Convention (race, religion, nationality, membership of a particular social group, political opinion). Regarding race, for example, it is feasible that internal displacement might arise as a result of discriminatory practices targeting a particular racial or religious group. However, in that case the nexus to the Refugee Convention would be based on the reasons for displacement (reasons of race or religion), rather than the fact of displacement itself. Regarding the category of particular social group, insofar as this author's research has revealed, being an IDP would not, in itself, make an individual a member of a particular social group. This argument was raised in the Australian case of *AOL15 v Minister for Immigration & Anor*, where the applicant argued, inter alia, that he feared harm in Sri Lanka because of his membership of a particular social group: IDPs.[147] The Federal Circuit Court found that this claim was 'a reference to his living circumstances, and not a claim to fear harm'.[148] Although the Court did not explicitly reject the contention that being an IDP constitutes membership of a 'particular social group', such rejection is implied by the fact that the applicant's claim to refugee status on this ground was unsuccessful.

In sum, therefore, the risk of internal displacement in the country of nationality or habitual residence will generally not bring an individual within the refugee definition. This is despite the fact that IDPs and refugees often find themselves in similar situations, facing similar harms, and with similar needs. In light of these similarities, the next section will assess whether the IDP/

144 *DXM16 v Minister for Immigration & Anor* [2018] FCCA 3675 (12 December 2018).
145 Hathaway, '*Law of Refugee Status*' (n 120) 112.
146 1400312 [2015] RRTA 309 (28 May 2015) [52].
147 [2017] FCCA 92 (2 February 2017).
148 ibid [26].

refugee distinction should be maintained or whether these two categories of forced migrants should be merged as a matter of law.

2.4.2 A Merging of the Categories of Internally Displaced Person and Refugee?

There has been some academic debate over whether the refugee and IDP categories should be merged, and there has been some compelling arguments made for such a merger.[149] As is clear from the preceding sections, there are many similarities between IDPs and refugees. Lee, for example, has argued that the crossing of international frontiers has been over-emphasized and that the requirement of border-crossing has lost its relevance in the post-Cold War era.[150] Furthermore, he states that prior to the conclusion of the Refugee Convention, there had been no agreement to define a refugee as a person being necessarily outside the country of their nationality and thus makes a case for 'reconsidering the use of the crossing of international borders as a prerequisite to systematic international protection and assistance of people forcibly displaced from their homes'.[151] From a practical perspective, it matters little to an individual to which category of forced migrant they belong, so long as they can access protection from harm. Focusing on the IDP/refugee distinction can therefore be unduly legalistic, ignoring the practical realities on the ground.

While operationally it may make little sense to distinguish between IDPs and refugees, legally their situations are very different.[152] As outlined above, international frontiers still regulate the areas of territorial sovereignty, and the practical similarities between the plight of IDPs and that of refugees do not change that fact. Moreover, the rights accorded to refugees are based on the fact that they are outside their country of origin and need basic entitlements to survive in a country where they do not have citizenship. These rights would not make sense if granted to an IDP in a domestic context.[153] Furthermore, to allocate a legal status to IDPs could result in further discrimination between IDPs

[149] An earlier version of this section was published in Bríd Ní Ghráinne, 'Internally Displaced Persons in International Refugee Law' in Satvinder S Juss, *Research Handbook on International Refugee Law* (Edward Elgar 2019).

[150] Luke Lee, 'Internally Displaced Persons and Refugees: Toward a Legal Synthesis?' (1996) 9 Journal of Refugee Studies 27, 30–38.

[151] ibid.

[152] James C Hathaway, 'Forced Migration Studies: Could We Agree Just to "Date"?' (2007) 20 Journal of Refugee Studies 48.

[153] Michael Barutciski, 'Tensions Between the Refugee Concept and the IDP Debate' (1998) 4(3) Forced Migration Review 11, 12; ibid 358.

and other human rights victims who are not displaced. In addition, Barutciski argues that merging the IDP/refugee categories could result in a watering-down of their respective existing protection standards:

> While the distinction between refugees and the internally displaced increasingly blurs as a result of the new interventionism, the present political context raises legitimate concerns that victims of displacement will be left with a form of protection that reflects the lowest common denominator. The reduced international commitment to external asylum means that refugees risk losing their privileged position with regard to protection, while the limited effectiveness of in-country protection indicates that the internally displaced will not actually be offered a new option of remaining in their homes. The resulting trade-off is not an equitable one.[154]

This author agrees with Barutciski and advocates that IDPs and refugees should continue to be governed by different protection regimes. However, that is not to say that the term IDP is not a useful concept. While the term does not grant legal status in any international legally binding instrument, the concept has succeeded in drawing international attention to a serious forced migration problem, and it assists in identifying and addressing the specific needs of IDPs. Having set out the main similarities and differences between IDPs and refugees, the next section will explain how these similarities and differences give rise to complementarity and conflict in the protection of these forced migrants.

2.4.3 Complementarity and Conflict between the Protection of Internally Displaced Persons and the Protection of Refugees

There are various ways in which the protection of IDPs may complement the protection of refugees and vice versa. First, protecting IDPs might lead to a reduction in the number of refugees. As aforementioned, many IDPs cross a border and become refugees. If protection was available in their own country, they may not have decided to cross a border in the first place.[155] In addition,

[154] Michael Barutciski, 'The Reinforcement of Non-Admission Policies and the Subversion of UNHCR: Displacement and Internal Assistance in Bosnia-Herzegovina (1992–94)' (1996) 8 International Journal of Refugee Law 49, 95 (hereafter Barutciski, 'The Reinforcement of Non-Admission Policies and the Subversion of UNHCR').

[155] UNHCR, 'The Protection of Internally Displaced Persons and the Role of UNHCR' (2007) [35] (hereafter UNHCR, 'The Protection of Internally Displaced Persons'); UNHCR, 'Internally Displaced Persons—The Role of the High Commissioner for Refugees' (20 June 2000) UN Doc EC/50/SC/INF:2 (hereafter UNHCR, 'Internally Displaced Persons—The Role of the High Commissioner for Refugees').

by assisting IDPs, individual organizations as well as the international community can gain a much better knowledge of the push factors of displacement, both internal and external, and can thus improve asylum management, especially concerning eligibility procedures.[156]

Moreover, sometimes it does not make sense to distinguish between IDPs and refugees when it comes to providing protection. Where refugees and displaced persons are generated by the same causes and surround a border, often the refugee problem cannot be addressed without first attending to the needs of IDPs. Internal conflicts of a secessionist nature may uproot people within national boundaries, which then become international borders. For example, in the Former Yugoslavia in the mid-1990s, the UNHCR decided to provide protection and assistance to the uprooted on the basis of humanitarian need, rather than refugee status. In such cases, IDPs are termed as such only in the short-term, and borders (which may shift) should not be the only factor in determining where to focus international assistance.[157] Refugees may also seek asylum in a state where there are IDPs, and both IDPs and refugees may be in need of the same type of humanitarian assistance and/or protection.[158] This was the case when refugees from Sierra Leone sought asylum in Liberia in the 1990s, where the two categories were practically indistinguishable from each other and, thus, the protection of IDPs was complementary protection of refugees and vice versa.[159] Relatedly, refugees are often repatriated to areas where internal displacement exists, and thus involvement with IDPs is essential for the purposes of maintaining a comprehensive approach to protection.[160] In such circumstances, it may be operationally difficult to distinguish between the refugees and internally displaced, as was the situation for UNHCR in the 1990s in Mozambique, Sierra Leone, Afghanistan, and Guatemala.[161]

That said, the literature to date has also raised some concerns regarding the negative impact IDP protection may have on refugee protection. For

[156] UNHCR, 'The Protection of Internally Displaced Persons' (n 155). It is also important to note that focusing attention on IDPs is not only for the purposes of reducing refugee flow: it provides protection to those who are unable or who have no desire to cross a border and claim refugee status.

[157] UNHCR, 'Internally Displaced Persons—The Role of the High Commissioner for Refugees' (n 155).

[158] UNHCR, 'Protection Aspects of UNHCR Activities on Behalf of Internally Displaced Persons' (17 August 1994) UN Doc EC/SCP/87 [39] (hereafter UNHCR, 'Protection Aspects of UNHCR Activities on Behalf of Internally Displaced Persons').

[159] UNHCR, 'Internally Displaced Persons—The Role of the High Commissioner for Refugees' (n 155).

[160] ibid. See also UNHCR, 'Protection Aspects of UNHCR Activities on Behalf of Internally Displaced Persons' (n 158) [15].

[161] UNHCR, 'Internally Displaced Persons—The Role of the High Commissioner for Refugees' (n 155).

example, UNHCR's primary mandate is directed towards protecting refugees and facilitating solutions to the refugee problem,[162] but it has been involved in IDP protection since the 1970s.[163] The UNHCR has highlighted some operational concerns stemming from the differences between the categories of IDP and refugee. More often than in refugee situations, IDP operations involve the UNHCR working in dangerous and unstable environments not controlled fully by national authorities.[164] IDP operations are also often in situations of international armed conflicts, where the UNHCR faces additional challenges such as logistical problems, negotiating access to victims, and staff security.[165] The UNHCR is in danger of being manipulated by both external powers as a substitute for political action and by the parties to the conflict who seek to divert humanitarian aid.[166] More generally, the UNHCR's involvement with IDPs could put further strain on what are already over-stretched UNHCR resources, which will inevitably affect the UNHCR's primary mandate, which focuses on refugees.[167] In addition, the UNHCR's assistance to IDPs may have unintended political consequences, such as by making it easier for the state to avoid fulfilling its protection obligations towards those on its territory if an international agency will do it instead.[168]

Three further aspects of conflict may arise. First, the primary motivation behind IDP discourse could be to serve the political interests of refugee-receiving states. In this sense, states could justify the closure of borders which prevents IDPs from fleeing the country and seeking asylum abroad.[169] The validity of

[162] UNGA, 'Statute of the Office of the United Nations High Commissioner for Refugees' (n 135).
[163] There has been significant debate on the benefits and pitfalls of UNHCR's involvement with IDPs. See Ben Hudson and Bríd Ní Ghráinne, 'Enhancing State-to-State Dialogue on Internal Displacement: Current Global Fora and Future Prospects' (2020) 39(4) Refugee Survey Quarterly 425; Richard Plender, 'The Legal Basis of International Jurisdiction to Act with Regard to the Internally Displaced' (1994) 6(3) International Journal of Refugee Law 345; Guy S Goodwin-Gill, 'Refugee Identity and Protection's Fading Prospect' in Frances Nicholson and Patrick Twomey (eds), *Refugee Rights and Realities: Evolving Concepts and Regimes* (CUP 1999) 220; Catherine Phuong, 'The Office of the United Nations High Commissioner for Refugees and Internally Displaced Persons' (2005) 24(3) Refugee Survey Quarterly 71; Guy S Goodwin-Gill, 'UNHCR and Internal Displacement: Stepping into a Legal and Political Minefield' in US Committee for Refugees (USCR) (ed), *World Refugee Survey 2000* (USCR 2000); Bradley, 'Unintended Consequences of Adjacency Claims' (n 135) 620; Bríd Ní Ghráinne, 'UNHCR's Involvement with IDPs—"Protection of that Country" for the Purposes of Precluding Application of the Refugee Convention?' (2015) 27(1) International Journal of Refugee Law 536.
[164] UNHCR, 'The Protection of Internally Displaced Persons' (n 155) [39].
[165] ibid [39].
[166] ibid [39].
[167] UNHCR, 'UNHCR's Expanded Role in Support of the Inter-Agency Response to Internal Displacement Situations' (8 June 2006) UN Doc EC/57/SC/CRP.18, 12 (hereafter UNHCR, 'UNHCR's Expanded Role in Support of the Inter-Agency Response to Internal Displacement Situations').
[168] Jennifer Hyndman, *Managing Displacement: Refugees and the Politics of Humanitarianism* (University of Minnesota Press 2000) 20.
[169] Barutciski, 'The Reinforcement of Non-Admission Policies and the Subversion of UNHCR' (n 154); UNHCR, 'UNHCR's Expanded Role in Support of the Inter-Agency Response to Internal Displacement Situations' (n 167).

these concerns is demonstrated by the increase in the last 30 years or so of state hostility towards refugees, which has been accompanied by the implementation of increasingly creative policies of deterrence such as off-shore and/or external processing of asylum-seekers, pushback policies at sea, the building of walls and fences, and the implementation of carrier sanctions.[170] It is therefore not surprising that the General Assembly has repeatedly asserted that activities on behalf of IDPs must not undermine the institution of asylum.[171] This concern is also reflected in Principle 15(c) of the Guiding Principles on Internal Displacement, which reaffirms the right of IDPs to seek asylum.[172]

Secondly, protection activities on behalf of IDPs could be seen as providing an 'Internal Protection Alternative', and thus those claiming asylum will not be recognized as refugees as lack of protection is a key criterion in order to fulfil the refugee definition.[173] Similarly, states might invoke the availability of IDP protection measures in countries of origin as a basis for deporting asylum-seekers whose claim for international protection has failed. For example, Turkey launched a cross-border operation in Northern Syria in October 2019, directed at pushing back Kurdish-led forces from the border and creating a 'safe zone'[174] for the purposes of resettling up to two million Syrian refugees.[175] Finally, protection activities on behalf of IDPs from agencies other than the UNHCR could trigger the application of Article 1D of the Refugee Convention, which would render the Refugee Convention inapplicable to those persons.[176]

[170] Ní Ghráinne, 'Safe Zones' (n 123); Bríd Ní Ghráinne, 'Left to Die at Sea: State Responsibility for the May 2015 Thai, Indonesian and Malaysian Pushback Operations' (2017) 10 Irish Yearbook of International Law 109 (hereafter Ní Ghráinne, 'Left to Die at Sea'); The Guardian, 'Denmark Passes Law to Relocate Asylum Seekers outside Europe' *The Guardian* (Copenhagen, 3 June 2021) <https://www.theguardian.com/world/2021/jun/03/denmark-passes-law-to-let-it-relocate-asylum-seekers-outside-europe> accessed 8 July 2021; Refugee Council of Australia, 'Offshore Processing' (*Refugee Council of Australia*) <https://www.refugeecouncil.org.au/offshore-processing/> accessed 8 July 2021; Patrick Kingsley, 'Migrants on Hungary's Border Fence: "This Wall, We Will Not Accept It"' *The Guardian* (22 June 2015) <https://www.theguardian.com/world/2015/jun/22/migrants-hungary-border-fence-wall-serbia> accessed 8 July 2021.

[171] UNGA Res 49/169 (23 December 1994) UN Doc A/RES/49/169; UNGA Res 50/152 (9 February 1996) UN Doc A/RES/50/152.

[172] Guiding Principles (n 2).

[173] UNHCR, 'UNHCR's Expanded Role in Support of the Inter-Agency Response to Internal Displacement Situations' (n 167).

[174] A safe zone is an area established in armed conflict for the purposes of protecting civilians—many of whom are IDPs—from attack. The idea is that those in the zone can live there safely, protected from the impacts of the conflict. Safe zones can take many forms, but often consist of areas in refugee-generating states that are protected by the military power of a foreign state or by an international organization. See Bríd Ní Ghráinne, 'The Syrian Safe Zone and International Law' (Policy Brief, Institute of International Relations Prague, 23 January 2021) <https://www.dokumenty-iir.cz/PolicyPapers/2020/SYRIAN_SAFE_ZONE_AND_INTERNATIONAL_LAW.pdf> accessed 8 July 2021 (hereafter Ní Ghráinne, 'The Syrian Safe Zone and International Law'); Ní Ghráinne, 'Safe Zones' (n 123).

[175] Ní Ghráinne, 'The Syrian Safe Zone and International Law' (n 174).

[176] UNHCR, 'UNHCR's Expanded Role in Support of the Inter-Agency Response to Internal Displacement Situations' (n 167).

In sum, there are numerous potential avenues for conflict when it comes to the protection of IDPs and refugees.

2.5 Conclusion

IDPs and refugees are similar in many ways, and there are many instances in which the protection of IDPs can complement refugee protection, and in which the protection of refugees can complement IDP protection. IDPs and refugees are also very different, particularly in light of the fact that a refugee has crossed a border whereas an IDP remains within the state. As such there are also substantial areas in which the protection of IDPs might in fact undermine or conflict with the protection of refugees.

A closer look at this latter issue is now well overdue. We have recently witnessed the highest level of displacement on record,[177] which has led to significant state hostility towards refugees,[178] and a focus on in-country protection to reduce refugee numbers. For example, states are increasingly invoking the doctrine of 'internal protection alternative', which precludes refugee status where there is a part of the refugee's country of origin where they can relocate and receive protection from persecution. In applying this concept, states have explicitly cited IDP protection measures (such as the availability of safe zones) as a basis for refusing refugee status.[179] Moreover, the urgent need for an analysis of how the protection of IDPs might conflict with refugee protection is underscored by the fact that Iran, Russia, and the USA have all considered establishing a 'safe zone' in Syria to reduce the need for IDPs to leave and seek asylum, with Turkey eventually following through with this idea.[180]

However, we do not yet know whether such actions of refugee-receiving states interpreting IDP protection measures as a substitute for asylum would actually be in breach of international law obligations. It is precisely this

[177] UNHCR, 'Figures at a Glance' (*UNHCR*) <https://www.unhcr.org/figures-at-a-glance.html> accessed 1 May 2019.

[178] Harold Honju Koh, *The Trump Administration and International Law* (OUP 2018); Shaun Walker, 'No entry: Hungary's Crackdown on Helping Refugees' *The Guardian* (Röszke, 4 June 2018) <https://www.theguardian.com/world/2018/jun/04/no-entry-hungarys-crackdown-on-helping-refugees> accessed 8 July 2021; Ní Ghráinne, 'Left to Die at Sea' (n 170); Ní Ghráinne, 'Covid-19, Border Closures, and International Law' (n 94).

[179] Katy Long, 'In Search of Sanctuary: Border Closures, "Safe Zones" and Refugee Protection' (2013) 26 Journal of Refugee Studies 458.

[180] BBC News, 'Syria War: Turkey Ready to Create "Safe Zone" for Kurds—Erdogan' *BBC News* (15 January 2019) <https://www.bbc.com/news/world-middle-east-46877308> accessed 8 July 2021; Aria Bendix, 'Safe Zones in Syria' *The Atlantic* (4 May 2017) <https://www.theatlantic.com/news/archive/2017/05/russia-iran-and-turkey-agree-on-safe-zones-in-syria/525486/> accessed 8 July 2021.

question that will be the concern of the following chapters. Chapter 3 will first provide essential background knowledge on the legal and institutional protection of IDPs, and chapters 4–6 will analyse to what extent the development and existence of this protection framework complements, conflicts with, or undermines the protection of refugees.

3
Legal and Institutional Protection of Internally Displaced Persons

3.1 Introduction

Although the total number of Internally Displaced Persons (IDPs) worldwide stands at 55 million,[1] it is only relatively recently that the issue of internal displacement has attracted international concern. Compared to other legal and institutional frameworks such as that of refugees, the IDP protection framework is still in its relative infancy. This chapter will explain the development of the current IDP protection framework. It identifies three key stages in this respect, which correspond with the chapter's structure: (i) the era of 'preventive protection' in the 1990s and early 2000s; (ii) the development of a distinct IDP legal framework from the 1990s onwards; (iii) the parallel development of an IDP institutional framework from the 1990s onwards. The chapter will argue that, despite these significant strides, the issue of refugee protection continues to dominate the international agenda, to the detriment of the IDP protection framework. Specifically, it is clear that the development of the IDP protection framework was significantly motivated by the desire to reduce refugee flows, and that the IDP legal and institutional framework is significantly weaker than that for refugees. Specific aspects of the IDP protection framework and how they relate to the refugee protection framework will be examined in subsequent chapters.

3.2 The Era of 'Preventive Protection'

As mentioned in chapter 2, the *travaux préparatoires* of the Refugee Convention illustrate that its drafters were not concerned with the provision of protection to those within their country of origin.[2] IDPs became of particular

[1] Internal Displacement Monitoring Centre, *Internal Displacement Index 2020 Report* (2020) 6.
[2] The *travaux préparatoires* indicate that a proposal to include IDPs in the refugee definition was rejected on the basis that the delegates viewed the existence of sufficient national protection as inconsistent

Internally Displaced Persons and International Refugee Law. Bríd Ní Ghráinne, Oxford University Press. © Ní Ghráinne 2022.
DOI: 10.1093/oso/9780198868446.003.0003

concern to the international community at a much later stage than refugees did. Sudan's internal displacement problem in 1972 was among the first to appear on the international agenda, when the Economic and Social Council requested that the UNHCR coordinate humanitarian assistance required for, inter alia, 'persons displaced within the country'.[3] This was followed over a decade later by Thailand's proposal that a study should be undertaken on the possible establishment of safety zones for refugees or IDPs as a way of lessening the refugee burden on the international community.[4] However, the IDP issue gained significant momentum in the post-Cold War era, when the recognition of refugees was no longer seen as a strategic political act which would highlight the failure of the country of origin to protect its nationals.[5] Chimni identifies this ideological shift as taking place in two overlapping stages.[6] First, the language of protection was replaced with the reality of restriction. In this sense, states employed creative means by which to limit entry of refugees onto their territory such as visa restrictions, pushback operations, walls, carrier sanctions, and engaging in restrictive interpretations of the Refugee Convention. Such restrictive measures are still in operation today.[7] Secondly, a new vocabulary entered refugee discourse, comprising terms such as 'refugee crisis',[8] 'preventive protection',[9] 'the right to remain',[10] 'buffer

with the concept of a refugee. See James C Hathaway, *The Law of Refugee Status* (Butterworths 1991) 29–31; *SZATV v Minister for Immigration and Citizenship* [2007] HCA 40 [49].

[3] UN Economic and Social Council Res 1705 (LIII) (27 July 1972) UN Doc E/RES/1705(LIII). See also UN Economic and Social Council Res 1655 (LII) (1 June 1972) UN Doc E/RES/1605(LII).

[4] BS Chimni, 'Incarceration of Victims: Deconstruction Safety Zones' in Najeeb Al-Nauimi and Richard Meese (eds), *International Legal Issues Arising under the United Nations Decade of International Law: Proceedings of the Qatar International Law Conference '94* (Martinus Nijhoff 1995) 852 (hereafter Chimni, 'Incarceration of Victims: Deconstruction Safety Zones').

[5] Bill Frelick, 'Preventing Refugee Flows: Protection or Peril' in *World Refugee Survey 1993* (US Committee for Refugees 1993) 5 (hereafter Frelick, 'Preventing Refugee Flows'); Chimni, 'Incarceration of Victims: Deconstruction Safety Zones' (n 4).

[6] Chimni, 'Incarceration of Victims: Deconstruction Safety Zones' (n 4).

[7] BBC News, 'Syrians Entering Lebanon Face New Restrictions' *BBC News* (Lebanon, 5 January 2015) https://www.bbc.com/news/world-middle-east-30657003 accessed 24 June 2021; Nick Thorpe, 'Hungary Deploys Army to Push Migrants Back to Syria' *BBC News* (Hungary, 14 July 2016) https://www.bbc.com/news/world-europe-36786438 accessed 29 June 2021; Bethan McKernan, 'Greece Extends Wall on Turkish Border as Refugee Row Deepens' *The Guardian* (Istanbul, 20 October 2020) https://www.theguardian.com/world/2020/oct/20/greece-extends-wall-on-turkish-border-as-refugee-row-deepens accessed 24 June 2021; BBC News, 'Denmark Asylum: Law Passed to Allow Offshore Asylum Centres' *BBC News* (3 June 2021) https://www.bbc.com/news/world-europe-57343572 accessed 5 July 2021.

[8] Alexander Peukert and others, 'To Allow or Refuse Entry: What Does the Law Demand in the Refugee Crisis at Europe's Internal State Borders?' (2017) 18(3) German Law Journal 618.

[9] Bill Frelick, 'Preventive Protection' and the Right to Seek Asylum: A Preliminary Look at Bosnia and Croatia' (1992) 4 International Journal of Refugee Law 439.

[10] James C Hathaway, 'Forced Migration Studies: Could We Agree Just to Date?' (2007) 20 Journal of Refugee Studies 349, 356.

zones',[11] 'relief corridors',[12] and 'safe zones'.[13] Attention thus turned to policies of containment with the goal of minimizing refugee outflows.

It was during this post-Cold War era that the UNHCR began to become involved with IDPs for the first time. This shift in momentum towards 'preventive protection' in the 1990s gave rise to a dilemma for the UNHCR—should it resist the concept of 'preventive protection' owing to the potential conflict with the right to leave and seek asylum, or should it take a functionalist approach, working with the policy set forth by states, who are the primary funders of the UNHCR and thus often designate the use and location of their donations?[14] The UNHCR ultimately opted for the latter approach, and originally defined preventive protection as:

> [t]he establishment or undertaking of specific activities inside the country of origin so that people no longer feel compelled to cross borders in search of protection and assistance, which may also include the establishment of safety zones or safe areas inside the country of origin where protection may be sought.[15]

Preventive protection may, as its name suggests, contribute to protecting IDPs in two respects. First, it ameliorates the conditions that force persons to flee their countries of origin in the first place. Second, it assists those who are unable or who have no desire to cross a border for the purposes of claiming international protection as a refugee. Nonetheless, the concept of 'preventive protection' is likely to be at least as much about states' interests in containing refugees as it is about assisting IDPs.[16] In the words of Long:

[11] Jonathan Zaragoza-Cristiani, 'Containing the Refugee Crisis: How the EU Turned the Balkans and Turkey into an EU Borderland' (2017) 52(4) Italian Journal of International Affairs 59; Erin Cunningham, 'US, Turkey Aim to Create Buffer Zone on Syrian Border. Nobody Knows How' *The Washington Post* (Istanbul, 13 August 2015) <https://www.washingtonpost.com/world/middle_east/us-said-it-will-create-a-safe-zone-on-syrian-border-but-nobody-knows-how/2015/08/12/4c7d0baa-37e4-11e5-ab7b-6416d97c73c2_story.html> accessed 24 June 2021.

[12] Geoff Gilbert and Anna Magdalena Rüsch, 'Creating Safe Zones and Safe Corridors in Conflict Situations: Providing Protection at Home or Preventing the Search for Asylum?' (Kaldor Centre for International Refugee Law, June 2017) https://www.kaldorcentre.unsw.edu.au/sites/kaldorcentre.unsw.edu.au/files/Policy_brief_Creating_safe_zones_and_safe_corridors.pdf accessed 24 June 2021.

[13] Bríd Ní Ghráinne, 'Safe Zones and the Internal Protection Alternative' (2020) 69(2) International and Comparative Law Quarterly 335.

[14] Erin Mooney in Frances Nicholson and Patrick M Twomey, *Refugee Rights and Realities: Evolving International Concepts and Regimes* (CUP 1999) 30; Jennifer Hyndman, *Managing Displacement: Refugees and the Politics of Humanitarianism* (University of Minnesota Press 2000) 19 (hereafter Hyndman, *Managing Displacement: Refugees and the Politics of Humanitarianism*).

[15] UNHCR, 'Report of the UNHCR Working Group on International Protection' (6 July 1992) 17–18.

[16] Hyndman, *Managing Displacement: Refugees and the Politics of Humanitarianism* (n 14) 27.

> the growth in the interest in IDP protection … [is] directly connected with the reality of border closure, and states' interests in circumventing rather than openly challenging the effect of such closures on refugees' rights to asylum and international protection.[17]

The following sub-sections will illustrate, by way of examples, how the concept of 'preventive protection' was implemented in practice. The examples are chosen to represent a wide diversity of circumstances, including geographical location, the perceived success of the operation in terms of lives saved, the intervening actor (eg states or international organizations), context (eg international or non-international armed conflict), legal basis for intervention (eg some were authorized by the UN Security Council (UNSC), some by the territorial state, some had neither UNSC nor territorial state authorization), and timespan (the examples range from 1990 to 2000). As will become apparent, although the circumstances under which preventive protection was implemented differed widely, all the below examples have two factors in common: the intervention was (at least partly) driven by humanitarian reasons and (at least partly) motivated by the desire to reduce and/or contain refugee flows.

3.2.1 Sri Lanka, 1990

The Eelam War is the name given to the second phase of armed conflict between the Sri Lankan Military and the separatist Liberation Tigers of Tamil Eelam (LTTE). This conflict began in 1990, after India had withdrawn from Sri Lanka and from peace talks between the government and the LTTE.[18] When the conflict began, UNHCR had almost completed a returnee operation in Sri Lanka. India was unwilling to host the refugees,[19] and the UNHCR was thus faced with the choice of abandoning those receiving reintegration assistance or looking after them in Sri Lanka and, in doing so, reducing the need for IDPs in Sri Lanka to leave and seek asylum abroad.[20] In November 1990, Open Relief Centres (ORCs) in Sri Lanka were established, which were 'temporary place[s]

[17] UNHCR Policy Development and Evaluation Service and Division of Operational Services, Katy Long, 'No Entry! A Review of UNHCR's Response to Border Closures in Situations of Mass Refugee Influx' (June 2010) UN Doc PDES/2010/07 [134] (hereafter Long, 'No Entry!').

[18] 'UNHCR's Operational Experience with Internally Displaced Persons', Office of the United Nations High Commissioner for Refugees, Division of International Protection, September 1994.

[19] CM Tiso, 'Safe Haven Refugee Programs: A Method of Combating International Refugee Crises' (1994) 8 Georgetown Immigration Law Journal 575 (hereafter Tiso, 'Safe Haven Refugee Programs').

[20] WD Clarance, 'Open Relief Centres: A Pragmatic Approach to Emergency Relief and Monitoring during Conflict in a Country of Origin' (1991) 3 International Journal of Refugee Law 320.

where displaced persons on the move can freely enter or leave and obtain essential relief assistance in a relatively safe environment'.[21] They had four main aims: (i) to prolong UNHCR's presence in the area in order to monitor developments regarding returnees; (ii) to assist returnees and IDPs by providing adequate water and food supplies, temporary shelter, and healthcare services;[22] (iii) to assist returnees and IDPs who may otherwise feel compelled to leave; and (iv) to promote conditions for voluntary repatriation.[23] The ORCs were seen as a test case for establishing the extent to which the international community would be prepared to see UNHCR undertake activities in a country of origin which would reduce the push factors of refugee outflows.[24]

The majority of studies on the ORCs have reported that they operated relatively safely, despite occasional evictions and security incidents.[25] By February 1991, more than 50,000 Sri Lankans were residing in the ORCs, and two months later, an average of 700–800 former refugees every 10 days were returning to Sri Lanka and seeking assistance from the programme.[26] In addition, Tamils were not debarred from seeking asylum outside the country because of the existence of the safe areas.[27] ORCs also enabled people who were living in nearby areas to temporarily seek refuge in the ORCs when threatened. Other IDPs resided on a more permanent basis while leaving only for short periods to check on their property and cultivate their land.[28] Tiso praises the ORCs highly, stating that 'the United Nations should build on the Sri Lankan experience as the operation has established many valuable precedents that the

[21] ibid.

[22] ibid.

[23] US Committee for Refugees, *Sri Lanka, Island of Refugees* (October 1991) 23 as cited in Chimni, 'Incarceration of Victims: Deconstruction Safety Zones' (n 4).

[24] Chimni, 'Incarceration of Victims: Deconstruction Safety Zones' (n 4) 846.

[25] Karin Landgren, 'Safety Zones and International Protection: A Dark Grey Area' (1995) 7 International Journal of Refugee Law 436 (hereafter Landgren, 'Safety Zones and International Protection'); Tiso, 'Safe Haven Refugee Programs' (n 19); Chimni, 'Incarceration of Victims: Deconstruction Safety Zones' (n 4); 'UNHCR's Operational Experience with Internally Displaced Persons', Office of the United Nations High Commissioner for Refugees, Division of International Protection, September 1994; Commission on Human Rights, 'Report of the Representative of the Secretary-General, Mr. Francis M. Deng, submitted pursuant to Commission on Human Rights resolutions 1993/95 and 1994/68' (2 February 1995) UN Doc E/CN.4/1995/50; UNHCR, 'Report of the United Nations High Commissioner for Refugees' (6 October 1993) UN Doc A/48/12.

[26] Tiso, 'Safe Haven Refugee Programs' (n 19).

[27] Chimni, 'Incarceration of Victims: Deconstruction Safety Zones' (n 4); Frelick, 'Preventing Refugee Flows' (n 5). Although the concept of the Internal Protection Alternative (IPA) was well-established in Australian jurisprudence at the time, Australian courts did not consider that the ORCs constituted an IPA. See *V94/01232 [1994] RRTA 324* (3 March 1994) (Australian Refugee Review Tribunal); *V93/00078 [1994] RRTA 606* (11 April 1994) (Australian Refugee Review Tribunal); *V94/02151 [1994] RRTA 2379* (4 November 1994) (Australian Refugee Review Tribunal). The IPA is analysed in detail in chapter 4.

[28] Tiso, 'Safe Haven Refugee Programs' (n 19).

United Nations should follow in future crisis situations'.[29] The British Refugee Council referred to the Madhu ORC as 'a genuine place of safety in the North, after attacks by both sides on other areas holding high concentrations of displaced people'.[30] However, Arulanantham and the Immigration and Refugee Board of Canada reported that many Tamil refugees fled the ORCs because the Sri Lankan government had seized individuals from within the camps, many of whom were tortured or never returned.[31]

3.2.2 Iraq, 1991

Saddam Hussein's belligerent actions in the late 1980s and early 1990s created significant fear among the Kurdish population in Iraq, especially after he launched a chemical attack on the Kurdish town of Halabjah in 1988.[32] Following encouragement from US President George W Bush, Kurdish rebels attempted to overthrow the government in 1991.[33] The rebellion failed and thousands fled out of fear of reprisals from Iraq.[34] Turkey quickly closed its borders because it viewed the Kurdish refugees as a political problem.[35] It relied on its geographic limitation to the 1951 Refugee Convention, arguing that it was only obliged to accept as refugees those having a well-founded fear of persecution as a result of events occurring in Europe.[36] At that time, there were more than 200,000 Kurdish IDPs trapped in the mountains at the Turkey–Iraq border, living in dire conditions.[37]

[29] ibid.

[30] Jennifer Hyndman, 'Preventive, Palliative, or Punitive? Safe Spaces in Bosnia-Herzegovina, Somalia, and Sri Lanka' (2003) 16 Journal of Refugee Studies 167, 168 (hereafter Hyndman, 'Preventive, Palliative, or Punitive?').

[31] Ahilan T Arulanantham, 'Restructured Safe Havens: A Proposal for Reform of the Refugee Protection System' (2000) 22(1) Human Rights Quarterly 1 (hereafter Arulanantham, 'Restructured Safe Havens'); Chimni, 'Incarceration of Victims: Deconstruction Safety Zones' (n 4) 847; Immigration and Refugee Board of Canada, 'Sri Lanka: Internal Flight Alternatives' (*Refworld*, 1 December 1992) https://www.refworld.org/docid/3ae6a83bc.html accessed 6 July 2021.

[32] Thomas E Ricks, 'Operation Provide Comfort: A Forgotten Mission with Possible Lessons for Syria' (*Foreign Policy*, 6 February 2017) https://foreignpolicy.com/2017/02/06/operation-provide-comfort-a-forgotten-mission-with-possible-lessons-for-syria/ accessed 6 July 2021.

[33] David E Clary, 'Operation Provide Comfort: A Strategic Analysis' (Thesis, Air War College, Air University 1994).

[34] Hikaru Yamashita, *Humanitarian Spaces and International Politics: The Creation of Safe Areas* (Ashgate 2004) (hereafter Yamashita, *Humanitarian Spaces and International Politics*).

[35] Long, 'No Entry!' (n 17) [101].

[36] Katy Long, 'In Search of Sanctuary: Border Closures, "Safe Zones" and Refugee Protection' (2013) 26 Journal of Refugee Studies 458, 476.

[37] Long, 'No Entry!' (n 17) [107].

Although UNHCR initially tried to persuade Turkey to open its borders,[38] the strategic importance of the Turkish border to the United States, United Kingdom, and France meant that these states were reluctant to condemn the Turkish border closure.[39] Notwithstanding the fact that Security Council Resolution 688 reaffirmed the 'sovereignty, territorial integrity, and political independence of Iraq and of all states in the area', the United States, United Kingdom, and France interpreted the resolution's reference to the 'massive flow of refugees towards and across international frontiers' as justifying the creation of a safe zone for Kurds in Iraq without Iraqi consent, which they termed 'Operation Provide Comfort'.[40] The operation was aimed at being short term because the leaders were unanimous from the start in their intention to hand over the operation to the UN as soon as possible.[41] Six camps were set up in April 1991, each to shelter between 60,000 and 65,000 people.[42] A no-fly zone (NFZ) was also set up to prevent further attacks on the displaced persons.[43] On 18 April 1991, Prince Sadruddin Aga Khan—the personal representative of the United Nations Secretary-General for Humanitarian Assistance Related to the Iraq–Kuwait Crisis—signed a memorandum of understanding with the Iraqi government allowing for the establishment of UN humanitarian centres within the country.[44] Towards the end of April, attention turned to the prospect for a mass 'voluntary' repatriation of Kurds from border areas, and UNHCR agreed to participate in the operation as a 'reluctant but pragmatic partner'.[45] The allied haven doubled its size and the UN subsequently took over the administra tion of the camps.[46]

The establishment the safe zone in Iraq has been criticized as legitimizing Turkey's decision to close its border and fundamentally compromising UNHCR's ability to insist upon the need for Turkey to grant asylum to Iraqi

[38] ibid [108].
[39] ibid (n 17) [109].
[40] UNSC Res 688 (5 April 1991) UN Doc S/RES/688; The US, UK, and France interpreted Security Council Resolution 688's reference to the 'massive flow of refugees towards and across international frontiers' as justifying the creation of a safe zone for Kurds in Iraq without Iraqi consent. This chapter argues that this was a misinterpretation of the resolution because (i) the resolution reaffirmed the 'sovereignty, territorial integrity, and political independence of Iraq' and (ii) UNSC resolutions authorizing the use of force usually do so explicitly. See UNSC Res 688 (5 April 1991), UN Doc S/RES/688.
[41] Yamashita, *Humanitarian Spaces and International Politics* (n 34).
[42] ibid.
[43] 'Moments in US Diplomatic History: Iraqi Kurds, Operation Provide Comfort, and the Birth of Iraq's Opposition' (Association for Diplomatic Studies and Training, 10 February 2016) https://adst.org/2016/02/iraqi-kurds-operation-provide-comfort-and-the-birth-of-iraqs-opposition/ accessed 6 July 2021.
[44] Long, 'No Entry!' (n 17) [115].
[45] ibid [120].
[46] As cited in Yamashita, *Humanitarian Spaces and International Politics* (n 34).

refugees.[47] Frelick notes that many Kurdish asylum claims were rejected on the basis of the existence of 'relatively safe areas' without sufficient enquiry as to whether the safe zone was *actually* safe.[48] Long also questions whether the establishment of the safe zone might have compromised the rights of IDPs to leave their own country and seek asylum.[49] The conformity of the operation with the UN Charter has also been questioned.[50] Having said this, the establishment of safe zones in Iraq has been described as the most successful of the security experiments that took place in the 1990s, as within six weeks of creation, the majority of IDPs had been able to leave the mountains and return to areas where it was easier to provide humanitarian relief.[51] Goodwin-Gill and McAdam cautiously leave open the possibility that returning an asylum-seeker to these camps may have been compatible with the 1951 Refugee Convention.[52]

It should be noted, however, that invoking this example as a precedent for the creation of future preventive protection measures should be done with caution. This is because the conditions for such an operation were particularly suitable in Iraq at that time. Iraqi military forces were badly damaged following the Gulf War, and because they would have had to cross much open country to attack the Kurds, they were vulnerable to air attack from the allied forces.[53] The Kurds themselves had strong fighting abilities, and it was clear that the US had an incentive to protect the Kurds so as not to take away from the Desert Storm victory.[54] In short, the conditions were unusually favourable to the preventive protection strategy.

3.2.3 Bosnia, 1992

As the former Yugoslavia began to disintegrate, the Republic of Bosnia and Herzegovina declared independence.[55] At that time, mainly Catholic Croats,

[47] Long, 'No Entry!' (n 17) [128].

[48] Frelick, 'Preventing Refugee Flows' (n 5).

[49] Long, 'No Entry!' (n 17) [122]; Phil Orchard, *Protecting the Internally Displaced: Rhetoric and Reality* (Routledge 2019) 123 (hereafter Orchard, *Protecting the Internally Displaced).*

[50] Chimni, 'Incarceration of Victims: Deconstruction Safety Zones' (n 4) 830.

[51] Hyndman, 'Preventive, Palliative, or Punitive?' (n 30); Long, 'No Entry!' (n 17) [130]; Yves Sandoz, 'Safety Zones for Internally Displaced Persons' in Najeeb Al-Nauimi and Richard Meese (eds), *International Legal Issues Arising under the United Nations Decade of International Law: Proceedings of the Qatar International Law Conference '94* (Martinus Nijhoff 1995) 917.

[52] Guy S Goodwin-Gill and Jane McAdam, *The Refugee in International Law* (OUP 2011) 219 (hereafter Goodwin-Gill and McAdam, *The Refugee in International Law*).

[53] Barry R Posen, 'Military Responses to Refugee Disasters' (1996) 21(1) International Security 72.

[54] Desert Storm was a 1991 bombing campaign that forced Iraq to end its occupation of Kuwait. See editors of Encyclopaedia Britannica, *25th Anniversary of Operation Desert Storm* (Encyclopaedia Britannica).

[55] 'Bosnia and Herzegovina' (*Nations Online*) https://www.nationsonline.org/oneworld/bosnia_herzegovina.htm accessed 6 July 2021;

Muslim Bosniaks, and Orthodox Serbs lived in the territory.[56] Bosnian Serbs objected to this declaration of independence. Supported by the Serbian government of Slobodan Milošević and the Yugoslav People's army, Serb forces attacked the newly declared Republic of Bosnia and Herzegovina. This was followed by a fierce struggle for territorial control, along with the ethnic cleansing of the non-Serb population from areas under Serb control; in particular, the Bosniak population of Eastern Bosnia, near the border with Serbia.[57]

By 1992, European states were firmly implementing non-admission policies vis-à-vis refugees from Bosnia.[58] In July 1992, a German call on governments to pledge to accept quotas of refugees was met with little support.[59] However, many states supported calls from Austria, the Netherlands, and Slovenia to establish safe zones in Bosnia.[60] The International Committee of the Red Cross stated that:

> As no third country seems to be ready, even on a provisional basis, to grant asylum to one hundred thousand Bosnian refugees … an original concept must be devised to create protected zones … which are equal to the particular requirements and the sheer scale of the problem.[61]

Thus 'safe areas' for IDPs were established primarily as an alternative for asylum,[62] which was explicitly acknowledged by states,[63] and many asylum

[56] Tony Barber, 'The Bosnia Crisis: Serbs, Croats and Muslims: Who Hates Who and Why: Tony Barber in Zagreb Traces the Ancient Roots of a Culture Clash that has Shattered what was Yugoslavia into Warring Pieces' *The Independent* (9 August 1992) https://www.independent.co.uk/news/world/the-bosnia-crisis-serbs-croats-and-muslims-who-hates-who-and-why-tony-barber-in-zagreb-traces-the-1539305.html accessed 6 July 2021.

[57] JR Lampe, *Bosnian War* (Encyclopedia Britannica).

[58] Mikhael Barutciski, 'The Reinforcement of Non-Admission Policies and the Subversion of UNHCR: Displacement and Internal Assistance in Bosnia-Herzegovina (1992–94)' (1996) 8 International Journal of Refugee Law 49 (hereafter Barutciski, 'The Reinforcement of Non-Admission Policies and the Subversion of UNHCR'); Nils Coleman, 'Non-Refoulement Revised Renewed Review of the Status of the Principle of Non-Refoulement as Customary International Law' (2003) 5(1) European Journal of Migration and Law 23.

[59] Frelick, 'Preventing Refugee Flows' (n 5).

[60] ibid, 9; Chimni, 'Incarceration of Victims: Deconstruction Safety Zones' (n 4) 839.

[61] ICRC, 'ICRC Position Paper: The Establishment of Protected Zones for Endangered Citizens in Bosnia and Herzegovina' (30 October 1992) https://casebook.icrc.org/case-study/bosnia-and-herzegovina-constitution-safe-areas accessed 6 July 2021.

[62] Leonardo Franco, 'An Examination of Safety Zones for Internally Displaced Persons as a Contribution toward Prevention and Solution of Refugee Problems' in Najeeb Al-Nauimi and Richard Meese (eds), *International Legal Issues Arising under the United Nations Decade of International Law: Proceedings of the Qatar International Law Conference '94* (Martinus Nijhoff 1995); Landgren, 'Safety Zones and International Protection' (n 25).

[63] Frelick notes that preventing refugee flows was also in Croatia's interest, because if everyone left Bosnia, who would fight the enemy? See Frelick, 'Preventing Refugee Flows' (n 5).

claims were refused on the grounds that 'safe areas' were available in Bosnia.[64] The United States suggested that assistance, even in the absence of adequate protection, could contribute to the goal of preventing the next wave of refugees.[65] Many states justified their refusal to accept refugees on the grounds that they would be contributing to ethnic cleansing, and also relied upon the 'right to remain' of those displaced by conflict.[66]

In two resolutions, the Security Council declared Srebrenica, Sarajevo, Bihać, Tuzla, Zeba, and Goražde as safe areas.[67] Although the Security Council acted under Chapter VII, no enforcement measures were clearly provided for. In addition, out of the 34,000 troops demanded by UNPROFOR, only 7,600 were provided.[68] Furthermore, the zones were not demilitarized, and the Bosnian army used them as training grounds and for launching attacks.[69] The Bosnian Serbs therefore perceived the safe areas as helping Bosnian forces to maintain territory.[70] Although the safe areas did save the lives of many IDPs, they have been perceived by many as a failure. Two safe havens fell to the Serbs, and Bosnian Serb forces entered Srebrenica in July 1995, following which more than 7,000 Muslims were killed.[71]

3.2.4 Somalia, 1992

During the Somali civil war in the early 1990s, Kenya became more hostile to Somali refugees as it feared infiltration by Somali militants.[72] The Security Council passed Resolution 794, which authorized a Unified Task Force of peacekeeping troops to undertake 'Operation Restore Hope'.[73] This entailed the creation of a preventive zone for IDPs within Somalia along the Kenyan border in order to slow the flow of potential refugees into Kenya and to encourage

[64] For example, German asylum adjudicators granted 59 asylum requests from Bosnians and denied 1,913. See ibid, 9; Barutciski, 'The Reinforcement of Non-Admission Policies and the Subversion of UNHCR (n 58); Arulanantham, 'Restructured Safe Havens' (n 31).

[65] Frelick, 'Preventing Refugee Flows' (n 5) 9.

[66] ibid; Landgren, 'Safety Zones and International Protection' (n 25).

[67] UNSC Res 819 (16 April 1993) UN Doc S/RES/819; UNSC Res 824 (6 May 1993) UN Doc S/RES/824.

[68] UNSC, 'Report of the Secretary-General pursuant to Security Council Resolution 959' (1994) UN Doc S/1994/1389.

[69] Sophie Haspeslagh, 'The Bosnian "Safe Havens"' (*Beyond Intractability*) https://www.beyondintractability.org/cic_documents/Safe-Havens-Bosnia.pdf accessed 6 July 2021, 2.

[70] ibid, 2.

[71] Jeffrey R Smith, *Srebrenica Massacre* (Encyclopedia Britannica 2014).

[72] Hyndman, 'Preventive, Palliative, or Punitive?' (n 30) 178.

[73] UNSC Res 794 (3 December 1992) UN Doc S/RES/794.

Somali refugees in Kenyan camps to return home.[74] The UNHCR stressed that 'prevention is not ... a substitute for asylum; the right to enjoy asylum, therefore, must continue to be upheld',[75] and Long stated that in-country protection was an entirely impracticable approach for a country such as Somalia in the midst of civil war.[76] Although some 12,000 Somali refugees had returned by June 1993 with the help of the UNHCR, the vast majority Guiding Principles are based on Kenyan camps.[77] By mid-1995 the programme had ended, with the majority of refugees remaining in Kenya.[78]

3.2.5 Rwanda, 1994

Between April and July 1994, an estimated 800,000 people were massacred in Rwanda.[79] Most of the victims were members of the Tutsi ethnic group. The massacre was instigated by Hutu extremists who took control of the Rwandan government and armed forces, and it has subsequently been widely recognized as a genocide.[80] The international community was slow to respond, and the Security Council eventually authorized the strengthening of a peacekeeping force—United Nations Assistance Mission in Rwanda (UNAMIR)—that was already present in Rwanda.[81] On 17 May 1994, Resolution 918 authorized the expansion of UNAMIR, which consisted of 5,500 troops, and renamed it UNAMIR II.

The French government later decided to launch a military operation in Rwanda in order to maintain a humanitarian presence there pending the arrival of UNAMIR II.[82] This was authorized by the UNSC in Resolution 929 on 22 June 1994, after it noted that the situation in Rwanda constituted a 'threat to international peace and security'.[83] The resolution welcomed the offer by France to work with the Secretary-General in establishing:

[74] ibid [10].
[75] UNHCR, 'EXCOM Note on International Protection' (25 August 1992) UN Doc A/AC.96/799, [26].
[76] Long, 'No Entry!' (n 17) [339].
[77] Hyndman, 'Preventive, Palliative, or Punitive?' (n 30) 178.
[78] ibid 179.
[79] BBC News, 'Rwanda Genocide: 100 Days of Slaughter' *BBC News* (4 January 2019) https://www.bbc.com/news/world-africa-26875506 accessed 6 July 2021.
[80] *Prosecutor v Nyiramasuhuko et al* (Judgment) ICTR-98-42-A (14 December 2015).
[81] UNSC Res 912 (21 April 1994) UN Doc S/RES/912.
[82] Carol McQueen, *Humanitarian Intervention and Safety Zones* (Palgrave 2005) (hereafter McQueen, *Humanitarian Intervention and Safety Zones*).
[83] UNSC Res 929 (22 June 1994) UN Doc S/RES/929.

> a temporary operation under national command and control aimed at contributing, in an impartial way, to the security and protection of displaced persons, refugees and civilians at risk in Rwanda, on the understanding that the costs of implementing the offer will be borne by the Member States concerned.[84]

France decided to use its mandate under Resolution 929 to create a *zone humanitaire sûre* (ZHS). The ZHS spanned one-fifth of south-western Rwanda and was maintained until the French left Rwanda as scheduled on 22 August 1994.[85] The ZHS was reported to have saved 13,000–15,000 Tutsi lives, mainly by protecting Tutsis in camps surrounded by hostile gendarmerie; and the general improvement in security in the south-west enabled a significant increase in humanitarian assistance.[86] It has also been credited as stemming the flow of refugees to Zaire, and thus saving many lives, given the conditions prevailing there.[87]

However, the operation has received significant criticism. Most of the Tutsis hiding in the bush were killed and the ZHS provided refuge to members of militias and the Rwandan interim government, which they failed to disarm.[88] In addition, the ZHS policy greatly eroded the Rwandan right to flee, as while thousands of IDPs were being killed in Kibeho IDP camp, France blocked the application of Rwandan's asylum demands on the grounds that they were being protected inside their own country.[89]

3.2.6 Afghanistan, 2000

During the Afghan civil war in the early 1990s, Pakistan's borders remained open to receive Afghan refugees. However, in the mid-1990s the World Food Programme and UNHCR ended food aid to refugee camps, resulting in mass migration to Pakistani cities and Pakistan's 2000 decision to close its border with Afghanistan in November.[90] According to the Pakistani government, assistance to refugees was creating a 'pull factor' that was attracting Afghan

[84] ibid.

[85] McQueen, *Humanitarian Intervention and Safety Zones* (n 82).

[86] ibid; Landgren, 'Safety Zones and International Protection' (n 25) 449.

[87] Chimni, 'Incarceration of Victims: Deconstruction Safety Zones' (n 4) 850.

[88] McQueen, *Humanitarian Intervention and Safety Zones* (n 82).

[89] James C Hathaway and R Alexander Neve, 'Making International Refugee Law Relevant Again: A Proposal for Collectivized and Solution-Oriented Protection' (1997) 10 Harvard Human Rights Journal 115, 136–37.

[90] Long, 'No Entry!' (n 17) [267].

refugees, worsening the situation within Pakistan.[91] Pakistan demanded that the international community increase its assistance and establish IDP camps within Afghanistan itself, arguing that Pakistan would only begin to accept refugees when it did so.[92] According to a joint NGO statement in 2001, NGOs started preparing for an IDP rather than a refugee crisis:

> Above all we want to prevent, if humanely possible, the population of Afghanistan becoming refugees by addressing their needs inside the country ... we are seriously concerned that the most immediate problem—the needs of the people inside Afghanistan—is not being adequately addressed ... It must be remembered that these potential refugees are currently trapped inside a closed country. All borders are closed and will probably remain so until the start of the conflict ... if they flee to Afghanistan's borders, our distribution systems will be seriously disrupted.[93]

Other states were also keen to encourage the establishment of IDP camps. Iran repeatedly stated that it believed the Afghan refugee population should be cared for in camps in Afghanistan and the Iranian Red Crescent Society established two camps on Afghan territory.[94] Although the border closure was not particularly effective (it was porous and guards were easily bribed), it signalled Pakistan's hostility towards Afghan refugees.[95] This stance continued throughout the displacement crisis that followed the start of US military action in Afghanistan post 9/11.[96]

3.2.7 Assessment of the Era of 'Preventive Protection'

Many of the examples of preventive protection outlined above—such as Iraq in 1991 and Sri Lanka in 1990—had positive humanitarian effects. For example, these operations probably ameliorated in some respect the suffering of those

[91] Daniel Langenkamp, 'The Victory of Expediency: Afghan Refugees and Pakistan in the 1990s' (2003) 27 The Fletcher Forum of World Affairs 229, 241.
[92] ibid 241.
[93] 'Working to Solve the Crisis in Afghanistan: A Statement by NGOs' (*Reliefweb*, 5 October 2001) https://reliefweb.int/report/afghanistan/working-solve-crisis-afghanistan-statement-ngos accessed 6 July 2021. NGOs represented: ACTED, ActionAid Pakistan, Action Contre la Faim, Aide Medicale Internationale, CARE International, Concern, DACAAR, Global Relief Foundation, Madera, MEDAIR, Mercy Corps, Ockenden International, Oxfam, SGAA, Save the Children US, Solidarites, Tearfund Ireland, Tearfund UK.
[94] Long, 'No Entry!' (n 17) [292].
[95] ibid [269].
[96] ibid [276].

remaining within a country's borders and/or proved a relatively safe place for refugees to return to. However, many of the so-called 'safe' areas established in the 1990s and early 2000s were anything but safe and were in fact targets of attack, such as in Bosnia and in Rwanda.

It is also clear that underlying all these operations was the deep desire of states to reduce the number of individuals claiming asylum on their territories. Although the establishment of 'safe zones' or 'safe havens' such as the examples outlined above became less and less common from the mid-2000s onwards, this practice was thrown back into the spotlight in October 2019 when Turkey established a safe zone in Syria. Once again, it was clear that this practice was motivated by the desire to decrease refugee flows, as this was explicitly stated by Turkey in its justification for the operation.[97] Once again, reports about the conditions in the safe zone indicate that they are not in any way safe.[98]

The era of 'preventive protection' and these high-profile operations did have one very positive outcome, even if for somewhat questionable reasons: the plight of IDPs was very firmly put on the international agenda. From the mid-1990s onwards, the international community's attention turned to the development of specific legal and institutional frameworks for the protection of IDPs. It is to these frameworks that the chapter now turns.

3.3 Development of a Legal Framework for Internally Displaced Persons

From the 1990s onwards, there was a gradual recognition that IDPs were no longer solely the concern of their own governments. Scholars, courts, and treaty monitoring bodies began to highlight provisions from various branches of public international law such as international human rights law, international criminal law, and humanitarian law that were particularly applicable in the displacement context.[99] IDP-specific soft law instruments were concluded, and two IDP-specific treaties were concluded in the African region. The following section will address each of these developments in turn.

[97] Bríd Ní Ghráinne, 'The Syrian Safe Zone and International Law' (*Institute of International Relations Prague*, 31 January 2020) https://www.iir.cz/brid-ni-ghrainne-the-syrian-safe-zone-and-international-law accessed 6 July 2021.

[98] ibid.

[99] Joan Fitzpatrick, 'Human Rights and Forced Displacement: Converging Standards' in Anne F Bayefsky and Joan Fitzpatrick (eds), *Human Rights and Forced Displacement* (Martinus Nijhoff 2000) 3; Walter Kälin, 'The Role of the Guiding Principles on Internal Displacement' [2005] Forced Migration Review 8, 8.

3.3.1 Relevant Branches of Public International Law

Public international law is divided into branches—such as humanitarian law, human rights law, and criminal law—each of which applies in specific contexts.[100] The key instruments of these branches of public international law existed long before the topic of IDPs was put on the international agenda, yet the complexity of reasons for which IDPs flee (ie conflict, natural and human-made disaster, development-induced displacement) as well as the fact that many IDPs become refugees has meant that various different branches of public international law contain provisions that are relevant to IDPs. This section will outline these various provisions and will illustrate—where relevant—how they have been interpreted by courts, scholars, and treaty monitoring bodies in more recent years in the context of internal displacement.

3.3.1.1 Human Rights Law

Several human rights treaties contain explicit prohibitions on internal displacement. However, these treaties are either regional in nature,[101] or apply to specific categories of IDPs (namely indigenous peoples).[102] There is thus no treaty of global geographical scope that prohibits internal displacement. However, many non-displacement-specific human rights treaties contain provisions that are particularly relevant to IDPs. A survey of the Universal Declaration of Human Rights (UDHR), together with the most widely ratified international and regional human rights treaties reveals a plethora of provisions that are relevant to IDPs. The following sections will set out to what extent these instruments offer: (a) protection from displacement; (b) protection

[100] Martti Koskenniemi, 'What is International Law For?' in Malcom Evans (ed), *International Law* (OUP 2014) 29; Anthea Roberts, *Is International Law International?* (OUP 2017).

[101] The Kampala Convention (art 3(1)(a)) and the Great Lakes Protocol on IDPs (art 3(1)) both oblige states to prevent arbitrary displacement: The 2009 African Union Convention for the Protection and Assistance of Internally Displaced Persons in Africa (adopted 23 October 2009, entered into foce 6 December 2012) 52 ILM 400 (Kampala Convention); Protocol on the Protection and Assistance to Internally Displaced Persons (adopted 30 November 2006, entered into force 21 June 2008) (Protocol on the Protection and Assistance to IDPs).

[102] Art 16 of the Indigenous and Tribal Peoples Convention, 1989 (No. 169) provides that the peoples to which the Convention applies shall not be removed from the lands which they occupy. Indigenous and Tribal Peoples Convention (No. 169) (adopted 27 June 1989, entered into force 5 September 1991) 1650 UNTS 383. Similarly, art 12 of the Indigenous and Tribal Populations Convention (No. 107) provides that: [t]he populations concerned shall not be removed without their free consent from their habitual territories except in accordance with national laws and regulations for reasons relating to national security, or in the interest of national economic development or of the health of the said populations. Indigenous and Tribal Populations Convention (No. 107) (adopted 26 June 1957, entered into force 2 June 1959).

during displacement; (c) protection after displacement; (d) the right to leave one's country and a corresponding right of entry of another country.[103]

Protection from Displacement in International Human Rights Law

Many treaties contain several provisions that give rise to an implied prohibition of internal displacement. These provisions include the right to freedom of movement;[104] the right to liberty and security of the person;[105] the right to private life, family, and home;[106] the right to property and/or peaceful enjoyment of possessions;[107] and the prohibition of cruel, inhumane, and degrading treatment.[108] Many courts and treaty monitoring bodies have explicitly found that internal displacement can violate one or more of these provisions. For example, the Human Rights Committee is of the view that freedom of movement includes 'protection against all forms of internal displacement',[109] and that forced evictions can be a violation of the right to privacy, family, home, and correspondence.[110] The Committee on Economic, Social, and Cultural

[103] It is important to note that some of these rights can be derogated from in an emergency. For example, art 4(2) of the International Covenant on Civil and Political Rights provides that some rights can be derogated from in an emergency, but no derogation can be made from arts 6, 7, 8 (paragraphs 1 and 2), 11, 15, 16, and 18. International Covenant on Civil and Political Rights (adopted 16 December 1966, entered into force 23 March 1976) 999 UNTS 171 (ICCPR).

[104] Art 12, ICCPR; art 5, Convention on the Elimination of Racial Discaimination (adopted 21 December 1965, entered into force 4 Janary 1969) 660 UNTS 195 (CERD); art 18, Convention on the Rights of Persons with Disabilities (adopted 24 January 2007, entered into force 3 May 2008) 2515 UNTS 3 (CRPD); art 15, Convention on the Elimination of All Forms of Discrimination Against Women (adopted 18 December 1979, entered into force 2 September 1981) 1249 UNTS 13 (CEDAW); art 2, European Convention for the Protection of Human Rights and Fundamental Freedoms (adopted 4 November 1950, entered into force 3 September 1953) 213 UNTS 221 (ECHR); art 22, American Convention on Human Rights (adopted 22 November 1969, entered into force 18 July 1978) 1144 UNTS 144 (ACHR); art 12, African Charter on Human and Peoples' Rights (adopted 27 June 1981, entered into force 21 October 1986) 21 ILM 58 (ACHPR).

[105] Art 9, ICCPR; art 9, International Covenant on Economic, Social, and Cultural Rights (adopted 16 December 1966, entered into force 3 January 1976) 993 UNTS 3 (ICESCR); art 26 CRC; art 14 CRPD; art 5 CERD; art 7, ACHR; art I, XVI American Declaration of the Rights and Duties of Man, OAS Res XXX adopted by the Ninth International Conference of American States (1948) reprinted in Basic Documents Pertaining to Human Rights in the Inter-American System OEA/Ser L V/II.82 Doc 6 Rev 1 at 17 (1992) (ADRDM); art 23, ACHPR; art 5 ECHR.

[106] Art 16, art 10 CRC; art 10 ICESCR; art 22, art 23 CRPD; art 17, art 23 ICCPR; art 8 ECHR; art V, VI, IX ADRDM; art 11 ACHR.

[107] Art 16 CEDAW; art 5 CERD; art 1, Protocol 1 to the European Convention for the Protection of Human Rights and Fundamental Freedoms (adopted 20 March 1952, entered into force 18 May 1954) ETS 9; art XXIII, ADRDM; art 21 ACHR.

[108] Art 7 ICCPR; art 37 CRC; art 15 CRPD; art 16, Convention against Torture and other Cruel, Inhuman or Degrading Treatment or Punishment (adopted 10 December 1984, entered into force 26 June 1987) 1465 UNTS 85 (CAT); art 5 ACHR; art 5 ACHPR; art 3, ECHR.

[109] UN Human Rights Committee, 'General Comment No. 27: Article 12 (Freedom of Movement)' (1999) UN Doc CCPR/C/21/Rev.1/Add.9, [7]; Martin Scheinin, 'Forced Displacement and the Covenant on Civil and Political Rights' in Anne Bayefsky and Joan Fitzpatrick (eds), *Human Rights and Forced Displacement* (Brill 2001) 66.

[110] UN Human Rights Committee, *Chiti v Zambia* Communication No 1303/2004 (2012) UN Doc CCPR/C/105/D/1303/2004; UN Human Rights Committee, *Naidenova v Bulgaria* Communication No. 2073/2011 (2012) UN Doc CCPRC/106/D/2073/2011 [15].

Rights has held that the right to adequate housing means that 'evictions should not result in individuals being rendered homeless or vulnerable to the violation of other human rights'.[111] The Committee against Torture has found that forced evictions and the demolition of housing resulting in internal displacement can amount to cruel, inhumane, or degrading treatment where such evictions are not carried out by public officials.[112] Finally, the African Commission on Human and Peoples' Rights found that the internal displacement by Sudan of indigenous tribes in Darfur violated numerous provisions of the Banjul Charter, including the obligation to respect the liberty and security of the person, the right to property, and family rights.[113] The European Court of Human Rights,[114] Inter-American Commission on Human Rights,[115] and Inter-American Court of Human Rights have also found that situations of internal displacement can give rise to violations of various provisions of international human rights law.[116]

Protection During Displacement in International Human Rights Law

There are a wide range of provisions in international treaties that offer protection during displacement, including the right to equality and the prohibition of discrimination,[117] the right to an adequate standard of

[111] Committee on Economic, Social, and Cultural Rights, 'General Comment no. 7: Article 11.1 (The Right to Adequate Housing: Forced Evictions)' (1997) UN Doc E/1998/22 [16].

[112] UN Committee against Torture, *Hajrizi Dzemajl et al. v Yugoslavia* (2002) UN Doc CAT/C/29/D/161/2000; UN Committee Against Torture, 'Report of the Committee Against Torture: Israel' (17 May 2002) UN Doc A/57/44, [52]–[53].

[113] *Sudan Human Rights Organisation & Centre for Housing Rights and Evictions (COHRE) v Sudan*, 209/03–296/05, African Commission on Human and People's Rights (13–27 May 2009).

[114] *Dogan v Turkey* App no 29361/07 (ECHR, 27 May 2010); *Dulas v Turkey* App no 25801/94 (ECHR, 30 January 2001); *Šekerović and Pašalić v Bosnia and Herzegovina* App nos 5920/04 and 67396/09 (ECHR, 8 March 2011); *Ayder and Others v Turkey* App no 23656/94 (ECHR, 8 January 2004); *Bilgin v Turkey* App no 23819/94 (ECHR, 16 November 2000); *Selcuk and Asker v Turkey* App no 12/1997/796/998-999 (ECHR, 24 April 1998); *Xenidin-Arestis v Turkey* App no 46347/99 (ECHR, 22 December 2005); *Demades v Turkey* App no 16219/90 (ECHR, 31 October 2003); *Yoyler v Turkey* App no 26973/95 (ECHR, 24 July 2003); *Mentes and Others v Turkey* App no 58/1996/677/867 (ECHR, 28 November 1997).

[115] *Ana Teresa Yarce et al v Columbia*, Inter-American Commission of Human Rights Report No 86/13 (4 November 2013).

[116] *Case of the Moiwana Community v Suriname*, Inter-American Court of Human Rights Series C No 124 (15 June 2005); *Case of the 'Mapiripán Massacre' v Colombia*, Inter-American Court of Human Rights Series C No 134 (15 September 2005); *La Granja, Ituango v Colombia*, Inter-American Commission of Human Rights Report No 5700 (2 October 2000); *Case of Yarce et al v Colombia*, Inter-American Court of Human Rights Series C No 325 (22 November 2016); *Case of the Members of the Village of Chichupac and neighbouring communities of the Municipality of Rabinal v Guatemala*, Inter-American Court of Human Rights Series C No 328 (30 November 2016); *Case of the Santo Domingo Massacre v Colombia*, Inter-American Court of Human Rights Series C Report No 259 (30 November 2012); *Case of Chitay Nech et al v Guatemala*, Inter-American Court of Human Rights Series C Report No 212 (25 May 2010).

[117] Art 26 ICCPR; art 3 ICESCR; art 5, art 12 CRPD; art 5 CERD; art 3, art 15 CEDAW; art 14 ECHR; art II ADRDM; art 24 ACHR; art 2 ACHPR.

living,[118] the right to adequate housing,[119] the right to health,[120] as well as some of the provisions mentioned above such as the prohibition of cruel, inhuman, and degrading treatment. Courts and treaty monitoring bodies have explained how some of these rights apply in the context of internal displacement. For example, the case before the African Commission on Human and People's Rights as mentioned above concerning the displacement of indigenous tribes in Darfur also found that the situation during displacement involved violations of inter alia, the right to be heard (Article 7); the right to enjoy the best attainable state of physical and mental health (Article 16); and the right of all peoples to economic, social and cultural development (Article 22).[121] The European Court of Human Rights has found that the conditions in Darfuri IDP camps are 'dire' and hence a violation of the prohibition of cruel, inhuman, and degrading treatment.[122]

Protection After Displacement in International Human Rights Law

Human rights treaties also provide for several provisions that are applicable in the post-displacement phase, such as the prohibition of discrimination and the right to an effective remedy.[123] Courts and treaty monitoring bodies have also explained how these rights apply in the post-displacement context. For example, General Recommendation XXII of the Committee on the Elimination of all Forms of Racial Discrimination sets out that the prohibition of discrimination entails the right of IDPs of voluntary and safe return to their homes and the right to restoration and compensation of property that was seized during displacement.[124] Moreover, the European Court of Human Rights,[125]

[118] Art 11 ICESCR; art 27 CRC; art 28 CRPD.

[119] Art 11 ICESCR; art 5 CERD.

[120] Art 12 ICESCR; art 25 CRPD; art 24 CRC; art 5 CERD; art 12 CEDAW; art XI ADRDM; art 16 ACHPR.

[121] *Sudan Human Rights Organisation & Centre for Housing Rights and Evictions (COHRE) v Sudan*, 209/03–296/05, African Commission on Human and People's Rights (13–27 May 2009). Other cases from the African Commission on Human and Peoples' Rights that have found a violation of the ACHPR in the context of internal displacement include *Abdel Hadi, Ali Radi & Others v Republic of Sudan*, 368/09, African Commission on Human and Peoples' Rights (22 October-5 November 2013); *Centre for Minority Rights Development (Kenya) and Minority Rights Group International on behalf of Endorois Welfare Council v Kenya*, 276/03, African Commission on Human and People's Rights (11–25 November 2009); *African Commission on Human and Peoples' Rights v the Republic of Kenya*, 006/12, African Court of Human and Peoples' Rights (26 May 2017).

[122] *Sufi and Elmi v United Kingdom* App nos 8319/07 and 11449/07 (ECHR, 28 November 2011).

[123] See note 118 on the prohibition of discrimination. The right to an effective remedy is encapsulated in the following provisions: art 2 ICCPR; art 6 CERD; art 14 CAT; art 2 CEDAW; art 13 ECHR; art 10 ACHR.

[124] UN Committee on the Elimination of Racial Discrimination, 'General Recommendation XXII (Article 5 and Refugees and Displaced Persons)' (1996) UN Doc A/51/18, Annex VIII [2(a)], [2(c)].

[125] *Ayder and Others v Turkey* App no 23656/94 (ECHR, 8 January 2004); *Bilgin v Turkey* App no 23819/94 (ECHR, 16 November 2000); *Selcuk and Asker v Turkey* App no 12/1997/796/998-999

the African Commission on Human and Peoples' Rights,[126] and the Inter-American Court of Human Rights have found violations of the right to an effective remedy in the post-displacement phase.[127]

The Right to Leave and Corresponding De Facto Right of Entry

Article 13(2) of the UDHR proclaims that: '[e]veryone has the right to leave any country, including his own'.[128] This right is part of customary international law and is also enshrined in Article 12(2) of the 1966 International Covenant on Civil and Political Rights (ICCPR).[129] As such, using IDP protection measures as part of a policy of refugee containment would—ipso facto—violate the right to leave one's country. This might be the case where for example a territorial state tries to prevent its citizens from leaving the country on the basis that they should seek protection in an IDP camp rather than seek asylum abroad.

However, the right to leave a country does not mean that an individual has a corresponding right to enter another country.[130] This is the case even where an individual is an asylum-seeker. Article 14(1) of the UDHR sets out the individual's right 'to seek and to enjoy in other countries asylum from persecution'. The drafting history of this article reveals that the drafters of the Declaration contemplated—but ultimately declined to adopt—any specific obligation on the state to grant asylum.[131] The Declaration thus does not give rise to an individual's right to asylum vis-à-vis the state of refuge or any state in particular. Moreover, although there is some support that the UDHR may

(ECHR, 24 April 1998); *Yoyler v Turkey* App no 26973/95 (ECHR, 24 July 2003); *Dogan v Turkey* App no 29361/07 (ECHR, 27 May 2010); *Dulas v Turkey* App no 25801/94 (ECHR, 30 January 2001).

[126] *Centre for Minority Rights Development (Kenya) and Minority Rights Group International on behalf of Endorois Welfare Council v Kenya*, 276/03, African Commission on Human and People's Rights (11–25 November 2009).

[127] IACtHR: *Case of the Moiwana Community v Suriname*, Inter-American Court of Human Rights Series C No 124 (15 June 2005); *Case of the 'Mapiripán Massacre' v Colombia*, Inter-American Court of Human Rights Series C No 134 (15 September 2005); *La Granja, Ituango v Colombia*, Inter-American Commission of Human Rights Report No 5700 (2 October 2000).

[128] Universal Declaration of Human Rights (adopted 10 December 1948 UNGA Res 217 A(III) (UDHR); art 11 CPRD.

[129] R Boed, 'The State of the Right of Asylum in International Law' (1994) 5 Duke Journal of Comparative and International Law 1, 6 (hereafter Boed, 'The State of the Right to Asylum in International Law'). See also art 10 CRC; art 18 CRPD; art 5 CERD; art 15 CEDAW; art 22 ACHR; art 12 ACHPR.

[130] María-Teresa Gil-Bazo, 'Asylum as a General Principle of International Law', (2015) 27(1) International Journal of Refugee Law 3, 10 (hereafter Gil-Bazo, 'Asylum as a General Principle of International Law').

[131] Boed, 'The State of the Right to Asylum in International Law' (n 129).

bind states on the basis of custom,[132] it has not been stated by commentators or states that Article 14 falls within customary international law.[133]

Taken together, Articles 12(2) and 14 of the UDHR mean that a state cannot prevent its nationals from leaving a country, but those nationals do not have a corresponding right to asylum vis-à-vis another state. However, they may nonetheless have a de facto right of entry in order to lodge an asylum claim. This is because asylum-seekers are protected by the prohibition of *refoulement* under Article 33 of the 1951 Refugee Convention (see below),[134] which prohibits their removal to a place where there is a real risk to their lives or freedoms.[135] The obligation to interpret this provision in good faith, in light of its object and purpose and in light of relevant human rights instruments, means that Article 33 gives rise to an implicit obligation to grant access to fair and effective asylum procedures, which in practice would probably mean a right of entry.[136] That is not to say that an individual's asylum claim would be successful, of course, or that their removal would necessarily constitute *refoulement*. Each claim must be considered on a case-by-case basis. Whether a risk of internal displacement upon return to the country of nationality could give rise persecution and/or refoulement is dealt with in more detail in chapter 4.

3.3.1.2 International Humanitarian Law

International humanitarian law also provides protection to the internally displaced. Its protection is more comprehensive during an international conflict as the Geneva Convention relative to the Protection of Civilian Persons in Time of War ('Fourth Geneva Convention') and Protocol Additional to the Geneva Conventions of 12 August 1949, and relating to the Protection of Victims of International Armed Conflicts ('Additional Protocol I') are applicable.[137]

[132] *Legal Consequences for States of the Continued Presence of South Africa in Namibia (South West Africa) Notwithstanding Security Council Resolution 276 (1970)*, 1971 ICJ 16, 57 (Advisory Opinion of June 21); at 76 (Ammoun, J, separate opinion).

[133] Hurst Hannum, 'The Status of the Universal Declaration of Human Rights in National and International Law' (1996) 25 Georgia Journal of International and Comparative Law 287, 346

[134] The obligation of non-refoulement can also be found in international human rights law. See Bríd Ní Ghráinne, 'Complementary Protection and Encampment' (2021) 21(1) Human Rights Law Review 54.

[135] Gil-Bazo, 'Asylum as a General Principle of International Law' (n 130) 13.

[136] Art 33(1), Vienna Convention on the Law of Treaties (adopted 23 May 1969, entered into forced 27 January 1980) 1155 UNTS 331; Mariagiulia Giuffré, 'Access to Asylum at Sea? Non-refoulement and a Comprehensive Approach to Extraterritorial Human Rights Obligations' in Violeta Moreno-Lax and Efthymios Papastavridis (eds), *'Boat Refugees' and Migrants at Sea: A Comprehensive Approach* (Brill 2016) 248; Bríd Ní Ghráinne, 'Left to Die at Sea: State Responsibility for the May 2015 Thai, Indonesian, and Malaysian Pushback Operations' (2017) 10 Irish Yearbook of International Law 109.

[137] 1949 Geneva Convention Relative to the Protection of Civilian Persons in Time of War ('Fourth Geneva Convention') (adopted 12 August 1949, entered into force 21 October 1950) 75 UNTS 287; 1977 Declaration on Territorial Asylum (Adopted by the Committee of Ministers on 18 November 1977 at the 278th Meeting of the Ministers' Deputies).

Article 49 of the former Convention prohibits individual or mass forcible transfers, and this provision forms part of customary international law.[138]

There are far fewer humanitarian law provisions applicable in non-international armed conflicts. Such limited coverage is regrettable, considering that the largest amount of IDPs is created during internal armed conflict and it is in that situation that the need for specific protection arises.[139] However, Common Article 3 of the Geneva Conventions ('Common Article 3')[140] is applicable in situations of 'armed conflict not of an international character'. It requires that parties to such a conflict shall be required to apply 'at a minimum' the following provisions:

> (1) Persons taking no active part in the hostilities, including members of armed forces who have laid down their arms and those placed 'hors de combat' by sickness, wounds, detention, or any other cause, shall in all circumstances be treated humanely, without any adverse distinction founded on race, colour, religion or faith, sex, birth or wealth, or any other similar criteria. To this end, the following acts are and shall remain prohibited at any time and in any place whatsoever with respect to the above-mentioned persons:
> (a) violence to life and person, in particular murder of all kinds, mutilation, cruel treatment and torture;
> (b) taking of hostages;
> (c) outrages upon personal dignity, in particular humiliating and degrading treatment;
> (d) the passing of sentences and the carrying out of executions without previous judgment pronounced by a regularly constituted court, affording all the judicial guarantees which are recognized as indispensable by civilized peoples.
> (2) The wounded and sick shall be collected and cared for.
> An impartial humanitarian body, such as the International Committee of the Red Cross, may offer its services to the parties to the conflict.

138 TMC Asser Instituut, *Yearbook of International Humanitarian Law* (TMC Asser Press 1998) 261.

139 Catherine Phuong, *The International Protection of Internally Displaced Persons* (CUP 2004) 41 (hereafter Phuong, *The International Protection of Internally Displaced Persons*).

140 1949 Geneva Convention for the Amelioration of the Condition of the Wounded and Sick in Armed Forces in the Field ('First Geneva Convention') (adopted 12 August 1949, entered into force 21 October 1950) 75 UNTS 31; Geneva Convention for the Amelioration of the Condition of Wounded, Sick and Shipwrecked Members of Armed Forces at Sea ('Second Geneva Convention') (adopted 12 August 1949, entered into force 21 October 1950) 75 UNTS 85; Geneva Convention Relative to the Treatment of Prisoners of War ('Third Geneva Convention') (adopted 12 August 1949, entered into force 21 October 1950) 75 UNTS 135; Fourth Geneva Convention.

The parties to the conflict should further endeavour to bring into force, by means of special agreements, all or part of the other provisions of the present Convention.

The application of the preceding provisions shall not affect the legal status of the parties to the conflict.

Common Article 3 has been declared by the International Court of Justice as forming part of customary international law,[141] and therefore applies regardless of whether the state in question is a party to the Geneva Conventions. Moreover, the guarantees applicable in non-international armed conflicts are expanded upon in Additional Protocol II to the Geneva Conventions.[142] It is composed of 28 articles, which contain more detailed provisions on fundamental guarantees, treatment of the wounded and sick, and the protection of the civilian population. Of particular relevance to IDPs is Article 17, which prohibits the forced movement of civilians. It is important to note that unlike Common Article 3, Additional Protocol II is only applicable in those states which are parties to it, which excludes many that have serious armed conflicts taking place on their territory. Even then, its threshold of applicability is higher than that of Common Article 3. Whereas Common Article 3 applies to any armed conflict occurring within a state, Article 1(1) of the Protocol II provides that it shall apply only to armed conflicts which:

> take place within the territory of [a state party] between its armed forces and dissident armed forces or other organized armed groups which, under responsible command, exercise such control over a part of its territory as to enable them to carry out sustained and concerted military operations and to implement this Protocol.

Therefore, while Additional Protocol II is useful in expanding the protection afforded by Common Article 3, it has a very limited field of applicability, confined essentially to conflicts in which both parties control parts of territory. It is therefore not surprising that the provisions applicable in non-international armed conflicts have been described as 'almost skeletal' when compared to the rules applicable to international conflicts.[143]

[141] *Military and Paramilitary Activities in and against Nicaragua* (*Nicaragua v United States of America*) (Merits) [1986] ICJ Rep 14, 104.

[142] Steve Peers, *EU Immigration and Asylum Law, Text and Commentary* (2nd rev edn, Martinus Nijhoff 2012).

[143] Christopher Greenwood, 'The Law of War (International Humanitarian Law)' in Malcolm D Evans (ed), *International Law* (2nd edn, OUP 2006) 807.

A further limitation of international humanitarian law is that neither the Geneva Conventions nor their Additional Protocols provide for any complaints or enforcement mechanism. Enforcement is primarily left to individual states by means of domestic jurisdiction. Violations of the most fundamental provisions of the Geneva Conventions and Additional Protocol I are known as 'grave breaches' of those treaties and all states have jurisdiction to prosecute persons accused of these crimes. In addition, the International Criminal Court and various international tribunals have jurisdiction to try war crimes and/or grave breaches of the Geneva Conventions. The remit of such jurisdiction will be expanded upon in more detail in the next section on international criminal law.

3.3.1.3 International Criminal Law

The United Nations International Criminal Tribunal for the Former Yugoslavia (ICTY) had jurisdiction to try grave breaches of the Geneva Conventions, which includes the forcible transfer of civilians.[144] The Tribunal also had the jurisdiction to try war crimes under Article 3,[145] which includes 'wanton destruction of cities, towns or villages or devastation not justified by military necessity'; 'attack, or bombardment, by whatever means, of undefended towns, villages, dwellings, or buildings'; and 'plunder of public or private property'. Article 4(2)(e) of the ICTY statute includes the forcible transfer of children as an action that may, under certain circumstances, constitute genocide. Article 5(h) and 5(i) list 'persecution' and 'other inhumane acts', respectively, as examples of crimes against humanity. The former requires discriminatory intent, and thus forced displacement coupled with this specific intent can constitute 'persecution' and, as such, qualify as a crime against humanity.[146] As for the latter, the Trial Chamber in the *Kupreškić et al.* judgment held that forcible displacement within or between national borders is included as an inhumane act under Article 5(i) defining crimes against humanity.[147]

The United Nations International Criminal Tribunal for Rwanda (ICTR) had jurisdiction to try grave breaches of the Geneva Conventions.[148] It

[144] UNSC, 'Statute of the International Criminal Tribunal for the Former Yugoslavia (as amended on 17 May 2002)' Res 827 (25 May 1993) UN Doc S/RES/827, art 2(g).

[145] ibid, art 3; *Prosecutor v Prlić et al* (Judgment) ICTY-04-74-A (29 November 2017); *Prosecutor v Popović et al* (Judgment) ICTY-05-88-A (30 January 2015).

[146] *Prosecutor v Radislav Krstić* (Judgment) ICTY-98-33-T (2 August 2001).

[147] *Prosecutor v Kupreškić et al* (Judgment) ICTY-95-16-T (14 January 2000) [566]. See also *Prosecutor v Ratko Mladic* (Judgment) ICTY-09-92-T (22 November 2017); *Prosecutor v Stanišić and Župljanin* (Judgment) ICTY-08-91-A (30 June 2016); *Prosecutor v Vlastimir Đorđević* (Judgment) ICTY-05-87/1-A (27 January 2014).

[148] UNSC, 'Statute of the International Criminal Tribunal for Rwanda' Res 955 (8 November 1994) UN Doc S/RES/955, art 4.

also included the forcible transfer of children as an act that may constitute genocide,[149] and the categories of 'persecutions on political, racial, and religious grounds' and of 'other inhumane acts' is included as a crime against humanity.[150]

Finally, the International Criminal Court (ICC) has jurisdiction to try 'the most serious crimes of concern to the international community as a whole'.[151] Three of these crimes are particularly relevant to IDPs: genocide, crimes against humanity, and war crimes. Specifically, Article 6(e) lists the forcible transfer of children as an act that may constitute the crime of genocide. In addition, Article 7(i)(d) lists the forcible transfer of a population as an act that may constitute a crime against humanity, and forcible transfer is defined as 'forced displacement of the persons concerned by expulsion or any other coercive acts from the area in which they are lawfully present, without grounds permitted under international law'.[152] Finally, war crimes may include the transfer of persons within or outside a particular territory and/or 'ordering the displacement of the civilian population for reasons related to the conflict, unless the security of the civilians involved or imperative military reasons so demand'.[153]

3.3.1.4 International Refugee Law

Finally, refugee law offers a useful example when developing a protection framework for the internally displaced. Refugee law cannot apply to IDPs because IDPs are displaced within the state, but it can nonetheless serve as a 'point of comparison' and 'might also inspire standard-setting for internally displaced persons'.[154] Many aspects of the key soft law instrument on internal displacement—the Guiding Principles on Internal Displacement, analysed in the next section of this chapter—were inspired by provisions of refugee law, including the Refugee Convention,[155] the Convention Governing the Specific

[149] Art 2 (e).

[150] Art 3 (h), (i).

[151] 1998 Rome Statute of the International Criminal Court (adopted 17 July 1988, entered into force 1 July 2002) 2187 UNTS 90 (Rome Statute), preamble.

[152] ibid art 7(2)(d); *Prosecutor v Dominic Ongwen* (Judgment) ICC-02/04-01/15 (7 May 2021); *Prosecutor v Bosco Ntganda* (Judgment) ICC-01/04-02/06 A A2 (30 March 2021).

[153] Rome Statute, arts 8(2)(a)(vii), 8(2)(b)(viii), 8(2)(e)(viii).

[154] UNECOSOC, 'Report of the Representative of the Secretary-General, Mr. Francis M. Deng, submitted pursuant to Commission on Human Rights Resolution 1995/57, Compilation and Analysis of Legal Norms' (22 February 1996) UN Doc E/CN.4/1996/52/Add.2 [33] (hereafter Deng, 'Compilation and Analysis of Legal Norms'); Phuong, *The International Protection of Internally Displaced Persons* (n 139) 47.

[155] Convention Relating to the Status of Refugees (adopted 28 July 1951, entered into force 22 April 1954) 189 UNTS 137 (Refugee Convention).

Aspects of the Refugee Problem in Africa ('OAU Convention'),[156] and UNHCR documents, such as the 1991 Guidelines on the Protection of Refugee Women and the 1994 Guidelines on the Protection and Care of Refugee Children.[157] Consequently, the influence of refugee law may be seen in many of the Guiding Principles. For example, the right of non-*refoulement* which is found in Article 33(1) of the Refugee Convention is set out in Principle 15,[158] notwithstanding that no right in the context of IDPs existed in international law.[159] In addition, the right of voluntary return of IDPs (Principle 28) was influenced by Article 5 of the 1969 OAU Convention. Finally, inspiration also came from ExCom,[160] in the formulation of the principle of family reunification (Principle 7), which was influenced, in part, by UNHCR ExCom Conclusion No. 24 (XXXII) – 1981, which states that 'every effort should be made to ensure the reunification of separated refugee families'.[161] The content and significance of the Guiding Principles is analysed in more detail in the next section.

3.3.2 The Guiding Principles on Internal Displacement

In 1992, IDPs worldwide numbered 25 million.[162] As outlined above, although some branches of public international law offer protection to IDPs, this protection varies according to circumstances and was not IDP-specific. Following a request from the UN Commission on Human Rights,[163] the UN Secretary-General appointed Mr Francis Deng as his Representative on Internally Displaced Persons in 1992. One of Mr Deng's tasks was to direct a team of experts in examining the existing legal protection for IDPs, which resulted in a

[156] Convention Governing the Specific Aspects of the Refugee Problem in Africa (adopted 10 September 1969, entered into force 20 June 1974) 1001 UNTS 45.

[157] UNHCR, 'Guidelines on the Protection of Refugee Women' (1991) UN Doc EC/SCP/ 67; UNHCR, 'Refugee Children: Guidelines on Protection and Care' (1994).

[158] UNCHR, 'Report of the Representative of the Secretary-General, Mr. Francis M. Deng, submitted pursuant to Commission resolution 1197/39. Addendum: Guiding Principles on Internal Displacement' (11 February 1998) UN Doc E/CN.4/1998/53/Add (hereafter 'Guiding Principles on Internal Displacement').

[159] Phil Orchard, 'Protection of Internally Displaced Persons: Soft Law as a Norm-Generating Mechanism' (2010) 36 Review of International Studies 281, 284.

[160] The Executive Committee of the High Commissioner's Programme (ExCom) meets in Geneva annually to review and approve UNHCR's programmes and budget, advise on international protection, and discuss a wide range of other issues with UNHCR and its intergovernmental and non-governmental partners.

[161] UNHCR EXCOM Conclusion No 24 (XXXII) 'Family Reunification' (1981).

[162] Francis Deng, 'As Conflict Rages Across the Globe, People are Not Protected in Their Own Country' (*MIT Centre for International Studies*, 4 June 2007) http://www.alternet.org/world/52544/?page=entire accessed 27 May 2014.

[163] UNCHR Res 1992/73 (5 March 1992) UN Doc E/CN.4/RES/1992/73.

report entitled the 'Compilation and Analysis of Legal Norms'.[164] The report concluded that there remained some gaps in IDP protection. It identified a need 'to restate general principles of protection in more specific detail', and finally, it advocated the creation of 'a future international instrument on the protection of the internally displaced'.[165]

The General Assembly heeded this suggestion, and together with the Commission on Human Rights it requested Mr Deng to create an 'appropriate' framework for the protection of IDPs.[166] The Representative decided to elaborate a set of 30 non-binding Guiding Principles. At first glance, it may have seemed preferable to draft a legally binding treaty. Nonetheless, in the specific context of IDPs, the decision to use a non-binding instrument was probably a wise one. When the Guiding Principles were being drafted, there was almost no governmental support for a convention and the decision to use a non-binding instrument may be seen as an attempt to mitigate sovereignty concerns.[167] Furthermore, the issue of IDPs was extremely sensitive as it concerned the internal affairs of states. Moreover, international organizations feared that a binding convention could undermine the Refugee Convention. There was concern that legally binding IDP protection could be used by governments as an excuse to deny asylum, citing an internal protection alternative (analysed in chapter 4) as a basis for which to deny refugee status.[168]

Additionally, with the number of IDPs outnumbering that of refugees, it was clear that the need for IDP protection was urgent. A non-binding instrument could be drafted in a much shorter space of time than a treaty, which could take decades.[169] It was feared that governments would use negotiations as an opportunity to water down their existing obligations by creating an IDP protection

[164] Guiding Principles on Internal Displacement (n 159).

[165] Deng, 'Compilation and Analysis of Legal Norms' (n 154).

[166] UNCHR Resolution 1996/52 (19 April 1996) UN Doc E/CN.4/RES/1996/52.

[167] Roberta Cohen, 'The Guiding Principles on Internal Displacement: An Innovation in International Standard Setting' (2004) 10 Global Governance: A Review of Multilateralism and International Organizations 459, 464 (hereafter Cohen, 'The Guiding Principles on Internal Displacement').

[168] ibid, 464; Phuong, *The International Protection of Internally Displaced Persons* (n 139) 39; Erika Feller, 'UNHCR's Role in IDP Protection: Opportunities and Challenges' [2006] Forced Migration Review 11; Goodwin-Gill and McAdam, *The Refugee in International Law* (n 52) 157. See also Council Directive 2004/83/EC of 29 April 2004 on minimum standards for the qualification and status of third country nationals or stateless persons as refugees or as persons who otherwise need international protection and the content of the protection granted [2004] OJ L304/12, which allows member states to take into account internal protection measures in determining eligibility for asylum.

[169] Alan E Boyle and Christine M Chinkin, *The Making of International Law* (OUP 2007) 214; Walter Kälin, 'How Hard is Soft Law? The Guiding Principles on Internal Displacement and the Need for a Normative Framework' (Roundtable Meeting, Ralph Bunche Institute for International Studies, CUNY Graduate Centre, 19 December 2001) 2 (hereafter Kälin, 'How Hard is Soft Law?'); David Fisher, 'Epilogue: International Law on the Internally Displaced Persons' in Paula Banerjee and others (eds), *Internal Displacement in South Asia: The Relevance of the UN's Guiding Principles* (SAGE 2005) 318.

framework that was weaker than those existing provisions applicable to the internally displaced.[170] The International Committee of the Red Cross (ICRC) believed it would be difficult to reach consensus on the term 'displaced persons' since the result would be the lowest common denominator, and this would be a depletion of existing IDP protection.[171] Additionally, governments could use the opportunity to weaken the development of norms as customary international law by denouncing their validity.[172]

Moreover, there was no guarantee that a treaty would be successful, or that it would attract the number of ratifications necessary for it to come into force.[173] This was the case for the Convention on the Protection of the Rights of All Migrant Workers and Members of their Families,[174] which only entered into force 12 years after its initial adoption by the General Assembly.[175]

Finally, it was felt that it was too early to draft a treaty on IDPs as it would entail a merging of human rights and humanitarian law.[176] Although some rights fall within the exclusive domain of international humanitarian law, some may be the sole concern of human rights and others may fall within the remit of both disciplines.[177] Accordingly, the distinction between both branches of law, notably, the presence of an armed conflict, is fundamental, and it was feared that many states would have opposed the combination of the two.[178]

The final outcome—the Guiding Principles on Internal Displacement—was thus a soft law instrument. The Guiding Principles helpfully set out a description of an IDP, as analysed in more detail in chapter 2. The Guiding Principles are then divided into five parts: (i) General Principles; (ii) Principles Relating to Protection from Displacement; (iii) Principles Relating to Protection During Displacement; (iv) Principles Relating to Humanitarian Assistance; and

[170] Jeff Crisp, 'Forced Displacement in Africa: Dimensions, Difficulties and Policy Considerations' (New Issues in Refugee Research, July 2006) http://www.unhcr.org/refworld/pdfid/4ff15cc42.pdf accessed 6 July 2021, 12.

[171] International Committee of the Red Cross, 'The ICRC and Internally Displaced Persons' (1995) 305 International Review of the Red Cross 182, 185; Jean-Phillippe Lavoyer, 'Refugees and IDPs: International Humanitarian Law and the Role of the ICRC' (1995) 305 International Review of the Red Cross 162, 170.

[172] Cohen, 'The Guiding Principles on Internal Displacement' (n 167) 464.

[173] Kälin, 'How Hard is Soft Law?'(n 169) 3.

[174] International Convention on the Protection of the Rights of All Migrant Workers and Members of their Families (adopted 18 December 1990, entered into force 1 July 2003) 2220 UNTS 39481.

[175] Migrant Workers Need Protection: UN Treaty Comes into Force' (*Human Rights Watch*, 30 June 2003) http://www.hrw.org/en/news/2003/06/30/migrant-workers-need-protection accessed 6 July 2021.

[176] Kälin, 'How Hard is Soft Law?'(n 169) 3

[177] *Legal Consequences of the Construction of a Wall in Occupied Palestinian Territory* (Advisory Opinion) [2004] ICJ Rep 136 [106]; Theodor Meron, *Human Rights in Internal Strife: their International Protection* (Grotius Publications 1987) 27.

[178] Kälin, 'How Hard is Soft Law?'(n 169) 4.

(v) Principles Relating to Return, Resettlement, and Reintegration. Principle 15 is of particular relevance to the theme of this book, as it states the right of IDPs to, inter alia, seek asylum in another country. This clearly shows that the drafters were concerned that IDP protection could be invoked by states as a way to contain refugee flows.

Many of the Guiding Principles are based on pre-existing rights under the branches of public international law outlined above, such as the prohibition of cruel, inhuman, and degrading treatment, and freedom of movement.[179] Other principles are clearly more innovative, in that they creatively reformulate pre-existing rights to a displacement-specific context and/or are not necessarily heavily supported by existing law at the time of drafting. A number of these principles merit highlighting. For instance, Principle 3 says that national authorities have the primary responsibility to protect IDPs but Principle 2 states that the Guiding Principles are directed to all authorities, not just states. This makes the Guiding Principles distinct from most of the instruments outlined above, which are mainly directed towards states. Principle 6 sets out a prohibition of arbitrary displacement, which, as set out in chapter 2, is not clearly set out in any globally binding legal instrument.

Principle 25 reiterates the duty of the state to provide humanitarian assistance to IDPs but notes that international humanitarian organizations and 'other appropriate actors' have the right to offer their services in support of IDPs. Such an offer shall not be regarded as an 'unfriendly act' and consent thereto 'shall not be arbitrarily withheld'. Principle 25 thus raises questions regarding to what extent humanitarian organizations can assist IDPs even without consent of the territorial state, but given that the drafters of the Guiding Principles were so careful to emphasize state sovereignty (eg in Principle 3), it is unlikely that they intended to imply the possibility of intervention. Principle 28 addresses the issue of durable solutions for IDPs, which had not at the time of drafting been addressed by any international instrument. It explicitly sets out two possible durable solutions for IDPs: voluntary return to their homes or places of habitual residence, or voluntary resettlement in another part of the country. I have argued elsewhere (with Ben Hudson) that Principle 28 also implicitly includes another solution: to resettle voluntarily in the location of displacement.[180] Many of these aforementioned principles had little or no basis

[179] Principle 11, Principle 14.

[180] Bríd Ní Ghráinne and Ben Hudson, 'The International Organisation for Migration's Engagement with the Guiding Principles on Internal Displacement' in Cathryn Costello, Megan Bradley, and Angela Sherwood (eds), *IOM Unbound? Obligations and Accountability of the International Organization for Migration in an Era of Expansion* (CUP, forthcoming 2022) (hereafter Ní Ghráinne and Hudson,

in pre-existing law. The next section will pay closer attention to this issue, in the context of the legal weight and current status of the Guiding Principles.

3.3.2.1 The Legal Weight and Current Status of the Guiding Principles on Internal Displacement

Under the leadership of Francis Deng, the then-Representative of the Secretary-General on Internally Displaced Persons, the Guiding Principles were submitted to the Human Rights Commission in 1998 and aimed to 'address the specific needs of internally displaced persons worldwide by identifying rights and guarantees relevant to their protection'.[181] They were concluded by experts (ie scholars and practitioners focusing on IDP issues) rather than states and have not been formally adopted by states in treaty form. In other words, the Guiding Principles are soft law and not, in themselves, legally binding under international law. In fact, some of the principles have little or no counterparts in existing law.[182] Take for example, Principle 15:

> Internally displaced persons have:
>
> ...
>
> (d) the right to be protected against forcible return to or resettlement in any place where their life, safety, liberty and/or health would be at risk.

Regarding paragraph (d), there is no provision of international law that applies the above principle to the internally displaced. Indeed, Walter Kälin, the former Representative of the Secretary-General on the Human Rights of Internally Displaced Persons acknowledged that this 'states a novel principle with no direct antecedent in existing instruments'.[183] Nonetheless, the drafters of the Guiding Principles found it appropriate to draw an analogy with Article 33(1) of the Refugee Convention. This provision encompasses the right of non-*refoulement*, that is, that no refugee may be expelled to territories where their life or freedom would be threatened on the basis of race, religion, nationality, membership of a particular social group, or political opinion.

'The International Organisation for Migration's Engagement with the Guiding Principles on Internal Displacement').

[181] Guiding Principles on Internal Displacement (n 158).

[182] Walter Kälin, one of the drafters of the Guiding Principles, stated that 'no new law in the strict sense of the word was created in *most* cases' (emphasis added). Walter Kälin, 'The Future of the Guiding Principles on Internal Displacement' (2006) Forced Migration Review 5, 5.

[183] Walter Kälin, 'Guiding Principles on Internal Displacement Annotations' (2008) 38 Studies in Transnational Legal Policy 69; Orchard, *Protecting the Internally Displaced* (n 49) 57.

Similarly, Principle 29 is also located in the grey area between *lex lata* and *lex ferenda*. The Principle deals with restitution for property loss and recognizes a duty of authorities to assist IDPs in recovering dispossessed property. When such recovery is not possible, 'competent authorities shall provide or assist those persons in obtaining appropriate compensation or another form of just reparation'. When the Guiding Principles were being drafted, the right to reclaim property was not clearly established in international law.[184] No explicit provision guaranteeing the right of restitution of property has been formulated in the main human rights instruments and the principle of compensation for property loss has been developed mainly by regional bodies, ie the European Court of Human Rights and the Inter-American Commission on Human Rights.[185] As noted by Williams, the entitlement to legal remedies for property confiscation was defined by international human rights law as a procedural right to a fair hearing, without identifying a specific right to restitution.[186] In fact, Principle 29 appeared to anticipate the development of the law, since, at the time of drafting, 'the question as to whether nationals are generally entitled to compensation for losses of their property . . . probably [had] to be answered in the negative'.[187] The fact that the drafters were unable to clarify the meaning of 'property' in the Guiding Principles further highlights the lack of legal provisions governing this area. Nonetheless, the drafters of the Guiding Principles concluded that a right to restitution existed, and Principle 29 provides for a right to compensation where recovery for dispossessed property is not possible.

However, the legal weight of the Guiding Principles is more nuanced than might appear at first glance. Although the Guiding Principles are technically a soft law instrument, most of the Guiding Principles have a significant foundation in pre-existing hard law obligations and do not, in fact, go beyond existing law.[188] For example, Principle 14 sets out the right of freedom of movement of IDPs, which is reflected in a plethora of existing treaties as explained in

[184] Phuong, *The International Protection of Internally Displaced Persons* (n 139) 64.

[185] ibid, 64. See also, for example, *Selcuk and Asker v Turkey* App no 12/1997/796/998-999 (ECHR, 24 April 1998); *Case of the 'Mapiripán Massacre' v Colombia*, Inter-American Court of Human Rights Series C No 134 (15 September 2005).

[186] Rhodri C Williams, 'Guiding Principle 29 and the Right to Restitution' (2008) Forced Migration Review 23, 23.

[187] R Hofmann, 'International Humanitarian Law and the Law of Refugees and Internally Displaced Persons' in *Law in Humanitarian Crisis* (Brussels 1995) 297 as cited in Phuong, *The International Protection of Internally Displaced Persons* (n 139) 64.

[188] Walter Kälin, 'The Guiding Principles on Internal Displacement—Introduction' (1998) 10 International Journal of Refugee Law 557, 562.

section 3.3.1.1. Thus, although technically a soft law document, the Guiding Principle do reflect—for the most part—binding obligations on states.

Moreover, despite technically being a soft law document, the Guiding Principles represented a 'benchmark'[189] and a 'watershed event' in IDP protection. In fact, in the 22 years or so of their existence, they have become the globally recognized standard on IDPs.[190] At the time of writing, approximately 42 states have developed law and policies on internal displacement, most of which were developed after the conclusion of the Guiding Principles and many of which refer to them either directly or indirectly (ie incorporate their substance without referring to the Guiding Principles explicitly).[191] The Constitutional Court of Colombia has even held that the national authorities are bound by the Guiding Principles,[192] and must carry out IDP protection 'in conditions that are compatible with full respect for the Guiding Principles'.[193] Moreover, the Guiding Principles have been continuously cited by resolutions of the General Assembly,[194] and in 2008, the General Assembly described the principles as 'the key international framework' for the protection of the internally displaced.[195] The Guiding Principles have also been referred to by the UN Security Council and UN Human Rights Council in drawing attention to the need to protect IDPs,[196] as well as in the reports by key stakeholders involved in the protection of IDPs including the UNHCR and the International

[189] John Holmes, 'Ten Years of the Guiding Principles' [2008] Forced Migration Review 3.

[190] John Bennett, 'Forced Migration within National Borders: The IDP Agenda' (1998) 1 Forced Migration Review 4, 5.

[191] Domestic incorporation has taken different forms. Some laws and policies merely cite the Guiding Principles, some explicitly endorse them, and/or some incorporate the definition and/or other individual Principles. See Orchard, *Protecting the Internally Displaced* (n 49) chapters 6–8; 'Global Database on IDPs Laws and Policies' (*Global Protection Cluster*) https://www.globalprotectioncluster.org/global-database-on-idp-laws-and-policies/ accessed 6 July 2021 (hereinafter 'Global Database on IDP Laws and Policies').

[192] *Constitutional Court Decision T-025* (2004); *Constitutional Court Decision SU-1150* (2000); *Constitutional Court Decision T-327* (2001).

[193] *Constitutional Court Decision T-178* (2005).

[194] UNGA Res 64/162 (18 December 2009) UN Doc A/RES/64/162; UNGA Res 66/165 (19 December 2011) UN Doc A/RES/66/165; UNGA Res 54/167 (25 February 2000) UN Doc A/RES/54/167. UNGA Res 58/177 (12 March 2004) UN Doc A/RES/58/177.

UNGA Res 58/177 (12 March 2004) UN Doc A/RES/58/177. UNGA Res 60/168 (7 March 2006) UN Doc A/RES/60/168; UNGA Res 62/153 (6 March 2008) UN Doc A/RES/62/153; UNGA Res 64/162 (18 December 2009) UN Doc A/RES/64/162; UNGA Res 66/165 (19 December 2011) UN Doc A/RES/66/165.

[195] UNGA Res 63/307 (30 September 2009) UN Doc A/RES/63/307.

[196] UNSC, 'Report of the Secretary-General to the Security Council on the Protection of Civilians in Armed Conflict' (8 September 1999) UN Doc S/1999/957; UN Human Rights Council 'Report of the Representative of the Secretary-General on the Human Rights of Internally Displaced Persons, Walter Kälin: addendum: high-level conference on "Ten Years of the Guiding Principles on Internal Displacement—achievements and future challenges" (Oslo, 16 and 17 October 2008): summary of the Conference Chair' (11 February 2009) A/HRC/10/13Add.3; Orchard, *Protecting the Internally Displaced* (n 49) 42.

Organisation for Migration (IOM).[197] Put simply although some principles may be better established in binding law than other principles, the Guiding Principles as a whole have 'shaped the global narrative on internal displacement'[198] and have become the primary reference point in the protection and assistance of IDPs.[199] The Guiding Principles also inspired the development of regional frameworks of IDP protection in Africa, which will be set out in more detail in the next section.

3.3.3 Regional Conventions on Internal Displacement

As aforementioned, at the time of the Guiding Principles' drafting there was little appetite for a binding international treaty on IDPs. Africa has nonetheless shown that creating binding regional frameworks is possible, with the conclusion of two major instruments: the 2006 Pact on Security, Stability and Development of the Great Lakes Region,[200] and the 2009 African Union Convention for the Protection and Assistance of Internally Displaced Persons in Africa.[201] Each of these instruments will be analysed in turn.

3.3.3.1 2006 Pact on Security, Stability and Development in the Great Lakes Region ('Great Lakes Pact')

In 2006 the Pact on Security, Stability and Development in the Great Lakes Region was signed by the 11 states of the International Conference of the Great Lakes Region (Angola, Burundi, the Central African Republic, Democratic Republic of Congo, Republic of Congo, Kenya, Rwanda, Sudan, Tanzania, Uganda, and Zambia).[202] It was subsequently ratified by all these states and entered into force in June 2008.

[197] UNHCR, 'Position Paper on Relocating Internally as a Reasonable Alternative to Seeking Asylum (The So-Called "Internal Flight Alternative" or "Relocation Principle")' (February 1999); IOM 'IOM Framework For Addressing Internal Displacement' (29 August 2017); Ní Ghráinne and Hudson, 'The International Organisation for Migration's Engagement with the Guiding Principles on Internal Displacement' (n 180).

[198] Romola Adeola, *The Internally Displaced Person in International Law* (Elgar 2020) 66.

[199] Orchard, *Protecting the Internally Displaced* (n 49) 51; Adama Dieng, 'Protecting Internally Displaced Persons: The Value of the Kampala Convention as a Regional Example' (2017) 99 International Review of the Red Cross 263 (hereafter Dieng, 'Protecting Internally Displaced Persons').

[200] 2006 Pact on Security, Stability and Development in the Great Lakes Region (Great Lakes Pact) 46 ILM 175.

[201] 2009 African Union Convention for the Protection and Assistance of Internally Displaced Persons in Africa (Kampala Convention) 52 ILM 400.

[202] Great Lakes Pact (n 200).

Two of the Pact's 10 protocols are relevant to the issue of internal displacement: the Protocol on the Protection and Assistance to Internally Displaced Persons, and the Protocol on the Property Rights of Returning Persons.[203] To a lesser extent, the Protocol on the Prevention and Suppression of Sexual Violence against Women and Children also deals with IDP protection, as there is a high level of sexual violence in situations where IDPs are found.[204]

The Great Lakes Pact as a whole is highly significant in the context of the Guiding Principles as it was the first multilateral instrument in the international community to explicitly prohibit arbitrary displacement and to bind member states to implement the Guiding Principles in their domestic legislation.[205] Article 6 of the Protocol on the Protection and Assistance to IDPs is particularly relevant. States Parties are obliged 'to adopt and implement the Guiding Principles as a regional framework for providing protection and assistance to internally displaced persons in the Great Lakes Region', to 'use the "Annotations of the Guiding Principles on Internal Displacement" as an authoritative source for interpreting the application of the Guiding Principles' and to 'enact national legislation to domesticate the Guiding Principles fully and to provide a legal framework for their implementation within national legal systems'.[206]

Kälin has noted that with this latter obligation, the Protocol's drafters have gone a step further than the Guiding Principles: 'This is very promising way to build consensus on the need to legally protect IDPs and on the content of such protection bottom-up; it could serve as an example for other regions.'[207] However, implementation of the Protocol is one of its key challenges,[208] evidenced by the fact that at present only six States Parties have introduced policies or legislation at the domestic level.[209]

203 Protocol on the Property Rights of Returning Persons (adopted 30 November 2006, entered into force 21 June 2008).

204 Protocol on the Prevention and Suppression of Sexual Violence against Women and Children (adopted 30 November 2006, entered into force 21 June 2008).

205 Art 3, art 6.

206 Protocol on the Protection and Assistance of IDPs.

207 Walter Kälin, 'The Great Lakes Protocol on Internally Displaced Persons: Responses and Challenges' (Speech at the Symposium on International Law in Post Conflict Situations: The Great Lakes Process, London School of Economics: International Humanitarian Law Project, London, 27 September 2007) 4.

208 Orchard, *Protecting the Internally Displaced* (n 49) 61.

209 Global Database on IDP Laws and Policies (n 191).

3.3.3.2 2010 Convention for the Protection and Assistance of Internally Displaced Persons in Africa ('Kampala Convention')

The trend of binding states at regional level has continued on the African continent.[210] In 2010 the African Union adopted the Convention for the Protection and Assistance of Internally Displaced Persons in Africa,[211] which was inspired by the conclusion of the Great Lakes Pact and which is also is broadly based on the Guiding Principles.[212] The Kampala Convention represents the regional instrument for the protection of the internally displaced. It was unanimously adopted by 46 African states and signed by 17 states. The Convention entered into force on 6 December 2012. At the time of writing (July 2021), the Convention has 31 States Parties.[213]

Unlike the Guiding Principles, which are formulated from the perspective of human rights of IDPs, the Kampala Convention is 'grounded on state responsibility and the responsibilities of other entities and actors'.[214] Its objectives are to promote and strengthen regional and national IDP protection measures, to establish a legal framework for the prevention of internal displacement and the

[210] Chaloka Beyani, 'Recent Developments in the African Human Rights System 2004–2004' (2007) 7(3) Human Rights Review 582; Chaloka Beyani, 'The Elaboration of a Legal Framework for the Protection of Internally Displaced Persons in Africa' (2006) 50(2) Journal of African Law 187.

[211] Kampala Convention.

[212] Chaloka Beyani, 'A View from Inside the Kitchen of the Kampala Convention: The Modernization of the International Legal Regime for the Protection of Internally Displaced Persons' (2020) LSE Working Papers http://eprints.lse.ac.uk/103693/4/SSRN_id3736788.pdf accessed 7 July 2021, 7 (hereafter, Beyani, 'A View from Inside the Kitchen of the Kampala Convention'; Brigitta Jakasa and Jeremy Smith, 'Africa: From Voluntary Principles to Binding Standards' [2008] Forced Migration Review 18, 18; Mehari T Maru, *The Kampala Convention and its Contribution to International Law: Legal Analyses and Interpretations of the African Union Convention for the Protection and Assistance of Internally Displaced Persons* (Eleven International Publishing 2014); Romola Adeola, *Development-Induced Displacement and Human Rights in Africa: The Kampala Convention* (Routledge Contemporary Africa 2021); Allehone Abebe, *The Emerging Law of Forced Displacement in Africa: Development and Implementation of the Kampala Convention on Internally Displaced Persons* (Routledge 2017); Walter Kälin, 'Consolidating the Normative Framework for IDPs' (2018) 30(2) International Journal of Refugee Law 314; Romola Adeola, 'The Impact of the African Union Convention on the Protection and Assistance of Internally Displaced Persons in Africa' (2019) 19 African Human Rights Law Journal 591; Romola Adeola, 'Xenophobia and Internal Displacement in Africa: Defining Protection and Assistance through the Kampala Convention' (2020) 27 South African Journal of International Affairs 493; Romola Adeola and Francis Viljoen, 'The Right Not to Be Arbitrarily Displaced in Africa' (2017) 25 African Journal of International and Comparative Law 459; Romola Adeola, 'The Kampala Convention and the Right not to be Arbitrarily Displaced' (2018) 59 Forced Migration Review 15.

[213] 'List of countries which have signed, ratified / acceded to the African Union Convention for the Protection and Assistance of Internally Displaced Persons in Africa (Kampala Convention)' (African Union, 18 June 2020) https://au.int/sites/default/files/treaties/36846-sl-AFRICAN%20UNION%20CONVENTION%20FOR%20THE%20PROTECTION%20AND%20ASSISTANCE%20OF%20INTERNALLY%20DISPLACED%20PERSONS%20IN%20AFRICA%20%28KAMPALA%20CONVENTION%29.pdf accessed 6 July 2021.

[214] Beyani, 'A View from Inside the Kitchen of the Kampala Convention' (n 212) 8; Dieng, 'Protecting Internally Displaced Persons' (n 199); Mike Asplet and Megan Bradley, 'Introductory Note to the African Union Convention for the Protection of Internally Displaced Persons in Africa "Kampala Convention"' (2013) 52 International Legal Materials 397.

protection of IDPs, and to set out the obligations of relevant actors regarding the prevention of internal displacement and assistance to IDPs in Africa.[215] It sets out the States Parties' general obligations, as well as their obligations relating to protection from internal displacement and their obligations relating to protection and assistance during displacement. The Kampala Convention also sets out the obligations of international organizations, humanitarian agencies, and the African Union; and contains provisions on IDPs' durable solutions and compensation, as well as registration and personal documentation. Crucially for the purposes of this work, the Kampala Convention explicitly refers to the relationship between IDP protection and refugee protection. Article XX states that:

> No provision in this Convention shall be interpreted as affecting or undermining the right of internally displaced persons to seek and be granted asylum within the framework of the African Charter on Human and Peoples' Rights, and to seek protection, as a refugee, within the purview of the 1969 OAU Convention Governing the Specific Aspects of Refugee Problems in Africa or the 1951 UN Convention Relating to the Status of Refugees as well as the 1967 Protocol Relating to the Status of Refugees.

Hence similar to the drafters of the Guiding Principles, the drafters of the Kampala Convention were very much mindful of the possibility that states might try to invoke this development in IDP protection as a ground for rejecting asylum claims.

The Kampala Convention represents three significant developments in IDP protection. First, when compared to the IDP description in the Guiding Principles, it explicitly recognizes more push factors of displacement.[216] In addition to the grounds set out in the Guiding Principles, the Kampala Convention also recognizes that internal displacement may occur based on policies of racial discrimination, as a method of warfare, as a result of harmful practices, and as a collective punishment. Explicit recognition of these factors is a helpful reminder to states that displacement can happen for a wide variety of reasons. However, like the Guiding Principles, the Kampala Convention's list of factors for displacement is not exhaustive and it states that internal displacement may be 'caused by any act, event, factor, or phenomenon of comparable gravity to all of the above and which is not justified under international law'.[217]

[215] Kampala Convention, art 2.
[216] Art IV (4).
[217] Art IV(4)(h).

Second, the Kampala Convention obliges parties to introduce domestic legislation on internal displacement.[218] Although the Great Lakes Pact contained a similar obligation, the geographical membership of the Kampala Convention is much wider as it is open to all African states. Yet the implementation of this provision has been somewhat disappointing with very few states introducing new legislation on IDPs since the Kampala Convention came into force in 2009.[219] Orchard suggests this might be because domestic processes to introduce legislation can be long and cumbersome, citing the Central African Republic, Democratic Republic of Congo, and Nigeria as examples of states which had IDP protection policies in draft forms for many years.[220] Beyani also points to the:

> difficulty faced by African States in applying the Kampala Convention and its modern aspects that combine State responsibility, the responsibility of international organisations, including the African Union, and those of non-state actors, particularly armed groups, in constitutionalised legal systems.[221]

Third, the Kampala Convention's monitoring and compliance mechanism represents the first such mechanism for IDPs. It establishes a Conference of State Parties to the Convention to monitor and review its implementation.[222] The Conference of State Parties finally held its first meeting in April 2017 and has now been formally constituted on an ongoing basis.[223] The State Parties also adopted a five-year Harare plan of action designed to establish a policy framework 'for the prevention, protection of and assistance to internally displaced persons ... at national level' and to strengthen regional and national measures to both prevent and eliminate the root causes of internal displacement and to improve durable solutions.[224] While UNHCR has welcomed the meeting, it

[218] Art III(2).

[219] Alfredo dos Santos Soares, 'Protecting Environmentally Displaced Persons under the Kampala Convention: A Brief Assessment' (2018) 9(1) Revista Catalana de Dret Ambiental 1.

[220] Orchard, *Protecting the Internally Displaced* (n 49); Beyani, 'A View from Inside the Kitchen of the Kampala Convention' (n 212).

[221] Beyani, 'A View from Inside the Kitchen of the Kampala Convention' (n 212) 18.

[222] Kampala Convention, art XIV.

[223] '1st meeting of conference of states parties to the Kampala Convention' (African Union, 5 April 2017) https://au.int/en/newsevents/20170403/1st-meeting-conference-states-parties-kampala-convention#:~:text=Harare%2C%20Zimbabwe%205%20April%202017,implementation%20of%20the%20Kampala%20Convention accessed 7 July 2021.

[224] 'Plan of action for the implementation of the Kampala Convention adopted by conference of states parties' (African Union, 6 April 2017) https://au.int/en/pressreleases/20170406/plan-action-implementationkampala-convention-adopted-conference-states accessed 6 July 2021.

also cautioned that the State Parties needed to 'take extra steps in putting in place national mechanism [sic] and policies for its implementation'.[225]

The Kampala Convention also commits States Parties to report on the measures taken in respect of the Convention's implementation when presenting their reports under the African Charter on Human and Peoples' Rights as well as the African Peer Review Mechanism.[226] Orchard is disappointed with the implementation of this obligation, however, and notes (in 2019), that of the 23 periodic reports submitted since the Kampala Convention came into force, only 11, or less than half, even mention IDPs.[227] In sum, although the Kampala Convention has 'modernised a somewhat soft static international legal framework relating to internally displaced persons',[228] there is much room for improvement regarding its implementation in practice.

3.3.4 Assessment of the Legal Framework of IDP Protection

The legal regime applicable to IDPs may therefore be summarized as follows. IDPs, owing to the fact that they have not crossed an international frontier, are primarily the responsibility of their own governments. Therefore, unlike refugees, they do not have an international legal status, although some regional conventions denote a legal status to IDPs.[229]

That is not to say that IDPs are without legal protection. IDPs are entitled to the protection of international human rights law, humanitarian law, and international criminal law. They are also protected by the Guiding Principles on Internal Displacement, a soft law document which is technically non-binding, but is based for the most part on hard law obligations and has been widely incorporated into domestic laws and policies and widely applied by key stakeholders in IDP protection.

Finally, the regional treaties on the protection of IDPs may be heralded as a welcome development in this area, especially by virtue of the fact that the traditional belief was that it would be extremely difficult, if not impossible, to draft a treaty dealing with the protection of IDPs. The Great Lakes Pact binds 11 countries with significant IDP problems, and the Kampala Convention has the

225 Orchard, *Protecting the Internally Displaced* (n 49).
226 Kampala Convention, art XIV.
227 Orchard, *Protecting the Internally Displaced* (n 49).
228 Beyani, 'A View from Inside the Kitchen of the Kampala Convention' (n 212) 2.
229 The term 'international legal status' is used in the sense of a status provided by a multilateral non-regional treaty.

potential to have a significant impact on the continent which is most affected by the IDP problem.

3.4 Institutional Framework for the Protection of Internally Displaced Persons

Unlike refugees, there is no specific agency dedicated to IDP issues. However, several mechanisms have emerged both within and outside the UN. The key developments in the institutional protection of IDPs will be dealt with in the following sections.

3.4.1 The Mandate of the Special Rapporteur of the Human Rights of Internally Displaced Persons

During the era of 'preventive protection' as outlined above, the position of Representative of the Secretary-General on Internally Displaced Persons was created. Francis M Deng first served in this position from 1992 to 2004, succeeded by Walter Kälin from 2004 to 2010 as the Representative of the Secretary-General on the Human Rights of Internally Displaced Persons. Chaloka Beyani held the position from 2010 to 2016, and the position is currently held by Cecilia Jiminez-Damary (appointed in 2016). The mandate of the Special Rapporteur was created to 'address the complex problem of internal displacement', 'work towards strengthening the international response to the complex problem of internal displacement', and 'engage in coordinated international advocacy and action' on behalf of the human rights of IDPs, 'while continuing and enhancing inclusive dialogue' with governments and other key stakeholders.[230] The methods employed by the Special Rapporteur include undertaking regular country missions to inquire into the treatment of IDPs and to make recommendations for solving ongoing problems.[231]

[230] 'Special Rapporteur on the Human Rights of Internally Displaced Persons' (*UN Human Rights Office of the High Commissioner*) https://www.ohchr.org/en/issues/idpersons/pages/idpersonsindex.aspx accessed 6 July 2021.

[231] 'About the mandate of the Special Rapporteur on the human rights of internally displaced persons' (*UN Human Rights Office of the High Commissioner*) https://www.ohchr.org/EN/Issues/IDPersons/Pages/Mandate.aspx accessed 6 July 2021.

3.4.2 The 'Collaborative Approach'

Before 2005, the international system in place for protecting IDPs was named the 'collaborative approach'. Under this system, all agencies shared the responsibility for responding to situations of internal displacement. This included the UNHCR, the United Nations Children's Fund ('UNICEF'), the World Food Programme (WFP), the World Health Organisation (WHO), the United Nations Development Programme (UNDP), the Office of the High Commissioner for Human Rights (OHCHR), the IOM, and NGOs. Although activities were coordinated by the Emergency Relief Coordinator, there was no accountability or locus of responsibility. In addition, there was no predictability of action as the different agencies were able to pick and choose which situations to act upon. A UNHCR report published in 2005 made it clear that the agency had been 'uncertain, inconsistent and unpredictable' in its policies towards IDPs.[232] That same year, the Secretary-General issued a report entitled 'Strengthening of the Coordination of Emergency Humanitarian Assistance of the United Nations', which identified 'significant capacity gaps' in areas such as shelter and camp management and protection. It recognized that the protection of civilians is primarily the responsibility of states, but also that 'the humanitarian system must work to fill protection gaps'[233] and that:

> partnerships within the system may be necessary to overcome those gaps in assistance—such as protection and camp management in situations involving IDPs—that do not enjoy leadership from any one agency.[234]

3.4.3 The 'Cluster Approach'

To address these concerns, the Inter-Agency Standing Committee agreed to a division of labour amongst the UN and other humanitarian agencies in 2005. The aims of the reform were to improve the predictability, timeliness, and effectiveness of humanitarian response; to provide leadership and accountability; and to address the responsibility gaps identified in the Secretary-General's

[232] Vanessa Matter and Paul White, UNHCR Evaluation and Policy Analysis Unit, 'Consistent and Predictable Responses to IDPs: A Review of UNHCR's Decision-Making Processes' (March 2005) UN Doc EPAU/2005/2.

[233] Secretary-General of the United Nations, *Strenghtening of the Coordination of Emergency Humanitarian Assistance of the United Nations* (A/60/87-E/2005/78 2005) 9.

[234] ibid 10.

report.[235] Named the 'cluster approach', nine different areas of humanitarian response were clustered together, and each was assigned a 'cluster lead'. For example, UNHCR and the IOM are co-leads for camp coordination and camp management (IOM in disaster and UNHCR in conflict situations), UNICEF is lead for water, sanitation and hygiene, and WHO is lead for health.[236] The cluster lead must set out the needs and organize planning, coordination, and reporting for the relevant situation. It is the first port of call and the provider of last resort in respect of each individual operation. The new 'cluster approach' was not in itself a mandate-giving mechanism, but a more clearly spelled-out role, based on the notion that governments have the primary role for protection of their citizens.[237] It is an arrangement through which the existing mandates of international organizations are brought together in a coordinated and predictable fashion.[238]

The cluster approach was applied for the first time following the 2005 earthquake in Pakistan.[239] Nine clusters were established within 24 hours of the earthquake. Since then, two evaluations on the cluster approach have taken place and it has been subjected to scholarly analysis.[240] The consensus is that, although leadership, accountability, and the effectiveness of aid delivery has increased, numerous problems remain. First, clusters have excluded national and local actors and have 'in several cases weakened national and local ownership capacities'.[241] Second, Dieng argues that the cluster approach had a tendency to focus on emergent crises to the detriment of protracted crises.[242] Third, Orchard argues that the cluster approach cannot replicate a single lead agency and there are still problems with coordination and leadership issues

[235] 'Cluster 2006 – Appeal for Improving Humanitarian Response Capacity' (United Nations Office for the Coordination of Humanitarian Affairs, 3 March 2006) https://www.humanitarianresponse.info/en/programme-cycle/space/document/cluster-2006-appeal-improving-humanitarian-response-capacity accessed 7 July 2021.

[236] 'What is the Cluster Approach?' (OCHA Services) https://www.humanitarianresponse.info/en/coordination/clusters/what-cluster-approach accessed 7 July 2021 (hereafter 'What is the Cluster Approach' (OCHA Services)).

[237] UNHCR Policy Development and Evaluation Service and Division of Operational Services, 'UNHCR's Expanded Role in Support of the Inter-Agency Response to Situations of Internal Displacement' (November 2006) UN Doc PDES/2006/06, 9.

[238] UNHCR, 'The Protection of Internally Displaced Persons and the Role of UNHCR' (2007) 4.

[239] 'What is the Cluster Approach' (OCHA Services) (n 236).

[240] Abby Stoddard and others, 'Cluster Approach Evaluation'(November 2007) https://www.humanitarianresponse.info/sites/www.humanitarianresponse.info/files/documents/files/Cluster%20Approach%20Evaluation%201.pdf accessed 7 July 2021; 'Cluster Approach Evaluation II Synthesis Report' (Global Public Policy Institute, 1 April 2010) https://www.gppi.net/2010/04/01/cluster-approach-evaluation-ii-synthesis-report accessed 6 July 2021 (hereafter 'Cluster Approach Evaluation II Synthesis Report').

[241] 'Cluster Approach Evaluation II Synthesis Report' (n 240); Dieng, 'Protecting Internally Displaced Persons' (n 199).

[242] Dieng, 'Protecting Internally Displaced Persons' (n 199).

within the clusters.[243] There is little coordination between the creation of domestic law and policies in some countries and the plans of the clusters, probably because of a lack of domestic actors within the cluster approach. This was emphasized by the UN Office for the Coordination of Humanitarian Affairs (OCHA) in 2017, which noted that 'IDPs are not often considered as a priority by concerned Governments, and complex institutional arrangements to deal with this issue in-country can impede progress'.[244] A final problem—which is not exclusive to the cluster approach but reflective of humanitarian assistance more generally—is that operations under the cluster approach have only limited accountability to the affected populations they are supposed to help, including IDPs.[245]

3.4.4 Responsibility to Protect and Humanitarian Intervention

A further key development in the institutional protection of IDPs concerns the doctrines of responsibility to protect ('R2P') and humanitarian intervention. These two doctrines developed in parallel to many of the developments outlined above, including the era of preventive protection and the development of a legal framework on behalf of IDPs.

The most significant expression of the R2P by states stems from the World Summit Outcome Document adopted in 2005. It presents R2P as two basic principles: first, that state sovereignty implies responsibility and the primary responsibility for the protection of its people lies with the state itself. Second, 'the international community, through the United Nations, also has the responsibility to use appropriate diplomatic, humanitarian and other peaceful means, in accordance with Chapters VI and VIII of the Charter, to help to protect populations from genocide, war crimes, ethnic cleansing and crimes against humanity'.[246] Since then, R2P has been relied upon by Ban Ki-Moon to take diplomatic steps following the wide-scale displacement in the wake of the post-election violence in Kenya in 2008.[247] In 2011, the Security Council expressly referred to the Libyan authorities' responsibility to protect its people in

[243] Orchard, *Protecting the Internally Displaced* (n 49).
[244] OCHA, 'Reduce and Address Displacement' https://agendaforhumanity.org accessed 14 July 2021.
[245] Orchard, *Protecting the Internally Displaced* (n 49).
[246] UNGA Res 60/1 (24 October 2005) UN Doc A/RES/60/1 [139].
[247] UNGA Report of the Secretary-General, 'Implementing the Responsibility to Protect' (2009) UN Doc A/63/677 [55].

resolutions which created an NFZ[248] and an arms embargo,[249] referred the situation to the ICC,[250] and imposed sanctions on certain individuals.[251] Although this concept is not legally binding, it has been used to justify actions by the international community to protect persons within a state's borders.

A parallel—and somewhat similar—concept is that of humanitarian intervention. It is similar to R2P in that it is concerned with the intervention of the international community in situations of mass suffering, which can include situations of mass internal displacement. However, humanitarian intervention is distinct from R2P because humanitarian intervention refers to the *unauthorized* application of armed force against a territorial state to protect people in that state from gross and systematic human rights violations. The term 'humanitarian intervention' does not encompass situations where the UNSC has authorized force, such as in Somalia (1992) and Rwanda (1994) (see section 3.2 above). This is because an intervention authorized by the UNSC does not need to be invoked pursuant to a purported 'right' to humanitarian intervention because such interventions fall within the enforcement powers of the UNSC.[252] Such intervention would more appropriately be associated with R2P.

Much ink has been spilled on whether a 'right' of humanitarian intervention exists under international law and these debates will not be addressed in detail here. Suffice it to say that the main positions are: (i) there is no 'right' of humanitarian intervention;[253] (ii) there is 'right' of humanitarian intervention;[254]

[248] UNSC Res 1973 (17 March 2011) UN Doc S/RES/1973.

[249] UNSC Res 1970 (26 February 2011) UN Doc S/RES/1970.

[250] ibid.

[251] ibid; UNSC Res 1973 (17 March 2011) UN Doc S/RES/1973.

[252] Dino Kritsiotis, 'The Arab Spring, Massive Violations of Human Rights and the Use of Force' 5(1) Amsterdam Law Forum 80 (2013).

[253] The 2000 Declaration of the South Summit by the G77 composed of about 130 member states declares that 'We reject the so-called "right" of humanitarian intervention, which has no legal basis in the United Nations Charter or in the general principles of international law': Group of 77 South Summit (G77, 10–14 April 2000) <http://www.g77.org/summit/Declaration_G77Summit.htm> accessed 6 July 2021; Nigel Rodley, 'Humanitarian Intervention' in M Weller (ed), *The Oxford Handbook of the Use of Force in International Law* (OUP 2015) (hereafter Rodley, 'Humanitarian Intervention'); Christian Henderson, *The Use of Force In International Law* (CUP 2018); Chris O'Meara, 'Should International Law Recognize a Right of Humanitarian Intervention?' (2017) 66 International and Comparative Law Quarterly 441; Vaughan Lowe and Antonios Tzanakopoulos, *Humanitarian Intervention* (Max Planck Encyclopedia of Public International Law 2012); Joel I Charney, 'Anticipatory Humanitarian Intervention in Kosovo' (1999) 93 American Journal of International Law 837; the views of Ian Browlie in 'Select Committee of Foreign Affairs Fourth Report' (*UK Parliament*, 2000) https://publications.parliament.uk/pa/cm199900/cmselect/cmfaff/28/2813.htm accessed 6 July 2021; Peter Hilpold, 'Humanitarian Intervention: Is there a Need for a Legal Reappraisal?' (2001) 12 European Journal of International Law 437.

[254] In the ICJ proceedings regarding the *Legality of the Use of Force* (by NATO in Yugoslavia), the UK and Belgium expressly relied on the doctrine of humanitarian intervention. See 'Written Proceedings' and 'Oral Proceedings' (*ICJ*, 1999) https://www.icj-cij.org/en/case/105 accessed 6 July 2021. See also Daniel Bethlehem, 'Stepping Back a Moment – The Legal Basis in Favour of a Principle of Humanitarian Intervention' (*EJIL Talk!*, 12 September 2013) http://www.ejiltalk.org/stepping-back-a-mom

(iii) humanitarian intervention is illegal but might sometimes be viewed as legitimate;[255] (iv) although there is no such 'right' at present, there exists some practice which might someday crystalize into a right of humanitarian intervention.[256]

Regardless of the legal debates or the legality of such a 'right', recent years have illustrated that some states are willing to use force in other states for purportedly humanitarian reasons in situations where there are large numbers of IDPs. In 2018, the UK, US, and France conducted air strikes in Syria, which according to the UK was, inter alia, 'to alleviate overwhelming human suffering'.[257] The UK, Belgium, Denmark, and Germany expressly relied on the right of humanitarian intervention to justify the 1999 bombing by NATO in Yugoslavia.[258] In 1991, the UK, France, and the USA established safe zones and NFZs in Iraq, which was justified by the UK as humanitarian intervention.[259]

Although this admittedly only represents a handful of states, it is significant that many of these actions were largely tolerated and/or supported by many states.[260] Although the intervening states explicitly invoke a 'right' of

ent-the-legal-basis-in-favour-of-a-principle-of-humanitarian-intervention/#more-9297 accessed 6 July 2021; Guglielmo Veridrame, 'The Law and Strategy of Humanitarian Intervention' (*EJIL Talk!*, 30 August 2013) https://www.ejiltalk.org/the-law-and-strategy-of-humanitarian-intervention/ accessed 6 July 2021; the views of Christopher Greenwood in 'Select Committee of Foreign Affairs Fourth Report' (*UK Parliament*, 2000) https://publications.parliament.uk/pa/cm199900/cmselect/cmfaff/28/2813.htm accessed 6 July 2021; Harold Koh, *The Trump Administration and International Law* (OUP 2019); W Michael Reisman, 'Unilateral Action and the Transformations of the World Constitutive Process: The Special Problem of Humanitarian Intervention' (2000) European Journal of International Law 11(1) 3.

[255] Bruno Simma, 'NATO, the UN and the Use of Force: Legal Aspects' (1999) 10 European Journal of International Law 1; Independent International Commission on Kosovo, 'The Kosovo Report' (2000) 4; Peter Hilpold, The Kosovo Case and International Law: Looking for Applicable Theories' (2009) 8(1) Chinese Journal of International Law 47.

For a critique of this position see Anthea Roberts, 'Legality v Legitimacy: Can Uses of Force be Illegal but Justified?' in Philip Alston and Euan Macdonald (eds), *Human Rights, Intervention and the Use of Force* (OUP 2008).

[256] For discussion, see Oliver Corten, 'Human Rights and Collective Security: Is There an Emerging Right of Humanitarian Intervention?' in Philip Alston and Euan Macdonald (eds), *Human Rights, Intervention and the Use of Force* (OUP 2008).

[257] Policy Paper 'Syria Action—UK Government Legal Position' (Prime Minister's Office, 14 April 2018) https://www.gov.uk/government/publications/syria-action-uk-government-legal-position/syria-action-uk-government-legal-position accessed 6 July 2021.

[258] Simon Chesterman, *Just War or Just Peace?* (OUP 2009); Harold Koh, 'The War Powers and Humanitarian Intervention' (2016) Yale Faculty Scholarship Series https://digitalcommons.law.yale.edu/cgi/viewcontent.cgi?article=6221&context=fss_papers accessed 7 July 2021; Dino Kritsiotis, 'The Kosovo Crisis and NATO's Application of Armed Force against the Federal Republic of Yugoslavia' (2000) 49 International and Comparative Law Quarterly 330.

[259] See section 3.2.

[260] Nicholas J Wheeler, *Saving Strangers: Humanitarian Intervention in International Society* (OUP 2000) 260 (hereafter Wheeler, *Saving Strangers*); Alonso Gurmendi Dunkelberg and others, 'Mapping States' Reactions to Syria Strikes' (*Just Security*, 22 April 2018) https://www.justsecurity.org/55157/mapping-states-reactions-syria-strikes-april-2018/ accessed 6 July 2021; Patrick Smyth, 'EU Endorses Attacks on Syria by US, UK and France' (*Irish Times*, 14 April 2018) https://www.irishtimes.com/news/world/europe/eu-endorses-attacks-on-syria-by-us-uk-and-france-1.3462219; accessed 7 July 2021.

humanitarian intervention and tried to justify their actions on other grounds (eg weak claims of authorization via UNSC resolutions,[261] or that the actions were in response to chemical weapons attacks)[262] they also referred to the significant human suffering in the states concerned.[263] The practice of these states cannot be taken as support for a 'right' of humanitarian intervention, but they nonetheless form part of a general willingness to intervene in situations of mass human rights violations with neither explicit UNSC authorization nor consent of the territorial state.[264]

In sum, therefore, there is a general acceptance that intervention in situations of mass suffering (including where there is mass internal displacement) can be legal when authorized by the Security Council (R2P). Some even go so far as to argue that such intervention can be legal even without UNSC authorization (humanitarian intervention). As set out in section 3.2, these concepts have been used to justify intervention in situations of, inter alia, mass suffering of IDPs in the past and might very well be invoked in respect of future operations on behalf of IDPs.

3.4.5 Additional Institutional Protection of Internally Displaced Persons

There are various human rights mechanisms within the UN system that offer various degrees of institutional protection for IDPs. Aside from the mandate of the Special Rapporteur, as mentioned above, there are three other particularly relevant mechanisms. The first is the UN Secretary-General's High Level Panel on Internal Displacement, which was established following a request by 57 UN member states in May 2019.[265] It was established to prompt action to prevent,

Humanitarian relief was provided by Turkey, Spain, Italy, and the Netherlands following the establishment of 'Operation Provide Comfort' in Iraq in 1991 by the UK, US, and France. Thomas E Ricks, 'Operation Provide Comfort: A Forgotten Mission with Possible Lessons for Syria' (*Foreign Policy*, 6 February 2017) https://foreignpolicy.com/2017/02/06/operation-provide-comfort-a-forgotten-mission-with-possible-lessons-for-syria/ accessed 7 July 2021.

[261] Wheeler, *Saving Strangers* (n 260) 262, 263.

[262] See the 2017 US air strikes on a Syrian airfield, which was justified as a response to chemical weapons attacks. 'Syria Missile Strikes: US Launches First Direct Military Action against Assad' (*The Guardian*, 7 April 2017) https://www.theguardian.com/world/2017/apr/06/trump-syria-missiles-assad-chemical-weapons accessed 7 July 2021.

[263] Clinton and his advisors argued that the West had a moral responsibility to stop the terrible atrocities taking place. See Wheeler, *Saving Strangers* (n 260) 265.

[264] Rodley, 'Humanitarian Intervention' (n 253).

[265] 'Terms of Reference: High Level Panel on Internal Displacement' (United Nations) https://www.un.org/internal-displacement-panel/sites/www.un.org.internal-displacement-panel/files/tor_of_the_panel.pdf accessed 7 July 2021.

respond to, and solve the world's internal displacement crises. Building on ongoing efforts within the humanitarian, development, and peace communities, the Panel will produce a final report which will identify bold, concrete, and practical recommendations for member states, the UN system, and other relevant stakeholders. The report is due in early 2021, but at the time of writing has not yet been published.

Second, internal displacement is often framed as a human rights issue,[266] which means that the UN's Universal Periodic Review (UPR) is also relevant to IDP protection. The UPR is held under the auspices of the UN Human Rights Council and is proclaimed to be 'a cooperative mechanism, based on interactive dialogue' between states, 'with the full involvement of the country concerned and with consideration given to its capacity-building needs'.[267] The UPR covers all human rights issues and IDP protection has been addressed via this forum. However, a recent study by Hudson and Ní Ghráinne found that internal displacement is scarcely discussed in this forum, particularly in relation to disaster-induced displacement.[268]

Third, IDP protection issues are sometimes addressed by the UN treaty-based institutions. Through the state reporting process and the issuance of General Comments, these institutions have highlighted issues of particular concern to IDP populations (as outlined in section 3.3.1 above).[269]

Finally, recent years have seen the development of several more ad hoc, informal channels at the global level specifically addressing internal displacement. Notable examples include the 'Guiding Principles 20',[270] the Internal Displacement Monitoring Centre, IOM Displacement Dialogues,[271] and the Platform on Disaster Displacement.[272] A detailed analysis of each respective endeavour is outside of the scope of this work, but such analyses are available elsewhere.[273]

[266] Phuong, *The International Protection of Internally Displaced Persons* (n 139) 235; Ben Hudson and Bríd Ní Ghráinne, 'Enhancing State-to-State Dialogue on Internal Displacement: Current Global Fora and Future Prospects' (2020) 39 Refugee Survey Quarterly 425 (hereafter Hudson and Ní Ghráinne, 'Enhancing State-to-State Dialogue on Internal Displacement').

[267] Hudson and Ní Ghráinne, 'Enhancing State-to-State Dialogue on Internal Displacement' (n 266).

[268] ibid.

[269] ibid.

[270] 'GP 20: Celebrating 20 Years of the Guiding Principles on Internal Displacement' (*Global Protection Cluster*) https://www.globalprotectioncluster.org/gp20/ accessed 7 July 2021.

[271] 'IDMC Expert Forum 2020: Internal Displacement in a Changing Climate' (*IDMC*) https://www.internal-displacement.org/expert_forum_2020 accessed 7 July 2021.

[272] 'Platform on Disaster Displacement' (*Disaster Displacement*) https://disasterdisplacement.org/what-we-do accessed 7 July 2021.

[273] Hudson and Ní Ghráinne, 'Enhancing State-to-State Dialogue on Internal Displacement' (n 266).

3.4.6 Reflection on Institutional Protection of Internally Displaced Persons

Unlike for refugees, there is no organization that is specifically dedicated to IDP issues. Although several mechanisms have developed on an ad hoc basis in the last few decades, a number of problems remain, such as the relative lack of discussion of IDP issues at the UPR. Moreover, although the reformed cluster approach has led to increased leadership, accountability, and the effectiveness of aid delivery, problems remain, such as the exclusion of local actors, the focus on emergent crises to the detriment of protracted crises, and remaining shortfalls in coordination and leadership issues. Moreover, two of the largest agencies involved in the protection and assistance of IDPs—the UNHCR and IOM—also have significant responsibility for the protection and assistance of refugees. The potential for IDP protection activities to be invoked as an alternative for refugee status means that by assisting IDPs, these organizations might be undermining their efforts on behalf of IDPs. I deal with the role of IOM and UNHCR in protecting IDPs elsewhere (the latter in chapter 5 of this book).[274]

It is therefore time to seriously consider creating a specific agency on internal displacement.[275] However, several caveats must be borne in mind. First, the negotiation of a new agency on IDPs would be subject to state negotiations and compromise, and thus might fall short of what is necessary to create an effective response to internal displacement. Second, it is important to carefully consider whether a global agency would be the best approach, or whether IDP protection issues might be better addressed at a regional level. Through the conclusion of specific treaties on IDPs, Africa has already shown us that what might seem impossible at an international level might very well be achievable at regional level. It is hoped that the possibility of creating a specific agency on IDPs will be addressed by the High Level Panel's report, which is due in 2021.

3.5 Conclusion

Significant strides have been made in the last few decades concerning the legal and institutional protection of IDPs. Notable achievements include: (1)

[274] Ní Ghráinne and Hudson, 'The International Organisation for Migration's Engagement with the Guiding Principles on Internal Displacement' (n 180).

[275] Miriam Bradley, 'UNHCR and Accountability for IDP Protection in Colombia' in Kirstin Bergtora Sandvik and Katja Lindskov Jacobsen (eds), *UNHCR and the Struggle for Accountability: Technology, Law and Results-Based Management* (Routledge 2016).

the development of the Guiding Principles on Internal Displacement, which although technically a non-binding document have nonetheless become the global standard of IDP protection and have been incorporated into laws and policies of many states around the world; (2) the development of regional IDP treaties in Africa, which oblige member states to incorporate the Guiding Principles into their domestic laws; (3) the creation of the position of the UN Special Rapporteur on Internal Displacement, which particularly through country visits has drawn significant attention to the plight of IDPs around the world; (4) the reformed cluster approach, which despite some remaining problems has nonetheless improved the coordination and leadership of the global response to internal displacement. However, this chapter has illustrated that many of these developments were motivated—at least in part—by a desire to contain refugee flows.

Moreover, it is clear that IDPs have been neglected when compared to refugees in both legal and institutional terms. Unlike for refugees, there is still neither a global treaty nor a dedicated agency for the protection of IDPs. The latest major endeavour of the international community to address the protection needs of forced migrants—the UN Global Compact on Refugees[276]—has been criticized for 'virtually ignoring'[277] IDPs,[278] and the relative lack of discussion of IDP issues during the UPR process is indicative of the current lack of priority given to internal displacement by states. Yet, the support of 57 states for the establishment of a UN High Level Panel on Internal Displacement offers some indication that momentum is slowly gathering behind IDP-specific initiatives. It is hoped that the Panel seizes this momentum to put forward bold and concrete recommendations for the UN and other stakeholders, and that these recommendations will be taken up by states. We—the IDP stakeholder community—await the publication of this report and the subsequent response of states with much anticipation.

[276] UN 'Report of the United Nations High Commissioner for Refugees: Part II Global Compact on Refugees' (2018) UN Doc A/73/12 (Part II).

[277] Elizabeth Ferris and Susan Martin, 'The Global Compacts on Refugees and for Safe, Orderly and Regular Migration: Introduction to the Special Issue' (2019) 57(6) International Migration 5. See also T Alexander Aleinikoff, 'The Unfinished Work of the Global Compact on Refugees' (2018) 30(4) International Journal of Refugee Law 611; Alfredo dos Santos, 'The (Un)Protection of Internally Displaced Persons under the Global Compact on Refugees' in Alexander Sungurov and others (eds), *Current Issues on Human Rights* (Dykinson 2020) 289; Hudson and Ní Ghráinne, 'Enhancing State-to-State Dialogue on Internal Displacement' (n 266).

[278] The Global Compact on Refugees (GCR) makes two references to IDPs: (i) it notes in para 12 that population movements may be of a composite character and may involve IDPs; (ii) in para 89 it directs states to 'take into account' the situation of IDPs when contributing resources and expertise to support countries of origin.

4

Internal Displacement and the Internal Protection Alternative

4.1 Introduction

The internal protection alternative (IPA) is based on the idea that if there is a safe place within the individual's state of nationality or habitual residence where they can relocate, they are not a refugee. For example, a decision-maker might accept that Jim has a prima facie claim for refugee status based on, inter alia, threats from a terrorist organization in his home village. Yet, the decision-maker might nonetheless conclude that Jim is not in fact a refugee because he has an IPA available to him: he can relocate to another province where he will be provided with protection from the persecution feared. Additional examples of the application of the IPA could include relocating from the countryside to the city where an individual is less likely to be found by their persecutors;[1] or relocating to an area where a clan, tribe, militia, or international organization could provide protection.[2] Today, the IPA concept is an inherent part of refugee status determinations in most States Parties to the Refugee Convention and has been incorporated into Article 8 of the 2011 Recast EC Qualification Directive.[3]

The IPA concept therefore lies at the nexus between the availability of internal protection and the need for international protection. Essentially, the IPA inquiry asks whether the availability of internal protection for a particular individual means that they are not a refugee. It directly pertains to the relationship between IDPs and refugees—and thus the focus of this book—in two main respects. First, an individual who is returned to an IPA in essence becomes an

[1] *KAB v Sweden*, App no 886/11 (ECHR, 5 September 2013).

[2] *DM (Majority Clan Entities can Protect) Somalia v Secretary of State for the Home Department* [2005] UKAIT 00150; *Elmi v Minister of Citizenship and Immigration* 1999 CarswellNat 390 [1999] FCH 336; Council Directive 2011/95/EU of the European Parliament and of the Council of 13 December 2011 on standards for the qualification of third-country nationals or stateless persons as beneficiaries of international protection, for a uniform status for refugees or for persons eligible for subsidiary protection, and for the content of the protection granted (recast) [2011] OJ L337/9, art 8, art 7(1)(b) (hereafter the Qualification Directive).

[3] Qualification Directive (n 2).

Internally Displaced Persons and International Refugee Law. Bríd Ní Ghráinne, Oxford University Press. © Ní Ghráinne 2022.
DOI: 10.1093/oso/9780198868446.003.0004

IDP—someone who is displaced within their country. The fact that an individual becomes an IDP, as well as the conditions facing IDPs in the proposed area of relocation, could be relevant considerations in determining whether that area is a valid IPA. Second, and conversely, IDP protection measures in a putative IPA could be viewed as negating the presence of a 'well-founded fear of being persecuted' necessary to qualify as a refugee, and/or result in the conclusion that the asylum-seeker is unable to show that protection is unavailable to them within the whole of their country of origin. In other words, the availability of protection to IDPs could support the finding of an IPA, resulting in the denial of refugee status.

Until now, these issues have not been addressed in the literature.[4] We therefore do not know whether and to what extent becoming an IDP on return is relevant to the IPA inquiry. Specifically, we do not know to what extent becoming an IDP is evidence in support of an IPA, or to what extent becoming an IDP is evidence against the finding of an IPA. This chapter aims to shed light on these issues and in doing so, will clarify the relationship between internal displacement and the IPA.

The chapter is formed of six sections. Section 4.2 will explain the relationship between the refugee definition and the IPA, and section 4.3 will explain the applicable criteria in the IPA inquiry. Section 4.4 will illustrate to what extent the possibility of becoming an IDP forms part of courts' assessment of the existence of an IPA. Section 4.5 will illustrate how the chapter's arguments regarding the IPA / internal displacement relationship are applicable also to the application of the cessation clauses. Section 4.6 will conclude.

The chapter's key argument is that the IDP label does not carry significant weight when determining whether a location qualifies as an IPA. Even though return to a situation of internal displacement might give rise to human rights violations, the fact that an individual will become an IDP on return does not rule a place out of being a valid IPA. This is the case even where that individual might have to live in an IDP camp or in a critical shelter arrangement, such as an unfinished or abandoned makeshift shelter, tent, mosque, or church, or squat in a government building. In fact, the broad nature of the IDP description (which covers a wide range of people and circumstances) can obfuscate the central issue at hand—namely whether the living conditions that the individual will be exposed to in that area are compatible with the IPA test. The

[4] A section of Kate Ogg's article examines returning to a camp environment in the context of IPA claims, but it does not deal with the issue of internal displacement more broadly. See Kate Ogg, 'Protection from "Refuge": On What Legal Grounds Will a Refugee be Saved from Camp Life?' (2016) 28(3) International Journal of Refugee Law 384 (hereafter Ogg, 'Protection from "Refuge"').

arguments made in this chapter are also relevant to the cessation of refugee status, but it is more unlikely that the cessation clauses will be found to apply where there is a situation of internal displacement.

4.2 The Nexus between the Refugee Definition and the Internal Protection Alternative

It is difficult to pinpoint the exact source of the IPA concept in international law. There is no mention of an IPA in the refugee definition and no explicit reference was made to its existence at the time of drafting.[5] This is not surprising, considering that the traditional assumption at the time was that state sovereignty extended over the whole of the state. It was hence presumed that an individual's ability to receive protection would not depend on whether they could relocate within the state. Nonetheless, states have held that there exists a nexus between the IPA and the refugee definition in two main respects.[6] The first is based on the definition's requirement that the fear of persecution must be 'well-founded'.[7] This has been interpreted to mean that the fear is not well-founded where the persecutory source of the fear could be avoided by relocating to a safe area within the country of origin.[8]

The second basis for the IPA lies in the notion of 'protection'.[9] The focus of the refugee definition is not upon protection in a particular region, but upon the more general notion of protection by that country.[10] If, within that country, obtaining its 'protection' is merely a question of relocating, it implies that inability or the unwillingness to return to the country of nationality is for reasons extrinsic to those set out in the Refugee Convention and that the claimant is therefore not a refugee. Rather than being 'basically at odds with fundamental

[5] *R v Secretary of State for the Home Department, Immigration Appeals Tribunal, Ex parte Anthonypillai Francis Robinson* [1998] QB 929 [10] (hereafter *R v Secretary of State for the Home Department*); *Januzi v Secretary of State for the Home Department* [2006] UKHL 5 [7], [2006] 2 AC 426, 440 (hereafter *Januzi v Secretary of State for the Home Department*); *Randhawa v Minister for Immigration, Local Government and Ethnic Affairs* [1994] 52 FCR 437, 440–41, 124 ALR 265 (Australian Federal Court) (hereafter *Randhawa v Minister for Immigration, Local Government and Ethnic Affairs*); *Decision of 28 April 2000, 96/21/1036-7* (Australian High Administrative Court).

[6] Bríd Ní Ghráinne, 'The Internal Protection Alternative and Human Rights Considerations—Irrelevant or Indispensable?' (2015) 27(1) International Journal of Refugee Law 29 (hereafter Ní Ghráinne, 'Internal Protection Alternative and Human Rights'). Sections 1, 2, 3.1 and 3.2 of this article are reproduced in this chapter, by permission of Oxford University Press.

[7] Convention Relating to the Status of Refugees (adopted 28 July 1951, entered into force 22 April 1954) 189 UNTS 137 (hereafter Refugee Convention), art 1(A)(2).

[8] *Januzi v Secretary of State for the Home Department* (n 5).

[9] *Refugee Appeal No 76044* [2008] NZRSAA 80 [110].

[10] *Randhawa v Minister for Immigration, Local Government and Ethnic Affairs* (n 5).

refugee protection principles',[11] the IPA is based on the notion of 'surrogate' international refugee protection, which means that a person is a refugee only when they are unable or unwilling to avail themselves of the protection of the country of nationality.[12]

Regardless of which part of the Refugee Convention the IPA concept is linked to, it is clear that the 'well-founded fear' and 'protection' elements are interconnected when it comes to the IPA concept.[13] In any event, states have placed an equal emphasis, if not a greater emphasis, on the publications of the UNHCR, in particular, the 1979 Handbook on Procedures and Criteria for Determining Refugee Status.[14] Paragraph 91 states:

> The fear of being persecuted need not always extend to the whole territory of the refugee's country of nationality. Thus in ethnic clashes or in cases of grave disturbances involving civil war conditions, persecution of a specific ethnic or national group may occur in only one part of the country. In such situations, a person will not be excluded from refugee status merely because he could have sought refuge in another part of the same country, if under all the circumstances it would not have been reasonable to expect him to do so.[15]

In sum, authorities in the field generally accept that the IPA is consistent with international refugee law.[16] This is because, as Hathaway explains, the

[11] UNHCR, 'An Overview of Protection Issues in Western Europe: Legislative Trends and Positions Taken by UNHCR' (1995) 1(3) European Series 1, 63; UNHCR, 'Position Paper on Relocating Internally as a Reasonable Alternative to Seeking Asylum (The So-Called "Internal Flight Alternative" or "Relocation Principle")' (February 1999) 2 (hereafter UNHCR, 'Position Paper on Relocating Internally').

[12] In addition, the other criteria of art 1A of the Refugee Convention would need to be met. *Canada (Attorney General) v Ward* [1993] 2 SCR 689 [25]; *Horvath (AP) v Secretary of State for the Home Department* [2001] 1 AC 489; *Refugee Appeal No 76044* [2008] NZRSAA 80 [102], 9; *Randhawa v Minister for Immigration, Local Government and Ethnic Affairs* (n 5).

[13] Andreas Zimmermann, *The 1951 Convention Relating to the Status of Refugees and its 1967 Protocol: A Commentary* (OUP 2010) 447 (hereafter Zimmermann, *Relating to the Status of Refugees and its 1967 Protocol: A Commentary*).

[14] *R v Secretary of State for the Home Department* (n 5) [12]; *A.E., F.E. v Secretary of State for the Home Department* [2003] EWCA Civ 1032, [2004] QB 531 [19]; *Januzi v Secretary of State for the Home Department* (n 5) [9]; *Randhawa v Minister for Immigration, Local Government and Ethnic Affairs* (n 5) 442.

[15] UNHCR, 'Handbook on Procedures and Criteria for Determining Refugee Status under the 1951 Convention and the 1967 Protocol relating to the Status of Refugees' (re-edited January 1992) UN Doc HCR/IP/4/Eng/REV.1 (hereafter UNHCR, 'Handbook on Procedures and Criteria for Determining Refugee Status').

[16] James C Hathaway, 'International Refugee Law: The Michigan Guidelines on the Internal Protection Alternative' (1999) 21 Michigan Journal of International Law 131 (hereafter Hathaway, 'Michigan Guidelines'); Guy S Goodwin-Gill and Jane McAdam, *The Refugee in International Law* (OUP 2011) (hereafter Goodwin-Gill and McAdam, *The Refugee in International Law*); Ní Ghráinne, 'Internal Protection Alternative and Human Rights' (n 6); Bríd Ní Ghráinne, 'Safe Zones and the Internal Protection Alternative', (2020) 69 International and Comparative Law Quarterly 335 (hereafter

Refugee Convention is designed only to provide a back-up source of protection or 'surrogate protection' to persons seriously at risk.[17] Most importantly, domestic courts, as frontline interpreters of the Refugee Convention, regularly apply the IPA in refugee status determination proceedings. Hence in practical terms, the IPA is firmly established as an implicit part of the refugee definition.

Finally, it is important to note that although there exist regional systems of refugee protection in both Africa and Latin America, the IPA is generally accepted to not be applicable to the two main refugee protection instruments in these regions—the 1969 OAU Convention Governing Specific Aspects of the Refugee Problem in Africa,[18] and the Cartagena Declaration, respectively.[19] In other words, an individual can be a refugee under these conventions even if there is a place within their country where they can relocate and receive protection. Having established the relationship between the IPA and the main refugee conventions, the next section will focus on the criteria applicable in the IPA analysis.

Ní Ghráinne, 'Safe Zones and the Internal Protection Alternative') (sections IV and V of this article are reproduced in this chapter, with permission from Cambridge University Press); Bríd Ní Ghráinne, 'The Internal Protection Alternative' in Cathryn Costello, Jane McAdam, and Michelle Foster (eds), *The Oxford Handbook of International Refugee Law* (OUP 2021) (hereafter Ní Ghráinne, 'The Internal Protection Alternative'); (sections 1–5 of this chapter have been reproduced here, by permission of Oxford University Press https://global.oup.com/academic/product/the-oxford-handbook-of-international-refugee-law-9780198848639?lang=en&cc=be).

[17] Hathaway, 'Michigan Guidelines' (n 16) 131.

[18] Art 1(2) of the OAU Convention provides that an individual is a refugee, inter alia, in connection with 'events seriously disturbing public order in *either part of the whole* of his country of origin or nationality' (emphasis added). Convention Governing the Specific Aspects of the Refugee Problem in Africa (adopted 10 September 1969, entered into force 20 June 1974) 1001 UNTS 45 (hereafter 'Convention Governing the Specific Aspects of the Refugee Problem in Africa'); Hugo Storey, 'The Internal Flight Alternative Test: The Jurisprudence Re-examined' (1998) 10 International Journal of Refugee Law 499, 502; Jessica Schultz, *The Internal Protection Alternative in Refugee Law* (Brill 2018) 162 (hereafter Schultz, *The Internal Protection Alternative*).

[19] While the Cartagena Declaration does not state that the reason for being outside the country of origin may have its locus 'in either part of the whole' of a country of origin, it does state the necessity 'of bearing in mind ... the precedent of the OAU Convention (article 1, paragraph 2)'. Colloquium on the International Protection of Refugees in Central America, Mexico and Panama, 'Cartagena Declaration on Refugees' (19–22 November 1984) (Cartagena Declaration). Although the declaration is not binding as a matter of international law, it has been incorporated into the domestic legislation of many states. See Michael Reed-Hurtado, 'The Cartagena Declaration on Refugees and the Protection of People Fleeing Armed Conflict and Other Situations of Violence in Latin America' (June 2013) UNHCR Legal Protection and Policy Research Series PPLA/2013/03.

4.3 Applicable Criteria in the Internal Protection Alternative Analysis

The fact that the IPA is not explicitly anchored in the Refugee Convention has led to wide divergence in the IPA's interpretation by states. This divergence is compounded by the fact that the Refugee Convention does not have a central binding monitoring or enforcement mechanism, capable of delivering authoritative interpretations of the Refugee Convention.[20] The criteria applied by states falls into two categories: (i) a handful of criteria that can be clearly derived from the text of the Refugee Convention—these criteria are applied by many states and represent the legally binding minimum standard; and (ii) additional criteria which do not have a solid footing in the text of the Refugee Convention. These criteria are applied by some states but do not have widespread acceptance, and thus do not yet have the status of binding international law. Both of these categories will be explained in more detail below and section 4 will illustrate how courts have applied these criteria in the context of internal displacement and the IPA inquiry.

4.3.1 Widely Accepted Criteria in the Internal Protection Alternative Analysis

This section will set out the three criteria that are generally accepted as forming part of the IPA inquiry: (i) the IPA must be accessible to the applicant; (ii) there must be effective protection from the original risk of persecution; and (iii) there must be no new risk of being persecuted or of *refoulement*.[21] It will also briefly set out how these criteria might be relevant in the context of internal displacement, which will be explained in further detail in section 4, which draws on relevant case law.

A note on methodology is helpful at this stage to explain how these criteria are derived. As aforementioned, the IPA is often considered to be an implicit part of the Refugee Convention. The 1969 Vienna Convention on the Law of Treaties (VCLT) provides that a treaty shall be interpreted in good faith in accordance with the ordinary meaning to be given to the terms of the treaty

[20] Art 38 of the Refugee Convention states that disputes between the parties shall be referred to the International Court of Justice for settlement. However individuals do not have standing before the ICJ and thus it is not an effective means by which to challenge the rejection of an asylum application.

[21] Ní Ghráinne, 'The Internal Protection Alternative' (n 16); Ní Ghráinne, 'Safe Zones and the Internal Protection Alternative' (n 16).

in their context and in the light of the treaty's object and purpose.[22] The first point of departure for determining the criteria for the IPA (and hence how the refugee definition is interpreted) is therefore the terms of the refugee definition itself as found in the Refugee Convention. As such, the three criteria mentioned below are primarily derived from the terms of the refugee definition.

The VCLT also provides that 'subsequent practice' should be taken into account when determining the meaning of a treaty.[23] Both judgments of domestic courts and the practice of regional systems created by states (such as the EU) constitute subsequent practice for the purposes of interpreting the IPA.[24] Finally, the VCLT also directs us to take into account 'other relevant rules of international law' when interpreting the meaning of a treaty.[25] Understanding how the IPA has been interpreted in other treaty regimes also helps us to understand how it should be interpreted in relation to the Refugee Convention. Thus, although the three criteria set out below are primarily derived from the terms of the Refugee Convention, the fact that they can be found in both case law and other rules of international law further supports the fact that they are binding criteria in the IPA inquiry.

The first binding criteria is that the IPA must be safely and legally accessible to the applicant.[26] In the words of the Canadian Federal Court of Appeal:

[22] Vienna Convention on the Law of Treaties (adopted 23 May 1969, entered into force 27 January 1980) 1155 UNTS 331, art 31(1).

[23] Art 31(3)(b).

[24] Oliver Dörr and Kristen Schmalenbach, *Vienna Convention on the Law of Treaties: A Commentary* (Springer 2012) 59.

[25] Art 31(3)(c).

[26] Joined cases C-175/08, C-176/08, C-178/08 and C-179/08 *Aydin Salahadin Abdulla (C-175/08), Kamil Hasan (C-176/08), Ahmed Adem, Hamrin Mosa Rashi (C-178/08) and Dler Jamal (C-179/08) v Bundesrepublik Deutschland* [2010] ECR I-1493 (hereafter *Aydin Salahadin Abdulla*); Qualification Directive (n 2) art 8; *Salah Sheekh v The Netherlands* App no 1948/04 (ECHR, 11 January 2007) (hereafter *Salah Sheekh v Netherlands*); *Sufi and Elmi v the United Kingdom* App nos 8319/07 and 11449/07 (ECHR, 28 November 2011) (hereafter *Sufi and Elmi v The United Kingdom*); *Al-Amidi v Minister for Immigration and Multicultural Affairs* 177 ALR 506; *Randhawa v Minister for Immigration, Local Government and Ethnic Affairs* (n 5); *Thirunavukkarasu v Canada (Minister of Employment and Immigration)* 1993 CarswellNat 160; 22 Imm LR (2d) 241 (Canadian Federal Court of Appeal) (hereafter *Thirunavukkarasu v Canada); Dirshe v MCI,* Decision No IMM-2124-96 (1997) (Canadian Federal Court of Appeal); *Hashmat v Canada (MEI)* [1997] FCJ No 598 (Canadian Federal Court); *Al-Amidi v Minister for Immigration and Multicultural Affairs* [2000] FCA 1081 (Federal Court of Australia); *Sathananthan v Canada (Minister for Citizenship and Immigration)* [1999] 4 FC 52 (Canadian Federal Court); *R v Secretary of State for the Home Department* (n 5); *R v Secretary of State for the Home Department, Immigration Appeals Tribunal, Ex parte Anthonypillai Francis Robinson* [1998] QB 929; (1993) *Neue Zeitschrift für Verwaltungsrecht* 1210, 1212 (German Federal Administrative Court); *Judgment of 29 May 2008 No 10 C 1107*, BVerwGE 131 (German Federal Administrative Court); *Judgment of 29 May 2008* 1B 97/06 (German Federal Administrative Court); *Matter of H,* Decision No 3276, 1996 (US Board of Immigration Appeals); *Refugee Appeal No 71684/99* [1999] (New Zealand Refugee Status Appeals Authority).

> An [internal protection alternative] cannot be speculative or theoretical only; it must be a realistic attainable option. Essentially, this means that the alternative place of safety must be realistically accessible to the claimant. Any barriers to getting there should be reasonably surmountable. The claimant cannot be required to encounter great physical danger or to undergo undue hardship in travelling there or in staying there. For example, claimants should not be required to cross battle lines where fighting is going on at great risk to their lives in order to reach a place of safety.[27]

The requirement that the IPA must be accessible flows from a 'good faith' interpretation of the Refugee Convention.[28] If the proposed IPA is not accessible, the applicant cannot be expected to seek protection from persecution there, and the applicant may qualify for international protection (ie they may be recognized as a refugee). In the IDP context, a relevant consideration might be whether IDPs are permitted to relocate in the proposed area, whether particular documentation is required to enter the proposed area, and whether the individual has access to such documentation.

Second, there must be effective protection in the proposed IPA from the original risk of persecution. This means that the relocation area must be an 'antidote'[29] to the persecution feared.[30] This criterion is uncontroversial because it is anchored in the text of the Refugee Convention. Article 1A provides that an individual is a refugee, inter alia, if that individual has a well-founded fear of persecution. It is generally accepted that if the fear of persecution can be remedied by relocating within the state, the individual does not qualify as a refugee.[31] However, if relocation would expose the individual to persecution,

[27] *Thirunavukkarasu v Canada* (n 26).

[28] VCLT (n 22) art 31(1).

[29] James C Hathaway and Michelle Foster, *The Law of Refugee Status* (OUP 2014) 334 (hereafter Hathaway and Foster, *The Law of Refugee Status*).

[30] *AH (Sudan) v Secretary of State for the Home Department* [2007] UKHL 49 (hereafter *AH (Sudan)*); *Judgment of 8 December 1998 No 9 C 17/98*, B VerwGE 108 (German Federal Administrative Court); *Ahmed v Canada (Minister of Employment and Immigration)* (1993) 156 NR 221 (FCA) (Canadian Federal Court of Appeal); *Rasaratnam v Canada* [1992] FC 706, 709–11 (Canadian Federal Court); *Salah Sheekh v Netherlands* (n 26).

[31] UNHCR, 'Handbook on Procedures and Criteria for Determining Refugee Status' (n 15), 15; Goodwin-Gill and McAdam, *The Refugee in International Law* (n 16); James Hathaway and Michelle Foster, 'Internal Protection/Relocation/Flight Alternative as an Aspect of Refugee Status Determination' (Global Consultation on International Protection, Expert Roundtable Discussion organised by the UNHCR, 2001) (hereafter Hathaway and Foster, 'Internal Protection/Relocation/Flight Alternative'); Jonah Eaton, 'The Internal Protection Alternative Under European Union Law: Examining the Recast Qualification Directive' (2012) 24(4) International Journal of Refugee Law 765 (hereafter Eaton, 'Examining the Recast Qualification Directive'); *Januzi v Secretary of State for the Home Department* (n 5); Qualification Directive (n 2) art 8; *Randhawa v Minister for Immigration, Local Government and Ethnic Affairs* (n 5); *Thirunavukkarasu v Canada* (n 26); *Daniel Martin Butler v Attorney General and Refugee Status Appeals Authority* [1999] NZAR 205; *Nalliah Karanakaran v Secretary of State for*

the area of relocation cannot be said to provide an antidote to the persecution feared and thus cannot qualify as an IPA. As such, the individual should be recognized as a refugee.

As set out in chapter 5, there is no definition of what constitutes persecution in the Refugee Convention. Indeed, it is generally accepted that the drafters of the Refugee Convention intentionally declined to define 'being persecuted' because they recognized the impossibility of exhaustively listing all the forms of maltreatment that might entitle persons to refugee status.[32] However, many different scholarly authorities propose a human rights interpretation of the term 'persecution',[33] and this approach is generally accepted in state practice.[34] It is nonetheless important to note that not all human rights violations will necessarily constitute persecution. Assessment will turn on factors including (i) the nature of the freedom threatened; (ii) the nature and severity of the restriction;[35] and (iii) the likelihood of the restriction eventuating in the individual case.[36] Examples of serious harm sufficient to ground a risk of being persecuted may include a risk to life, the risk of torture or cruel, inhuman, or degrading treatment, or punishment, slavery, risk of beatings, or other physical violence, and the risk of violation of socio-economic rights.[37] The conditions facing IDPs in a proposed IPA might be relevant when determining whether there is a risk of 'serious harm' and hence a risk of persecution.

the Home Department [2000] 3 All ER 449; *SZATV v Minister for Immigration and Citizenship* [2007] HCA 40.

[32] Hathaway and Foster, *The Law of Refugee Status* (n 29); See also UNHCR, 'Handbook and Guidelines on Procedures and Criteria for Determining Refugee Status under the 1951 Convention and the 1967 Protocol Relating to the Status of Refugees' (December 2011) UN Doc HCR/1P/4/ENG/REV.3 [51].

[33] Zimmermann, *Relating to the Status of Refugees and its 1967 Protocol: A Commentary* (n 13); Goodwin-Gill and McAdam, *The Refugee in International Law* (n 16); Hathaway and Foster, *The Law of Refugee Status* (n 29).

[34] For example, the European Union's Qualification Directive has explicitly adopted the human rights approach by defining 'an act of persecution' as an act that is 'sufficiently serious by its nature or repetition as to constitute a severe violation of basic human rights, in particular the rights from which derogation cannot be made' or an 'accumulation of various measures, including violations of human rights'; Qualification Directive (n 2) art 9(1)(a).

[35] For example, the Qualification Directive (n 2) notes that the violation(s) must be 'sufficiently serious by its nature or repetition'; art 9(1)(a).

[36] Goodwin-Gill and McAdam, *The Refugee in International Law* (n 16). See also Hathaway and Foster, *The Law of Refugee Status* (n 29).

[37] Goodwin-Gill and McAdam, *The Refugee in International Law* (n 16); Schultz, *The Internal Protection Alternative* (n 18); *Shi Chen v Holder* [2010] 604 F.3d 324 (Seventh Circuit, United States Court of Appeals); *M93 of 2004 v Minister for Immigration & Anor* [2006] FMCA 252 (Federal Magistrates Court of Australia); *BG (Figi)* [2012] NZIPT 800091 (New Zealand Immigration and Protection Tribunal); *BVerwG* [2013] 10 C 23.12 (German Federal Administrative Court).

The third generally accepted criterion is that there must be no new risk of being persecuted or of *refoulement*.[38] This criterion is uncontroversial because, as set out above, lack of protection from persecution is one of the criteria for establishing refugee status, and *refoulement* is prohibited by Art 33(1) of the Refugee Convention. In essence, this criterion prohibits the return of every individual who could face a new risk of persecution, or where there are substantial grounds for believing that they would be in danger of torture, inhuman or degrading treatment, or punishment if returned to a particular IPA.[39] In addition, there must be no risk of 'chain' or 'constructive' *refoulement*, that is, an applicant should not be returned to an inadequate IPA where the conditions there are so unreasonable that an applicant may in desperation return to the territory of her persecutors or another area where there is a real risk of serious harm.[40] For example, poor socio-economic conditions such as lack of food, shelter, housing, and/or medical care—even if they do not amount to persecution—could rule out an area from being a lawful IPA. Once again, the conditions facing IDPs in a specific area might be a relevant factor in determining whether there is a risk of refoulement, and hence whether it is a valid IPA.

4.3.2 Divergent Criteria in the Internal Protection Alternative Analysis

There are a number of additional criteria that are applied by some states in the IPA inquiry. It is not entirely clear if these criteria are used to expand upon or interpret the criteria as set out above, or if they are additional stand-alone criteria in the IPA inquiry. In any event, they are not binding as they do not have widespread support in state practice and are not clearly derived from the terms of the Refugee Convention. Yet from a practical perspective it is important

38 ECRE, 'Actors of Protection and the Application of the Internal Protection Alternative, National Report—Belgium' (2014); Hathaway and Foster, *The Law of Refugee Status* (n 29); Reinhard Marx, 'The Criteria of Applying the "Internal Flight Alternative" Test in National Refugee Status Determination Procedures' (2002) 14 International Journal of Refugee Law 179 (hereafter Marx, 'The Criteria of Applying the "Internal Flight Alternative" Test'); Schultz, *The Internal Protection Alternative* (n 18); Ní Ghráinne, 'The Internal Protection Alternative and Human Rights' (n 6); Eaton, 'Examining the Recast Qualification Directive' (n 31); Kay Hailbronner and Daniel Thym (eds), *EU Immigration and Asylum Law* (Hart 2016); Zimmermann, *Relating to the Status of Refugees and its 1967 Protocol: A Commentary* (n 13); *Sufi and Elmi v the United Kingdom* (n 26); *Salah Sheekh v Netherlands* (n 26).

39 Goodwin-Gill and McAdam, *The Refugee in International Law* (n 16).

40 Hathaway and Foster, *The Law of Refugee Status* (n 29); *Sufi and Elmi v the United Kingdom* (n 26); Eaton, 'Examining the Recast Qualification Directive' (n 31); Zimmermann, *Relating to the Status of Refugees and its 1967 Protocol: A Commentary* (n 13).

to outline them here, as states have the final say on the interpretation of the Refugee Convention regardless of whether that interpretation is accurate.

First, some states apply the criterion that the conditions in the IPA should be reasonable and/or not unduly harsh. However, there is disagreement amongst these states—as well as amongst scholars and practitioners—about the meaning of these terms. For example, although there is a general understanding that the Refugee Convention is part and parcel of the broader international human rights law framework and that human rights law must be taken into account when interpreting the Refugee Convention,[41] there is disagreement about how far human rights considerations should inform the meaning of these terms and the IPA inquiry more generally. Some argue that the availability of basic norms of civil, political, and socio-economic rights should inform the IPA inquiry,[42] but there is a lack definition of what these standards entail. There is also considerable uncertainty regarding the meaning of effective protection from persecution and how it applies in the IPA analysis.[43] Relevant factors include whether the risk of persecution is 'permanently eradicated',[44] and/or whether there is a legal system in operation for the detection, prosecution, and protection of acts of persecution or serious harm.[45] Finally, some courts and scholars are of the view that conditions in the proposed IPA should 'satisfy the affirmative, yet relative, standards set by' the Refugee Convention's definition of protection, namely Articles 2–33.[46] This concept of protection entails a duty of non-discrimination vis-à-vis citizens or other residents of the asylum country and refugees regarding a list of rights,[47] including general provisions, administrative measures, rights relating to juridical status, and rights relating to gainful employment. However, this approach has been criticized on the basis that

[41] UNHCR, 'UNHCR and Human Rights: A Policy Paper Resulting from Deliberations in the Policy Committee on the Basis of a Paper Prepared by the Division of International Protection' (6 August 1997) UN Doc AHC/97/325l; Alice Edwards, 'Human Rights, Refugees and the Right "to Enjoy" Asylum' (2005) 17 International Journal of Refugee Law 293, 297; Erika Feller, 'International Refugee Protection 50 Years On: The Protection Challenges of the Past, Present and Future' (2001) 83 International Review of the Red Cross 581, 582; Marx, 'The Criteria of Applying the "Internal Flight Alternative" Test' (n 38) 206; James Hathaway (ed), *Human Rights and Refugee Law*, vols I and II (Edward Elgar 2015); Bruce Burson and David James Cantor (eds), *Human Rights and the Refugee Definition: Comparative Legal Practice and Theory* (Brill Nijhoff 2016).

[42] UNHCR, 'Guidelines on International Protection: "Internal Flight or Relocation Alternative" within the Context of Article lA(2) of the 1951 Convention and/or 1967 Protocol relating to the Status of Refugees' (23 July 2003) UN Doc HCR/GIP/03/04 [28].

[43] Qualification Directive (n 2); *Aydin Salahadin Abdulla* (n 26).

[44] *Aydin Salahadin Abdulla* (n 26) [73].

[45] ibid [73]; Qualification Directive (n 2). See also the jurisprudence and literature cited in chapter 5.

[46] Hathaway, 'Michigan Guidelines' (n 16) 139; *Refugee Appeal No 71684/99* [2000] INLR 165 (New Zealand Refugee Status Appeals Authority) [57].

[47] Hathaway and Foster, *The Law of Refugee Status* (n 29) 44.

it purports to use refugee rights to consider the situation of citizens in their country of origin, which goes against the object and purpose of the Refugee Convention.[48]

Given the focus of this chapter, it is also pertinent to note that the Guiding Principles have been advocated as a potential yardstick by which to measure the adequacy of protection standards in a proposed IPA.[49] This in principle seems appropriate because, as aforementioned, if an asylum-seeker is forced to relocate to a safe place within their country of origin, they will, in effect, become internally displaced. The Guiding Principles are the global standard for protection of IDPs and thus have the potential to provide a helpful recapitulation of the human rights applicable to persons who have been forced to relocate, framed with specific reference to their needs.[50]

However, the use of the Guiding Principles to determine the adequacy of human rights protection in a proposed IPA suffers from many of the same shortcomings outlined above with other approaches, namely a lack of consensus about what these standards entail. Another problem with using the Guiding Principles as a benchmark for IPA determination is that the protections set out in the Guiding Principles are quite far-reaching. Situations that would violate the Guiding Principles would include the denial of the right to visit the grave sites of deceased relatives (Principle 16), lack of access to essential sanitation facilities (Principle 18), the inability to receive a passport (Principle 20), and arbitrary confiscation of property (Principle 21). Ruling out a proposed location from being an IPA on the basis of risks inconsistent with the Guiding Principles could go far beyond what was intended by the drafters of the 1951 Refugee Convention as the risk of such harms would not create an entitlement to refugee status.[51] In other words, if a proposed location is not an IPA because the conditions there are incompatible with the Guiding Principles (eg an individual cannot visit the grave sites of deceased relatives), and the individual is therefore a refugee, such an interpretation would conflict with the terms of the Refugee Convention, which sets out a very narrow definition of refugee.

[48] Ní Ghráinne, 'The Internal Protection Alternative and Human Rights' (n 6) 40; Ninette Kelley, 'Internal Flight/Relocation/Protection Alternative: Is it Reasonable?' (2002) 14 International Journal of Refugee Law 4, 35; *Januzi v Secretary of State for the Home Department* (n 5).

[49] Elizabeth Ferris, 'Internal Displacement and the Right to Seek Asylum' (2008) 27(3) Refugee Survey Quarterly 76, 88; Hathaway and Foster, 'Internal Protection/Relocation/Flight Alternative' (n 31) 45.

[50] Hathaway and Foster, 'Internal Protection/Relocation/Flight Alternative' (n 31) 43.

[51] ibid, 44.

Perhaps the biggest problem with using the Guiding Principles as a potential standard for IPA determination is that it is not clear whether some of the Guiding Principles are in fact hard law. As the legal standing of the Guiding Principles is discussed in detail in chapter 2, it is unnecessary to do so again here. However, suffice it to say that Principle 15 (concerning the prohibition of internal *refoulement*), Principle 25 (humanitarian assistance), and Principle 29 (restitution for property loss) have a questionable basis in international law and, indeed, Walter Kälin (the former Representative of the UN Secretary-General on the Human Rights of Internally Displaced Persons) could only go so far as to say that 'no new law in the strict sense of the word was created [by the Guiding Principles] in *most* cases' (emphasis added).[52] Thus some of the Guiding Principles are not binding on states, and may go beyond what states are willing to accept in practice. Consequently, the Guiding Principles are not an appropriate standard by which to measure the existence of an IPA.

The second additional criterion that is applied by some states in the IPA analysis regards the issue of non-state actors of persecution. Some jurisdictions apply a presumption that the IPA is inapplicable where the state is the agent of persecution.[53] This is because the state is presumed to act throughout the territory of a country,[54] making it difficult, if not impossible, for a persecuted individual to avoid detection by the state. This presumption may be rebutted where there is compelling evidence of the ability to deliver durable protection in the proposed IPA, and/or where the threat is one that emanates from local government authorities rather than throughout the state, and/or where the threat is from a 'rogue' agent of the state.[55]

Third, there is considerable disagreement over whether non-state actors can qualify as actors of protection for the purposes of establishing an IPA. Although some argue that the term 'protection' in the refugee definition refers only to lack of state protection,[56] there have been some suggestions in the literature and in case

[52] Walter Kälin, 'The Future of the Guiding Principles on Internal Displacement' [2006] Forced Migration Review 5, 5.

[53] *Chahal v United Kingdom* No 70/1995/576/662 (ECHR, 11 November 1996) [95]–[107]; *Minister for Immigration and Multicultural Affairs v Jang* [2000] FCA 1075. Hathaway and Foster note that 'some decision-makers have taken the view that whether or not the persecutor is the state is completely irrelevant'. See Hathaway and Foster, 'Internal Protection/Relocation/Flight Alternative' (n 31) 28.

[54] Zimmermann, *Relating to the Status of Refugees and its 1967 Protocol: A Commentary* (n 13).

[55] *Thirunavukkarasu v Canada* (n 26).

[56] Bríd Ní Ghráinne, 'UNHCR's Involvement with IDPs – "Protection of that Country" for the Purposes of Precluding Refugee Status?' (2014) 26 International Journal of Refugee Law 536, 538–42 (hereafter Ní Ghráinne, 'UNHCR's Involvement with IDPs'); James C Hathaway and Hugo Storey, 'What is the Meaning of State Protection in Refugee Law? A Debate' (2016) 28 International Journal of Refugee Law 486, 486 (Hathaway's position).

law that a modern-day interpretation of the Refugee Convention permits refugee status to be denied where effective protection is available from non-state actors such as international organizations, NGOs, shelters, or clans.[57] In addition, the EU Qualification Directive provides that international organizations can be actors of protection. This issue is highly relevant in the context of internal displacement because—as set out in chapter 3—many non-state actors are involved in protecting IDPs through the cluster arrangement. Even if non-state actors can, prima facie, constitute actors of protection, questions remain about whether non-state actors are able to offer sufficient protection from persecution. This issue is addressed in more detail in chapter 5 in the context of the UNHCR's involvement with IDPs.[58]

Fourth, it is not clear whether an IPA must be durable.[59] Many states require that an IPA must be durable,[60] and Article 7 of the EU Qualification Directive requires that protection must be 'non-temporary'. Although neither the Directive nor the CJEU have given any further guidance on the meaning of 'non-temporary' as per Article 7, the term has been examined in the context of cessation of refugee status. In the case of *Abdulla*, the CJEU held that protection is of a 'non-temporary' nature when it can be said that the factors which formed the basis of the refugee's fear of persecution may be regarded as

[57] *AM & AM (armed conflict: risk categories) Somalia CG* [2008] UKAIT 00091 [160]; *Salah Sheekh v Netherlands* (n 26) [36]; Qualification Directive (n 2) art 7; Hugo Storey, 'What Constitutes Persecution? Towards a Working Definition' (2014) 26 IJRL 272 481; James C Hathaway and Hugo Storey, 'What is the Meaning of State Protection in Refugee Law? A Debate' (2016) 28 International Journal of Refugee Law 486, 486 (Storey's position); Maria O'Sullivan, 'Acting the Part: Can Non-State Entities Provide Protection Under International Refugee Law?' (2012) 24 International Journal of Refugee Law 85, 98–108; Leyla Gayibova, 'The Evolutive Interpretation of the Term "Protection of that Country" in Article 1(2)A of the Convention Relating to the Status of Refugees' (Thesis, University of Sheffield 2017).

[58] See also Ní Ghráinne, 'UNHCR's Involvement with IDPs' (n 56) 536 and literature cited therein.

[59] *Aydin Salahadin Abdulla* (n 26); Committee Against Torture, *SS v Netherlands* (Communication No 191/2001) UN Doc CAT/C/30/D/191/2001 (hereafter *SS v Netherlands*); *Sufi and Elmi v The United Kingdom* (n 26); *Judgment of 24 February 2011* No 10 C 310 (German Federal Administrative Court); *Salah Sheekh v Netherlands* (n 26); Schultz, *The Internal Protection Alternative* (n 18); *AH (Sudan)* (n 30); Gina Clayton, 'Even If… The Use of the IPA in Asylum Decisions in the UK' (*Asylum Aid*, 1 July 2014) <https://www.refworld.org/docid/53c8d6024.html> accessed 3 September 2019 (hereafter Clayton, 'The Use of the IPA'); UNHCR, 'Position Paper on Relocating Internally' (n 11); Qualification Directive (n 2); Eaton, 'Examining the Recast Qualification Directive' (n 31) 784; European Council on Refugees and Exiles, 'ECRE Information Note on the Council Directive 2004/83/EC of 29 April 2004 on Minimum Standards for the Qualification of Third Country Nationals and Others in Need of International Protection' (2004) (hereafter European Council on Refugees and Exiles, 'ECRE Information Note').

[60] *AH (Sudan)* (n 30); Clayton, 'The Use of the IPA' (n 59); UNHCR, 'Position Paper on Relocating Internally' (n 11); Qualification Directive (n 2); *Aydin Salahadin Abdulla* (n 26); *Salah Sheekh v Netherlands* (n 26); European Council on Refugees and Exiles, 'ECRE Information Note' (n 59); *SS v Netherlands* (n 59). Schultz considers that the durability of protection is a baseline criterion. Durability is not viewed as a stand-alone baseline criterion in this chapter because (i) it is unclear what its added value is aside from its relevance in assessing accessibility, effective protection from the original risk of persecution, and no new risk of refoulement; and (ii) durability is not widely applied as a stand-alone criterion in state practice. See Schultz, *The Internal Protection Alternative* (n 18) 241.

having been permanently eradicated.[61] This implies that the body providing protection need not be present permanently, but rather that it has the ability to completely eradicate the persecution feared. Once again, this issue might be relevant to the wide range of actors that are involved in IDP protection and will be explored in more detail in chapter 5.

In sum, although there is some divergence on how the IPA should be applied, there is consensus regarding three criteria. In order to be an IPA, the proposed place of relocation: (i) must be accessible to the applicant; (ii) must provide effective protection from the original risk of persecution; and (iii) must not present a new risk of being persecuted or of *refoulement*. These criteria are cumulative so a failure to meet any one of these criteria means that there is not a valid IPA. It is worth noting that this author does not necessarily agree that this low threshold should be the yardstick by which a lawful IPA is measured,[62] but accepts that the terms of the Refugee Convention itself and the actual practice of states, as set out in the 1969 VCLT, are amongst the most important barometers in establishing the minimum binding criteria applicable in the IPA inquiry. It is also important to note that these criteria are used as part of the general assessment into the validity of a proposed IPA, namely whether the return of *any* individual there would be a violation of the Refugee Convention. A decision-maker generally also takes into account individual circumstances (such as the reason for flight, gender, health, etc), which may be highly pertinent in refugee status determination proceedings and lead to a more restrictive understanding of what qualifies as a lawful IPA.[63]

The following section will assess how courts have squared the risk of exposure to internal displacement with the IPA criteria. The focus will be on the binding minimum criteria as outlined above, but reference will be made to the additional criteria where relevant.

4.4 The Relationship between Internal Displacement and the Internal Protection Alternative Analysis

The fact that an individual will become an IDP is particularly relevant to the second and third of the binding criteria as outlined above; there must be

[61] *Aydin Salahadin Abdulla* (n 26) [73].
[62] For example, poor socio-economic conditions in the proposed relocation would not necessarily preclude it from being a lawful IPA.
[63] VCLT (n 22) arts 31, 31(3)(b).

effective protection from the original risk of persecution, and there must be no new risk of being persecuted or of *refoulement*. As aforementioned, when assessing whether there is effective protection from the original risk of persecution, a relevant factor might be the standard of protection (or lack thereof) available to IDPs in the proposed IPA. In addition, when assessing the risk of *refoulement,* a relevant factor might be the living conditions in the proposed IPA for IDPs and whether those conditions are so unreasonable that an IDP may in desperation return to the territory of their persecutors or another area where there is a real risk of serious harm. The situation of internal displacement in a proposed IPA might also be relevant to the 'divergent criteria', as set out above. For example, a decision-maker might inquire as to whether the living conditions facing IDPs are compatible with applicable human rights standards and/or whether they are unreasonable or unduly harsh. A state which accepts that protection in an IPA can be provided by non-state actors might give particular weight to the protection activities of the non-state actors of protection on behalf of IDPs. Finally, those states that apply a durability criterion to the IPA analysis might put particular weight on the question of whether a camp for IDPs can offer durable protection from persecution.

When courts analyse whether a proposed area is a viable IPA, they tend to first set out the criteria that they deem applicable to the IPA inquiry, and then analyse whether the conditions in the proposed IPA—taken together—satisfy those criteria. It is therefore difficult to ascertain which particular aspects of a situation of internal displacement are relevant to which particular criteria in the IPA analysis. Yet the below survey of IPA case law yields three important observations on the relationship between internal displacement and the IPA. A significant amount of this case law stems from common law countries, as these jurisdictions tend to frequently engage in the IPA analysis in relation to areas where there are large amounts of IDPs and produce detailed reasoning in their decisions.

First, it is unclear whether someone who is returned to their country and is expected to relocate to an IPA should automatically be considered as an IDP. Further analysis of the IDP definition can be found in chapter 2, but it suffices for now to say that this author argues that such an individual should be regarded as an IDP. This is because they are in essence forced to live in another part of their state, and because the description of IDP as set out in the Guiding Principles is broad enough to encompass such individuals. However, the relevant jurisprudence does not seem to be so definitive on this issue. For example, the Refugee Protection Division of the Immigration and Refugee Board of

Canada found that a claimant was not an IDP 'as traditionally defined in that she was not forced to flee her home in one region of Iraq and move to another due to the conflict. Rather, she would be relocating from Canada.'[64] On appeal the Federal Court found that this analysis was 'flawed' and noted that the claimant had been displaced a number of times within Iraq prior to moving to Canada.[65] The Federal Court did not clarify, however, whether its categorization of the claimant as an IDP was based on this fact of previous internal displacement within Iraq or whether their return from Canada could, in itself, mean that they were an IDP on return to Iraq. The UK Upper Tribunal has also not been very clear in its approach to this issue. It has noted that a relevant factor in determining the existence of a valid IPA is whether there is support available for the individual 'bearing in mind there is some evidence that returned failed asylum seekers are provided with the support generally given to IDPs'.[66] It is clear here that the Tribunal sees IDPs and returnees as two distinct categories of forced migrant, but it is not clear whether the Tribunal considers that a returnee can also be an IDP, or rather that a returnee is different from an IDP but can nonetheless benefit from support provided to IDPs.

In any event, the debate surrounding whether someone who returns to an IPA from abroad is an IDP is somewhat moot as courts and state authorities have repeatedly found that a risk of becoming an IDP will not, in itself, rule a particular location out as being a valid IPA.[67] A 2018 Australian Department of Foreign Affairs and Trade report stated that 'there are no legal impediments to internal relocation in Nigeria ... Nigeria has as many as three million internally displaced persons (IDPs) due to the insurgency in northeast and internal conflicts in the middle belt states.'[68] A case before the Refugee Appeal Division of the Canadian Immigration and Refugee Board found that although the appellant referred at length in his submission to the 'general situation and circumstances of those in IDP camps in Puntland ... the hardship associated with dislocation and relocation is not the kind of undue hardship that renders an [IPA] unreasonable.'[69] Consequently, the

[64] [32], Refugee Protection Division case cited in *Alkhoury v Canada (Citizenship and Immigration)* [2020] FC 153 [23].

[65] ibid [24].

[66] *AA (Article 15(c)) Iraq CG v Secretary of State for the Home Department* [2015] UKUT 00544 (IAC) [15]. See also *AS (Safety of Kabul) Afghanistan CG* [2018] UKUT 00118 (IAC) (hereafter *AS (Safety of Kabul)*), which noted at para 168 that 'returnees were in a similar position to those who had been internally displaced, with access to shelter, secure tenure, food, and economic security all remaining critical for some time after they have settled'.

[67] *AS (Safety of Kabul)* (n 66); *Sufi and Elmi v the United Kingdom* (n 26); *Salah Sheekh v Netherlands* (n 26).

[68] UK Home Office, *Country Policy and Information Note Nigeria: Internal Relocation* (Version 1.0, 2019) [5.2.2].

[69] *X (Re)* [2015] CanLII 66980 (CA IRB) [43].

appellant was found to have a valid IPA in Somalia, even though he might well end up in a situation of internal displacement.

Conversely, the presence of a large number of IDPs in a particular location can sometimes be perceived as *supporting* the finding of an IPA in that location. Essentially, courts might perceive the location as relatively safe because IDPs have sought protection and/or better prospects there. For example, in considering whether Kabul was a potential IPA, the UK Upper Tribunal attached 'some weight to the fact that Kabul remains a destination of choice for returnees ... IDPs and economic migrants given that it has greater economic prospects than other areas'.[70]

Put simply, therefore, the fact that someone will be an IDP on return to an IPA does not have a significant bearing on the overall decision of whether an IPA exists. In addition, the prospect of being an IDP can be interpreted both in favour and against the viability of a proposed IPA. Consequently, an individual's refugee claim might well be rejected even if they will become an IDP if returned to an IPA.

Second, regardless of whether the returnee is considered an IDP in the proposed place of relocation, courts have tended to take into account the conditions facing IDPs in that particular place when determining whether an IPA exists.[71] In fact, the Federal Court of Canada found that regardless of whether the individual is considered to be an IDP upon return, the conditions in the proposed place of relocation for IDPs must be taken into account in assessing the validity of a proposed IPA.[72] A similar finding was made by the UK Upper Tribunal, which held that when assessing whether there is a viable IPA:

> it is necessary to take into account (both in assessing 'safety' and 'reasonableness') not only the level of violence in that city but also the difficulties experienced by that city's poor and also the many Internally Displaced Persons (IDPs) living there, these considerations will not in general make return to Kabul unsafe or unreasonable.[73]

Third, although courts tend to tend to take into account the conditions facing IDPs when determining whether a proposed area is an IPA, they have acknowledged that not all IDPs will find themselves in similar circumstances.

[70] *AS (Safety of Kabul)* (n 66) [225].
[71] ibid; *Sufi and Elmi v The United Kingdom* (n 26).
[72] *Alkhoury v Canada (Citizenship and Immigration)* [2020] FC 153.
[73] *AK (Article 15(c)) Afghanistan CG v Secretary of State for the Home Department* [2012] UKUT 00163 (IAC) [B(iv)] (UK Upper Tribunal); affirmed in *AS (Safety of Kabul)* (n 66) [2].

For example, the term 'IDP' can cover 'a wide range of people and circumstances: the refugee returnee, the IDP returnee,[74] the urban poor, economic migrants and pastoralists who moved to urban centres having lost their livestock'.[75] In *MOJ & Ors (Return to Mogadishu) Somalia CG* [2014], the Upper Tribunal of the UK Immigration and Asylum Chamber noted that 'there may well be IDPs in Mogadishu who are far wealthier than "settled" inhabitants of the area'[76] while at the same time 'protection mechanisms fall short for those living in IDP camps at or close to levels of destitution'.[77] It went on to state that:

> A person may be settled in a reasonable standard of accommodation with access to food aid, resources provided by others such as remittances from abroad or a livelihood to provide for himself, yet retain the categorisation of an IDP because, at some point in the past, possibly many years ago, he left his home to move somewhere else. Such a person will not, in our judgment, face any enhanced level of risk as compared with any other settled citizen who is not classed as an IDP ... However, a person who has no option but to live in one of Mogadishu's IDP camps in a tent or makeshift shelter is in a wholly different position. Despite the positive assessment adopted by the respondent of living conditions in some IDP camps, there is ample evidence that conditions in many IDP camps are appalling.[78]

The Upper Tribunal noted that it should not be presumed that someone who is returned to an IPA will necessarily be without resources or access to them, and that the analysis should be done on a case-by-case basis.

As such, courts have tended to look beyond the IDP label and pay close attention to the likely conditions a particular individual will find themselves in if they are an IDP in the proposed IPA. Courts have noted a number of factors which will influence the standard of living conditions (or lack thereof) which an individual will face if returned to a proposed IPA. These factors include the availability of family and social support,[79] clan protection,[80] and financial resources;[81] their chances of securing

[74] It is not clear what the court meant by 'the refugee returnee' and the 'IDP returnee'. These terms are not defined in international law.

[75] *MOJ & Ors (Return to Mogadishu) Somalia CG v Secretary of State for the Home Department* [2014] UKUT 00442 (IAC) [228] (hereafter *MOJ & Ors*) [228].

[76] ibid [228].

[77] ibid [364].

[78] ibid, [410]–[411].

[79] ibid; *AAH (Iraqi Kurds – internal relocation) Iraq CG* UKUT 00212 (IAC) (hereafter *AAH (Iraqi Kurds- internal relocation)*; *Sufi and Elmi v The United Kingdom* (n 26).

[80] *MOJ & Ors* (n 75); *Sufi and Elmi v The United Kingdom* (n 26).

[81] *AAH (Iraqi Kurds – internal relocation)* (n 79).

employment;[82] and their access to documentation, which may be required to access basic rights or secure employment.[83] A court is more likely to find that a particular location is a valid IPA where an individual can live in a private setting, such as with a family member or in rented accommodation. In fact, most IDPs end up in such living arrangements.[84]

Some cases have examined the prospect of an IDP living in a 'critical shelter arrangement' such as an 'unfinished or abandoned makeshift shelter, tent, mosque, church or squatting in a government building'.[85] The UK Upper Tribunal has tended to find that such arrangements may constitute an IPA depending on the conditions within the 'critical shelter arrangement'. For example, the case of *AAH (Iraqi Kurds—internal relocation) Iraq CG UKUT 00212 (IAC)* found that there was a valid IPA available for the appellant, even though they would probably live in a 'critical shelter arrangement'.[86] The Upper Tribunal said whether this arrangement could be said to be 'unduly harsh' would depend 'on whether or not he is able to secure sufficient income to obtain basic necessities such as food, clean water and clothing'.[87] The Upper Tribunal concluded that:

> He will be able to lead what is in general for Iraq today a relatively 'normal' life. His accommodation will be far from ideal, but we find that he will be able to feed and clothe himself. He will be able, as he has done here, to establish a private life in the form of friendships with others, be it locals or other IDPs in his area. It is not reasonably likely that he will become destitute or that his human dignity will be otherwise compromised to an unacceptable extent.[88]

There is divergence on whether an IDP camp can be an adequate IPA.[89] Some courts have engaged in rigorous assessment of the conditions in IDP camps, finding that such camps cannot qualify as an IPA.[90] Other decisions have found

[82] ibid.
[83] *SMO, KSP & IM (Article 15(c); identity documents Iraq CG* [2019] UKUT 40O (IAC) (hereafter *SMO, KSP & IM*); *AAH (Iraqi Kurds – internal relocation) Iraq CG* UKUT 00212 (IAC).
[84] Brookings–LSE Project on Internal Displacement, 'Under the Radar: Internally Displaced Persons in Non-Camp Settings' (October 2013) https://www.brookings.edu/wp-content/uploads/2016/06/Under-the-radarIDPs-outside-of-camps-Oct-2013.pdf accessed 25 June 2021.
[85] *SMO, KSP & IM* (n 83) [E(27)(iii)]; *AH Sudan* (n 30).
[86] [146].
[87] ibid [146].
[88] ibid [148]. See also *SMO, KSP & IM* (n 83); *AH Sudan* (n 30); *Januzi v Secretary of State for the Home Department* (n 5); *AS (Safety of Kabul)* (n 66).
[89] Ogg, 'Protection from "Refuge"' (n 4).
[90] *X (Re)* [2015] CanLII 66980 (CA IRB) (Canadian Immigration and Refugee Board); *Sufi and Elmi v The United Kingdom* (n 26); *V04/16820 [2004] RRTA 523* (27 July 2004) (Refugee Review Tribunal of Australia); *V04/17373 [2005] RRTA 50* (22 April 2005) (Refugee Review Tribunal of Australia); *Abdillahi v Canada (Citizenship and Immigration)* [2015] FC 1202 (Federal Court of Canada); *X (Re)*

that a camp can be an IPA,[91] but have qualified this finding by stating that removal to a camp environment could nonetheless be a violation of human rights law, specifically Article 3 of the European Convention on Human Rights. For example, in *MOJ*, the Court stated that:

> While it is likely that those who do find themselves living in inadequate makeshift accommodation in an IDP camp will be experiencing adverse living conditions such as to engage the protection of Article 3 of the ECHR, we do not see that it gives rise to an enhanced [risk of refoulement] since there is an insufficient nexus with the indiscriminate violence which, in any event, we have found to be not at such a high level that all civilians face a real risk of suffering serious harm ... The fact that we have rejected the view that there is a real risk of persecution or serious harm or ill treatment to civilians or returnees in Mogadishu does not mean that no Somali national can succeed in a refugee or humanitarian protection or Article 3 claim. Each case will fall to be decided on its own facts.[92]

Thus, although courts tend to accept that the likelihood of becoming an IDP is a relevant factor in the IPA inquiry, it does not seem to have a significant bearing on their overall decision. In fact, the likelihood of becoming an IDP will not necessarily rule a location out from being an IPA even where an individual will be exposed to very poor living conditions by virtue of having to live in an IDP camp or 'critical shelter arrangement'.

4.5 Analogies to the Cessation of Refugee Status

Before concluding this chapter, it is important to note that the arguments made in this chapter also have broader relevance to the issue of cessation of refugee status. Article 1C of the Refugee Convention provides an exhaustive list of the circumstances under which refugee status can cease.[93] Similar cessation clauses are also found in the 1969 OAU Convention (Article 1(4)(e)) and in the

[2013] CanLII 96324 (CA IRB) (Canadian Immigration and Refugee Board); *X (Re)* [2016] CanLII 105360 (CA IRB) (Canadian Immigration and Refugee Board).

[91] *AH Sudan* (n 30).
[92] *MOJ & Ors* (n 75) [420]–[422].
[93] Georgia Cole, 'The End of Refugee Status: Cessation and Durable Solutions' in Cathryn Costello, Michelle Foster, and Jane McAdam (eds), *The Oxford Handbook of International Refugee Law* (OUP 2021).

Statute of the Office of the United Nations High Commissioner for Refugees (Paragraph 6(a)(e)).[94] Although there are six cessation clauses in the Refugee Convention, Articles 1C(5) and 1C(6) of the Refugee Convention (and their analogous provisions in other instruments) are particularly relevant to this chapter because they concern the conditions in the country of nationality or habitual residence. These grounds provide that an individual is no longer a refugee because the circumstances under which they were recognized as a refugee have ceased to exist.[95]

There are two main parallels between the IPA concept and the cessation clauses. First, some commentators have suggested that an analogy should be drawn between cessation clauses and the IPA inquiry when examining the conditions that must be satisfied for an IPA to exist.[96] This is because both cessation of refugee status and the IPA inquiry concern the definition of a refugee under Article 1 of the Refugee Convention and both entail consideration of the adequacy of protection in the refugee's country of origin. In other words, cessation is a 'mirror image'[97] of a decision determining refugee status. In fact, some courts have found that an IPA is not only relevant by analogy to the cessation inquiry, but that the new availability of an IPA in the country of origin can in principle be a basis for cessation of refugee status.[98]

[94] UNGA, 'Statute of the Office of the United Nations High Commissioner for Refugees', Annex to Res 428/V (14 December 1950) UN Doc A/RES/428(V) [6]; Convention Governing the Specific Aspects of the Refugee Problem in Africa (n 18).

[95] Art 1(C) of the Refugee Convention (n 7) states that: 'This Convention shall cease to apply to any person falling under the terms of section A if:

> . . .
>
> (5) He can no longer, because the circumstances in connexion with which he has been recognized as a refugee have ceased to exist, continue to refuse to avail himself of the protection of the country of his nationality; Provided that this paragraph shall not apply to a refugee falling under section A(1) of this article who is able to invoke compelling reasons arising out of previous persecution for refusing to avail himself of the protection of the country of nationality;
>
> (6) Being a person who has no nationality he is, because of the circumstances in connexion with which he has been recognized as a refugee have ceased to exist, able to return to the country of his former habitual residence;
>
> Provided that this paragraph shall not apply to a refugee falling under section A (1) of this article who is able to invoke compelling reasons arising out of previous persecution for refusing to return to the country of his former habitual residence.

[96] Marx, 'The Criteria of Applying the "Internal Flight Alternative" Test' (n 38) 190; Joan Fitzpatrick, 'The End of Protection: Legal Standards for Cessation of Refugee Status and Withdrawal of Temporary Protection' (1998–1999) 13 Georgetown Immigration Law Journal 343, 362; Maria O' Sullivan, 'Territorial Protection: Cessation of Refugee Status and Internal Flight Alternative Compared' in Satvinder S Juss, *The Ashgate Research Companion to Migration Law, Theory, and Policy* (Routledge 2013) (hereafter O'Sullivan, 'Territorial Protection').

[97] *Secretary of State for the Home Department v MA (Somalia)* [2018] EWCA Civ 994 (Court of Appeal of England and Wales) (hereafter *MA (Somalia)*).

[98] *SB (refugee revocation; IDP camps) Somalia* [2019] UKUT 00358 (IAC) (UK Upper Tribunal) (hereafter *SB*); ibid.

Second, the criteria applied in the IPA inquiry and in the application of Articles 1C(5) and (6) are very similar. Three aspects must be examined before cessation is determined: the change must be of a fundamental character, the change must be of an enduring nature, and there must be restoration of protection in the country of nationality.[99] This may take the form of the ending of hostilities; a complete political change and/or the return to a situation of peace and stability. There is clearly some overlap between the IPA criteria and the criteria for the application of Articles 1C(5) and (6) of the Refugee Convention. For example, if there is a risk of persecution in an area it can neither be an IPA nor be invoked as a ground for cessation of refugee status (because restoration of protection logically implies that there is no risk of persecution).

In light of these considerations, the arguments of this chapter in respect of the IPA / internal displacement relationship also hold in respect of the cessation clauses / internal displacement relationship. For example, both the IPA concept and the cessation clauses envisage that the individual may become an IDP on return, but this factor will not have a significant bearing on the outcome of a court's decision. In respect of the IPA, the individual will certainly become an IDP as the individual is expected to relocate in another area of their country. In respect of the cessation clauses, the individual might also be expected to relocate to a part of the territory of the state. For example the ECJ confirmed that Article 7 of the 2011 Recast Qualification Directive, which concerns protection provided by non-state actors, including international organizations, also applies to cessation under Article 11(1)(e) of the Qualifying Directive.[100] This is significant as, due to the reference in Article 7(1) to protection being provided in a 'substantial part of a territory', the effect of the ECJ judgment is that cessation of refugee status can occur even if the change of circumstances have only occurred in part of the territory.[101] Hence the application of both the IPA concept and the cessation clauses may lead to the individual in question becoming an IDP. Like the IPA inquiry, the fact that an individual will be an IDP on return will not, generally speaking, have a decisive influence on the application of the cessation clauses. For example, in a recent cessation decision in

[99] UNHCR, 'Guidelines on International Protection: Cessation of Refugee Status under Article 1C(5) and (6) of the 1951 Convention relating to the Status of Refugees (the "Ceased Circumstances" Clauses)' (10 February 2003) UN Doc HCR/GIP/03/03 [10]; UNHCR, 'Discussion Note on the Application of the "Ceased Circumstances" Cessation Clauses in the 1951 Convention' (20 December 1991) UN Doc EC/SCP/1992/CRP.1 [11]; *MA (Somalia)* (n 97); Hathaway and Foster, *The Law of Refugee Status* (n 29); Maria O'Sullivan, *Refugee Law and Durability of Protection* (Routledge 2019).

[100] *Aydin Salahadin Abdulla* (n 26) [75].

[101] O'Sullivan, 'Territorial Protection' (n 96) 211; *SB* (n 98).

the UK, the Court of Appeal of England and Wales found that return to an IDP camp would not in principle preclude the applicant's removal to Somalia.[102]

Moreover, as argued in respect of the IPA analysis above, the fact that there are many IDPs in a particular area and/or protection available to IDPs might support the contention that that area is now safe and that the cessation clauses are applicable. Conversely, a situation of internal displacement might lead to the opposite conclusion as it might point to the existence of ongoing persecution. Each case will have to be considered on its own merits.

Although the IPA and cessation inquiries are similar in many respects, it is important to emphasize that the standard required for a valid IPA cannot be simply transferred wholesale to the cessation inquiry. This is because the bar for finding that refugee status has ceased is even higher than for finding that there is an IPA. Cessation clauses are only applied to persons that have previously been recognized as refugees and thus have been recognized to have a well-founded fear of persecution in their country of nationality. The issue under consideration in respect of cessation is whether the circumstances under which such persecution arose have now changed to such an extent that persecution is no longer feared and protection is now available from the country of nationality.[103] This can be contrasted to the IPA, a concept which has not been included in the Refugee Convention and the existence of which is examined in the context of refugee status determination proceedings where the persecution feared cannot be said to exist throughout the country of origin. The standard of protection in the country of origin necessary to trigger the application of cessation clauses should be higher than that leading to the application of the IPA concept, as a well-founded fear of persecution has already been found to exist in the former case.

In sum, therefore, there are significant parallels between the IPA concept and the cessation clauses. By extension, the observations made in this chapter on the relationship between the IPA inquiry and internal displacement are also relevant when applying the cessation clauses in the context of internal displacement. However, it should be borne in mind that the standard of protection necessary to trigger the application of the cessation clauses is higher than that in the IPA inquiry. As such, the fact that an individual will become an IDP on return, the existence of a significant number of IDPs in a proposed relocation area, and/or the support available to IDPs in a particular area will be given

102 *SB* (n 98). This finding was made in relation to art 3 of the European Convention on Human Rights.

103 Hathaway and Foster, *The Law of Refugee Status* (n 29).

even less weight in the determination of the cessation of refugee status than they might be given in the IPA inquiry.

4.6 Conclusion

The IPA's widespread adoption by states has meant that—in practical terms at least—the IPA is now firmly part of the inquiry as to whether someone qualifies as a refugee. After many decades of divergent practice, there finally seems to be some consensus surrounding three core criteria applicable in the IPA inquiry: (i) the IPA must be accessible to the applicant; (ii) there must be effective protection from the original risk of persecution; and (iii) there must be no new risk of being persecuted or of *refoulement*. However, one question that has not been addressed in the literature until now is to what extent exposure to a situation of internal displacement is relevant to the IPA analysis. In addition, if becoming an IDP is relevant to the IPA analysis, to what extent is it evidence in favour or evidence against finding an IPA?

As this chapter has illustrated, the fact that an individual will be an IDP if returned to a putative IPA will not, generally speaking, have a decisive influence on whether a particular location is deemed to be a valid IPA. One explanation for this approach is the fact that the description of IDP in the Guiding Principles is very broad, capturing an extremely wide range of individuals in a wide range of circumstances. As set out in chapter 2, there is no requirement of a well-founded fear of persecution in order to fall within the IDP description, and the fact that an individual is an IDP may—but will not necessarily—mean that their human rights have been violated. In fact, the description of an IDP in the Guiding Principles would be likely to capture everyone who has been forced to return to an IPA because they are, in essence, forced to relocate within their country. If becoming an IDP would rule out a particular location as an IPA, this would mean that no asylum-seeker has an IPA available to them. Yet there is a general consensus that the IPA principle *is* compatible with the Refugee Convention. Hence it must be legal, at least in some situations, to return an individual to an IPA even if that means they will become an IDP.

What this means in practice is that refugee status can be denied even where it will condemn an individual to becoming another—arguably more vulnerable—type of forced migrant: an IDP. In fact, some courts have found that an IPA is valid even if an individual would have to live in a 'critical shelter arrangement' or an IDP camp. It is difficult to square this reasoning with the applicable criteria in the IPA inquiry, particularly the requirement that there must be no risk of persecution or refoulement in the proposed IPA. We know that conditions in IDP camps and in critical shelter arrangements can be dire,[104] and hence might well reach the threshold of human rights violations and/or serious harm captured in the meaning of persecution and/or refoulement.

It is therefore proposed here that the IDP label is not particularly helpful when determining whether a location qualifies as an IPA. The broad nature of the IDP description can obfuscate the central issue before the court—namely whether the living conditions that the individual will be exposed to on return are compatible with the IPA inquiry. Whether an individual is an IDP is a relevant consideration, but what is more relevant is where the individual falls on the spectrum of internal displacement. For example, an IDP who can live with relatives and has access to employment is likely to be significantly better off than an IDP who is forced to live in destitution in an IDP camp. The fact than an individual becomes an IDP on return is thus a relevant, but not central issue in the IPA analysis. The focus instead should firmly rest on whether the IPA is accessible to the applicant, whether there is effective protection from the original risk of persecution in the proposed IPA, and whether there is a new risk of being persecuted or of *refoulement*. The most relevant issue to the analysis is not whether a person is an IDP but rather whether the conditions they are exposed to as an IDP are compatible with these criteria.

Finally, this chapter has indicated how the arguments relating to the IPA and internal displacement might also apply to the cessation clauses. Similar to the IPA context, the existence of a situation of internal displacement in the proposed relocation area will not have a decisive bearing on the outcome of a case. However, because the bar for finding that refugee status has ceased is even higher than for finding that there is an IPA, it is more unlikely that the cessation clauses will be found to apply where there is a situation of internal displacement.

[104] *Sufi and Elmi v The United Kingdom* (n 26); Bríd Ní Ghráinne, 'Complementary Protection and Encampment' (2021) 21(1) Human Rights Law Review 54.

5

The UN High Commissioner for Refugees' Involvement with Internally Displaced Persons: Undermining International Refugee Law?

5.1 Introduction

As outlined in chapter 3, the UN High Commissioner for Refugees (UNHCR) is a major player in the protection and assistance of IDPs. Its international protection function has evolved significantly from being 'almost as a surrogate for consular and diplomatic protection' to including 'ensuring the basic rights of refugees and their physical safety and security'.[1] By the end of 2020, the UNHCR was providing protection and assistance to IDPs in 34 states, including in Colombia (8.3 million IDPs), Syria (6.7 million IDPs), DRC (5.2 million IDPs), Yemen (4 million IDPs), and Somalia (3 million IDPs).[2]

Although this effort on behalf of IDPs is a welcome development, the concern has been raised that the UNHCR might be undermining the institution of asylum.[3] Specifically, the in-country protection that the UNHCR offers to

[1] 'UNHCR's Protection Mandate' in UNHCR Global Report 2011 <http://www.unhcr.org/3dafdd0014.pdf> accessed 2 July 2021. Article 8 of the UNHCR statute provides that 'the High Commissioner shall provide for the protection of refugees falling under the competence of his Office by: (a) Promoting the conclusion and ratification of international conventions for the protection of refugees, supervising their application and proposing amendments thereto; (b) Promoting through special agreements with Governments the execution of any measures calculated to improve the situation of refugees and to reduce the number requiring protection; (c) Assisting governmental and private efforts to promote voluntary repatriation or assimilation within new national communities; (d) Promoting the admission of refugees not excluding those in the most destitute categories, to the territories of States; (e) Endeavouring to obtain permission for refugees to transfer their assets and especially those necessary for their resettlement; (f) Obtaining from Governments information concerning the number and conditions of refugees in their territories and the laws and regulations concerning them; (h) Establishing contact in such manner as he may think best with private organizations dealing with refugee questions; (i) Facilitating the co-ordination of the efforts of private organizations concerned with the welfare of refugees.' United Nations General Assembly, 'Statute of the Office of the United Nations High Commissioner for Refugees' (14 December 1950) A/RES/428(V) (hereafter UNGA, Statute of the UNHCR).

[2] UNHCR, *Global Trends: Forced Displacement in 2020* (2021) (hereafter UNHCR, *Global Trends 2020*).

[3] See section 5.2.

Internally Displaced Persons and International Refugee Law. Bríd Ní Ghráinne, Oxford University Press. © Ní Ghráinne 2022.
DOI: 10.1093/oso/9780198868446.003.0005

IDPs might be interpreted as 'protection of that country' under the Refugee Convention and may thus be used by states to deny refugee status. Such a conflict would be particularly problematic for the UNHCR, as its primary mandate is refugee protection and facilitating solutions to the refugee problem.[4]

For the first time, this chapter will explore whether the UNHCR's activities on behalf of IDPs could be undermining, in legal terms, the institution of asylum.[5] It will examine whether, and if so under which circumstances, in-state protection afforded by the UNHCR to IDPs constitutes 'protection of that country' under the Refugee Convention and may thus be used by refugee-receiving states as a reason to deny refugee status.[6] Insofar as this author's research has revealed, this argument has not (yet) been made by states in asylum determination proceedings and the concept of non-state actor of protection is a relatively new one in refugee law.[7] The arguments raised in this chapter are therefore pre-emptive but are nonetheless pertinent, particularly in light of the fact that Article 7 of the 2011 Recast EU Qualification Directive provides that for the purposes of determining refugee status, protection against persecution may be provided by 'parties or organisations, including international organisations, controlling the state or a substantial part of the territory of the state'.[8] In addition, the UNHCR might be seen to be 'controlling the state or a substantial part of the territory of the state' if, for example, it were acting as an agent of the host state, if it were acting on the territory of a so-called 'failed state', or if it were acting in pursuance of a Security Council resolution.

This chapter will be formed of seven sections. This first introductory section has set out the chapter's scope and aims. Section 5.2 will explain how the UNHCR came to be involved with IDPs and will outline the UNHCR's responsibilities under the cluster approach of IDP protection. Section 5.3 will explain how international law generally and refugee law specifically has evolved

[4] UNGA, Statute of the UNHCR (n 1); Ben Hudson and Bríd Ní Ghráinne, 'Enhancing State-to-State Dialogue on Internal Displacement: Current Global Fora and Future Prospects' (2020) 39(4) Refugee Survey Quarterly 425 (hereafter Hudson and Ní Ghráinne, 'Enhancing State-to-State Dialogue').

[5] Previous versions of parts of this chapter were published in Bríd Ní Ghráinne, 'UNHCR's Involvement with IDPs—"Protection of that Country" for the Purposes of Precluding Application of the Refugee Convention?' (2015) 27(1) International Journal of Refugee Law 536. Parts (sections 2 and 3) of this article are reproduced in this chapter by permission of Oxford University Press.

[6] IDP protection measures provided by an international organization could also be viewed as negating the presence of a 'well-founded fear of being persecuted' necessary to qualify as a refugee, and/or result in the conclusion that the asylum-seeker is unable to show that protection is unavailable to them within the whole of their country of origin. See chapter 4, section 4.1.

[7] However, Storey argues that protection can encompass 'situations where the government is supported by international organizations', in James C Hathaway and Hugo Storey, 'What is the Meaning of State Protection in Refugee Law? A Debate' (2016) 28(3) International Journal of Refugee Law 480, 17 (hereafter Hathaway and Storey, 'The Meaning of State Protection in Refugee Law').

[8] Art 7(1)(b).

in response to the growing power and influence of non-state actors such as the UNHCR. Section 5.4 will involve a textual analysis of the 1951 Refugee Convention to determine whether protection offered by international organizations is compatible with the term 'protection of that country' in the refugee definition. Section 5.5 will examine to what extent state practice sheds light on this issue. Section 5.6 will draw from the analysis in sections 5.3 to 5.5 to assess to what extent the UNHCR's activities on behalf of IDPs might constitute 'protection of that country' within the meaning of the Refugee Convention. This section will argue that the UNHCR is not capable in law or in fact of providing 'protection of that country'. Section 5.7 will conclude.

5.2 The UN High Commissioner for Refugees' Involvement with Internally Displaced Persons

As set out in chapter 3, various organizations have a role to play in protecting and assisting IDPs. These include the International Organisation for Migration (IOM),[9] the UN Office of the High Commissioner for Human Rights (OHCHR),[10] and the United Nations Children's Fund ('UNICEF').[11] However, the focus of this chapter will be on the UNHCR's role as it is the only organization within the cluster approach whose primary mandate focuses specifically on refugees,[12] and thus serves as the best case study for this book's core focus, namely the relationship between the protection of IDPs and international refugee law.

The UNHCR is a subsidiary organ of the United Nations which was established by the General Assembly under Article 22 of the Charter of the United Nations.[13] The mandate of the UNHCR primarily derives from its statute, which makes no explicit reference to the protection of persons aside from

[9] Bríd Ní Ghráinne and Ben Hudson, 'The International Organisation for Migration's Engagement with the Guiding Principles on Internal Displacement' in Cathryn Costello, Megan Bradley, and Angela Sherwood (eds), *IOM Unbound? Obligations and Accountability of the International Organization for Migration in an Era of Expansion* (CUP forthcoming 2022) [39]; Megan Bradley, *The International Organization for Migration: Challenges, Commitments, Complexities* (Routledge 2020).

[10] 'Areas of Activity' (*Office of the United Nations High Commissioner for Human Rights*, OHCHR) <https://www.ohchr.org/EN/Issues/IDPersons/Pages/Activity.aspx> accessed 12 July 2021.

[11] UNICEF and the Internal Displacement Monitoring Centre, 'Protecting and Supporting Internally Displaced Children in Urban Settings' <https://www.unicef.org/reports/protecting-and-supporting-internally-displaced-children-urban-settings> accessed 12 July 2021.

[12] UNCHR's primary mandate is refugee protection and facilitating solutions to the refugee problem. UNGA, Statute of the UNHCR (n 1).

[13] Charter of the United Nations (adopted 26 June 1945, entered into force 24 October 1945) 1 UNTS XVI.

refugees as defined in paragraph 6 and, by way of extension, those recognized as such under the 1951 Refugee Convention.[14] That is not to say that the protection of persons other than refugees is necessarily incompatible with the mandate of the UNHCR. The mandate of the UNHCR must be understood in the light of every succeeding General Assembly resolution dealing with the work of the UNHCR. Over the course of its history, resolutions of the General Assembly have expanded the UNHCR's competence beyond 1951 Refugee Convention refugees to also include refugees as defined in the Convention Governing the Specific Aspects of Refugee Problems in Africa[15] and the Cartagena Declaration on Refugees,[16] as well as other categories of persons such as stateless persons, repatriating refugees, IDPs, and populations affected by war. In addition, the UNHCR no longer solely makes reference to refugees, but often to 'persons of concern to UNHCR'.[17] Of these various groups of 'persons of concern', IDPs form the largest.[18]

5.2.1 The Evolution of UNHCR's Mandate Towards Internally Displaced Persons

Paragraph 9 of the UNHCR's Statute recognizes that the High Commissioner 'may engage in such activities ... as the General Assembly may determine, within the limits of the resources placed at his disposal'.[19] However, Goodwin-Gill cautioned in 2000:

> [Paragraph 9] is not a blank cheque for everything and anything else and especially not a formal, legal basis for activities that compromise [the UNHCR's] primary function of providing international protection to refugees and trespass on the jurisdiction of other actors.[20]

[14] UNGA, Statute of the UNHCR (n 1) [6].
[15] Convention Governing the Specific Aspects of Refugee Problems in Africa (adopted 10 September 1969, entered into force 20 June 1974) (OAU Convention).
[16] Colloquium on the International Protection of Refugees in Central America, Mexico and Panama, 'Cartagena Declaration on Refugees' (adopted 19–22 November 1984).
[17] 'Persons of Concern to UNHCR' (*UNHCR*) <https://www.unhcr.org/ph/persons-concern-unhcr> accessed 12 July 2021.
[18] UNHCR, *Global Trends 2020* (n 2).
[19] UNGA, Statute of the UNHCR (n 1) [6].
[20] Guy S Goodwin-Gill, 'UNHCR and Internal Displacement: Stepping into a Legal and Political Minefield' [2000] US Committee for Refugees, World Refugee Survey 26, 28.

In addition, Paragraph 3 of the Statute provides that the UNHCR 'shall follow policy directives given to him by the General Assembly or the Economic and Social Council'. The UNHCR also considers the advice of the Executive Committee of the High Commissioner's Programme (ExCom), a subsidiary organ of the General Assembly and the governing body of the UNHCR.[21] In addition, Paragraph 2 of the Statute provides that the work of the UNHCR 'shall be of an entirely non-political character; it shall be humanitarian and social and shall relate, as a rule, to groups and categories of refugees'.

A series of UN General Assembly resolutions has encouraged UNHCR involvement with IDPs, dating from as far back as 1972, where the Economic and Social Council called on the UNHCR to extend assistance both to refugees returning to southern Sudan and 'other displaced persons'.[22] Explicit reference to IDPs is found in General Assembly Resolution 48/116 (1993), commending the UNHCR for its work with IDPs.[23] This sentiment was restated in Resolution 53/125 (1998) by which the General Assembly:

> reaffirms its support for the High Commissioner's efforts, on the basis of specific requests from the Secretary-General or the competent principal organs of the United Nations, and with the consent of the concerned state, and taking into account the complementarities of the mandates and expertise of other relevant organisations, to provide humanitarian assistance and protection to persons displaced within their own country in specific situations calling for the Office's particular expertise, especially where such efforts could contribute to the prevention or solution of refugee problems.[24]

ExCom has also welcomed the UNHCR's activities in favour of IDPs. In its Conclusion No 75 (XLV) of 1994, it endorsed the UNHCR's expanding role in this area and referred to Resolution 48/116 as an 'appropriate framework for the involvement of the High Commissioner in situations of internal displacement'.[25] It also elaborated on elements of this resolution, such as the close relationship between internal displacement and refugee phenomena, the expertise of the UNHCR in this area and the need for close collaboration between the UNHCR and other stakeholders.[26] The 2009 African Union (AU)

[21] Hudson and Ní Ghráinne, 'Enhancing State-to-State Dialogue' (n 4).
[22] UN Economic and Social Council Res 1705 (LIII) (27 July 1972) UN Doc E/RES/1705(LIII).
[23] UNGA Res 48/116 (20 December 1993) UN Doc A/RES/48/116.
[24] UNGA Res 53/125 (9 December 1998) UN Doc A/RES/53/125 (hereafter UNGA Res 53/125 (9 December 1998).
[25] UNHCR Conclusion No 75 (XLV) 'Internally Displaced Persons' (1994).
[26] ibid.

Convention for the Protection and Assistance of Internally Displaced Persons in Africa ('Kampala Convention') also recognizes the UNHCR's protection expertise and the AU's invitation to the Office to continue and reinforce its role in the protection and assistance of IDPs.[27]

5.2.2 Criteria for UNHCR's Involvement with Internally Displaced Persons

The UNHCR has stated that before it becomes involved in an IDP operation, the following criteria must be satisfied: (i) there must be a request from the UN Secretary-General or competent organ of the UN (such as the Economic and Social Council); (ii) consent must be received from the state concerned and, where applicable, from other entities in a conflict; (iii) there must be access to the affected population; (iv) there must be adequate security for staff of the UNHCR and affected populations; (v) there must be clear lines of accountability, with the ability to intervene directly on protection matters; and (vi) there must be adequate resources and capacity.[28] The basis of the UNHCR's involvement with IDPs can be summarized in UN General Assembly Resolution 53/125 (1998), which reiterates:

> support for the role of the Office of the High Commissioner in providing humanitarian assistance and protection to internally displaced persons, on the basis of specific requests from the Secretary-General or the competent organs of the United Nations and with the consent of the State concerned, taking into account the complementarities of the mandates and expertise of other relevant organisations . . .[29]

The resolution also underlines that 'activities on behalf of internally displaced persons must not undermine the institution of asylum'.[30]

Today, the UNHCR's involvement with IDPs is formalized under the 'cluster approach', which is set out in more detail in chapter 3.[31] Under the cluster

[27] African Union Convention for the Protection and Assistance of Internally Displaced Persons in Africa (adopted 23 October 2009, entered into force 6 December 2012) (Kampala Convention).

[28] UNHCR 'Internally Displaced Persons—The Role of the High Commissioner for Refugees' (6 March 2000) EC/50/SC/INF.2, 2.

[29] UNGA Res 53/125 (9 December 1998) (n 24).

[30] ibid.

[31] Miriam Bradley, *Protecting Civilians in War: The ICRC, UNHCR, and Their Limitations in Internal Armed Conflicts* (OUP 2016) (hereafter Bradley, *Protecting Civilians in War*).

approach, the UNHCR agreed to assume global cluster leadership for protection and co-leadership for camp coordination/management and emergency shelter.[32] The UNHCR also joined as a member in several other clusters, such as water/sanitation/hygiene (led by UNICEF), logistics (led by the World Food Programme), and early recovery (led by the UN Development Programme). Today, the UNHCR's involvement with IDPs focuses the engagement of operations where the UNHCR has a comparative advantage and cluster leadership as spelled out in the Operational Guidelines for the UNHCR's Engagement in Situations of Internal Displacement.[33]

The UNHCR was (and still is) an obvious candidate for protection activities on behalf of IDPs for three reasons. First, as set out in chapter 2, IDPs often become refugees. Thus protecting and assisting IDPs may prevent refugee flows, and the prevention of refugee flows is a solution to the 'refugee problem'.[34] According to the UNHCR, it has an interest in protecting all those who, had they crossed an international border, would have had a claim to international protection. This interest arises because of the similarity between such IDPs and refugees, the causes and consequences of their displacement, and their humanitarian needs.[35] Second, refugees and IDPs are often found side by side and in the same predicament. If the UNHCR is protecting and assisting the refugees in a particular location, then, ethically, it should also protect and assist the IDPs.[36] Third, the UNHCR has vast experience with both forced migrants generally and IDP specifically. It has decades of experience with uprooted populations, a mandate encompassing protection and assistance, and has been involved in IDP operations since the 1960s.[37] In 2005—the year the cluster approach was introduced—Walter Kälin, the then-Representative of the Secretary-General on the Human Rights of Internally Displaced Persons stated that:

[32] The UNHCR co-leads the Global Shelter Cluster with International Federation of Red Cross and Red Crescent Societies (IFRC) and the Global Camp Coordination Camp Management Cluster (CCCM) with International Organisation for Migration (IOM). See 'Internally Displaced Persons' (*UNHCR*) <https://www.unhcr.org/internally-displaced-people.html> accessed 12 July 2021; Miriam Bradley, 'UNHCR and Accountability of IDP Protection in Colombia' in Kristin Bergtora Sandvik and Katja Lindskov Jacobsen (eds), *UNHCR and the Struggle for Accountability: Technology, Law, and Results-Based Management* (Routledge 2016).

[33] UNHCR, 'Operational Guidelines for UNHCR's Engagement in Situations of Internal Displacement' (1 February 2016) UNHCR/OG/2016/2 (hereafter UNHCR, 'Operational Guidelines').

[34] Bradley, *Protecting Civilians in War* (n 31).

[35] UNHCR, 'The Role of the High Commissioner for Refugees' (n 28) 3.

[36] Bradley, *Protecting Civilians in War* (n 31); Miriam Bradley, 'Unintended Consequences of Adjacency Claims: The Function and Dysfunction of Analogies between Refugee Protection and IDP Protection in the Work of UNHCR' (2019) 25(4) Global Governance 620 (hereafter Bradley, 'Unintended Consequences of Adjacency Claims').

[37] Bradley, *Protecting Civilians in War* (n 31).

> it is obvious that UNHCR is the organisation with the most experience and capacity to protect and assist persons displaced by armed conflict who are in camps or to organise IDP returns in safety or dignity after the end of conflict. Indeed, it is difficult to understand why there should not be at least a presumption that the High Commissioner for Refugees should assume responsibility in such situations.[38]

In its most recent policy on engagement with IDPs, the UNHCR committed itself 'to leverage fully the synergies between [their] engagement with refugees, internally displaced people, returnees, stateless people and others affected by humanitarian crises'.[39]

In sum, there are a variety of practical, normative, and political reasons driving the UNHCR's involvement with IDPs. Although it may seem that the UNHCR was given a new responsibility for IDPs under the cluster approach, in reality it is merely operating under its existing mandate of protecting IDPs. Yet the cluster approach cemented the UNHCR's role as one of the most significant international players in IDP protection.[40] The UNCHR is now the global cluster lead for protection, which is the biggest gap in the safeguarding of IDPs. More generally, the UNHCR had a much larger involvement with IDPs in the past, when it was, by its own admission, not 'as consistent and predictable' in its support to IDPs as compared to its support to refugees[41] and only intervened on behalf of IDPs on a case-by-case basis.

However, the UNHCR's involvement with IDPs has given rise to significant criticism.[42] Bradley has suggested that one additional underlying motivation for the UNHCR's involvement with IDPs was the 'increasingly restrictive asylum policies and practices'[43] adopted by western states in the 1980s and 1990s. She notes that:

[38] Interview with Prof Walter Kälin (2005) 23 Forced Migration Review 4, 6.

[39] UNHCR, 'Policy on UNHCR's Engagement in Situations of Internal Displacement' (18 September 2019) UNHCR/HCP/2019/1, 4 (hereafter UNHCR, 'Policy on UNHCR's Engagement').

[40] See also the Transformative Agenda, available at https://interagencystandingcommittee.org/iasc-transformative-agenda accessed 7 July 2021.

[41] UNHCR, 'Policy on UNHCR's Engagement' (n 39) 6.

[42] Other arguments include the potential diversion of resources from refugee protection, that in-country presence in armed conflict results in the politicization of the UNHCR and its frequent instrumentalization by parties to conflict; that increased engagement in countries of origin—and associated compromising of principles—weakens the UNHCR's moral authority to push states to meet their obligations in refugee protection, and hence serves to erode the institution of asylum. See Bradley, 'Unintended Consequences of Adjacency Claims' (n 36), Bradley, *Protecting Civilians in War* (n 31) chapters 1–3.

[43] Miriam Bradley, *Protecting Civilians in War* (n 31).

> As a consequence of the increasing reluctance of states to accept refugees, IDP protection came to be seen as both a humanitarian solution and as a means to contain would-be refugees in their countries of origin . . . The financial and political dependence of UNHCR on states . . . ensured that the policy pursued by UNHCR has reflected the global move towards containment.[44]

As such, there is a danger that the UNHCR's activities on behalf of IDPs might be interpreted as 'protection of that country' for the purposes of the refugee definition. In other words, states might reject refugee claims on the basis that an individual could receive protection from the UNHCR as an IDP in their own state. This would mean that by assisting IDPs, the UNHCR could be undermining its mandate towards refugees. The following sections will assess whether such an interpretation is legally compatible with the terms of the 1951 Refugee Convention. The analysis begins with section 5.3, which will illustrate how international law generally and refugee law specifically has evolved in response to the growing power and influence of non-state actors such as the UNHCR.

5.3 Non-State Actors in International Law and Refugee Law

At the time the 1951 Refugee Convention was drafted, states were the sole repositories of power in international law, international relations, and political theory. However, modern scholarship has challenged this view and it is no longer presumed that states have exclusive control of their territories. Non-state actors (NSAs) such as international organizations, corporations, peoples, and NGOs are now seen as major players in both the domestic and international legal spheres.[45] Multinational corporations—some of which have annual turnovers that rival the GDPs of states—produce vaccines in the fight to stem the COVID-19 pandemic; peoples pursuing their right to self-determination can

[44] ibid.

[45] Gunnar Folke Schuppert, 'The Changing Role of the State Reflected in the Growing Importance of Non-State Actors' in Gunnar Folke Schuppert (ed), *Global Governance and the Role of Non-State Actors* (Nomos 2006); Jean d'Aspremont (ed), *Participants in the International Legal System: Multiple Perspectives on Non-State Actors in International Law* (Routledge 2011); Sufyan Droubi and Jean d'Aspremont (eds), *International Organisations, Non-State Actors, and the Formation of Customary International Law* (Manchester University Press 2020); Anthea Roberts and Sandesh Sivakumaran, 'Lawmaking by Nonstate Actors: Engaging Armed Groups in the Creation of International Humanitarian Law' (2012) 37(1) Yale Journal of International Law 107; Cedric Ryngaert and Math Noortmann (eds), *Non-State Actor Dynamics in International Law: From Law-Takers to Law-Makers* (Routledge 2010).

cause states to alter their boundaries, recognize new entities, lose some degree of their effective control; international organizations can sometimes authorize military interventions; and non-state armed groups are active in the majority of armed conflicts around the world and have an immense impact on the estimated 66 million people living under their control.[46] The exponential growth of NSAs throughout the twentieth century coupled with the collapse of space and time brought about by the information revolution means that the influence of NSAs in global affairs is likely to become even greater.[47] International law has responded to this reality by recognizing that, in certain circumstances, NSAs have international legal personality making them the bearers of rights and obligations in international law.[48]

Modern international refugee law has also evolved in response to the growing power and influence of NSAs. An example of this may be seen in the interpretation of the term 'persecution' by domestic courts. A growing number of states now subscribe to the 'protection' theory, which maintains that persecution is not confined to actions of state authorities, but may also emanate from NSAs where the state is unable, or able but unwilling, to protect the individual from such persecution.[49] This stems from the conception of international

[46] Annyssa Bellal, Pascal Bongard, and Ezequiel Heffes, 'Research Brief. From Words to Deeds: A Research of Armed Non-State Actors' Practice and Interpretations of International Humanitarian and Human Rights Norms' (2019). Available at: https://www.geneva-academy.ch/joomlatools-files/docman-files/From%20Words%20to%20Deeds%20A%20Research%20of%20Armed%20Non-State%20Actors%E2%80%99%20Practice%20and%20Inter.pdfm accessed 18 March 2021; 'Communities facing conflict, climate change and environmental degradation walk a tightrope of survival' (*International Committee of the Red Cross*, 17 September 2020) <https://www.icrc.org/en/document/communities-facing-conflict-climate-change-and-environmental-degradation-walk-tightrope> accessed 18 March 2021.

[47] Alan Boyle and Christine Chinkin, *The Making of International Law* (OUP 2007).

[48] William Thomas Worster, 'Relative International Legal Personality of Non-State Actors' (2016–2017) 42 Brooklyn Journal of International Law 207; Roland Portmann, *Legal Personality in International Law* (CUP 2010).

[49] Maria O'Sullivan, 'Acting the Part: Can Non-State Entities Provide Protection Under International Refugee Law?' (2012) 24(1) International Journal of Refugee Law 85, 88 (hereafter O'Sullivan, 'Acting the Part'); *Januzi v Secretary of State for the Home Department* [2006] UKHL 5, [2006] 2 AC 426 [66]; Erika Feller, 'International Refugee Protection 50 Years On: The Protection Challenges of the Past, Present and Future' (2001) 83 International Review of the Red Cross 581, 594; Susan Kneebone, 'Moving Beyond the State: Refugees, Accountability and Protection' in Susan Kneebone (ed), *The Refugees Convention 50 Years on: Globalisation and International Law* (Ashgate 2003) (hereafter Kneebone, 'Refugees, Accountability and Protection'); Volker Turk, 'Non-State Actors of Persecution' in Vincent Chetail and others, *Switzerland and the International Protection of Refugees: a Colloquium of the Graduate Institute of International Studies, Geneva, in collaboration with the Office of the United Nations High Commissioner for Refugees = La Suisse et la Protection Internationale des Réfugiés: Colloque de l'Institut Universitaire de Hautes Études Internationales, Géneve, en Collaboration avec le Haut Commissariat des Nations Unies pour les Réfugiés* (Kluwer Law International 2002); Walter Kälin, 'Non-State Agents of Persecution and the Inability of the State to Protect' (2001) 15 Georgetown Immigration Law Journal 415; Pia Zambelli, 'Knowing Persecution When We See It: Non-State Actors and the Measure of State Protection' (2020) 32(1) International Journal of Refugee Law 28. For a more general discussion on the meaning of 'persecution', see Hugo Storey, 'What Constitutes Persecution? Towards a Working Definition' (2014) 26(2) International Journal of Refugee Law 272.

refugee protection as surrogate to national protection, in the sense that refugee protection is only applicable where protection is not available in the country of origin.[50] The 'protection' theory may be contrasted to the 'accountability' theory, which posits that only actions that are attributable to the state may constitute 'persecution' for the purposes of the refugee definition.[51]

In recent years, the acceptance by domestic courts that NSAs may be actors of persecution has been mirrored by the factual reality of NSAs providing protection to persons within their countries of origin. Clans, militias, international organizations, and NGOs have been perceived as providing sufficient protection such that would obviate the need for international protection as encapsulated in the Refugee Convention. For example, the Canadian Federal Court held in *Elmi v MCI* [1999] that in the situation of a complete breakdown of the state such as that which occurred in Somalia, a clan is capable of providing protection since it is acting as the 'de facto government agent of protection' in a particular area and because clan members 'traditionally look after one other'.[52] The European Court of Human Rights also seems to have accepted that clans may be able to provide sufficient protection from persecution.[53] In addition, since the emergence of the doctrines of 'responsibility to protect' and 'humanitarian intervention' in the last few decades,[54] there has been an increasing acceptance that protection is not solely the responsibility of the state and that, in certain circumstances, the responsibility to protect a population within a state's borders may shift to the international community. Further analysis of these doctrines appears in chapter 3.

The proposition that protection provided by NSAs should be recognized as 'protection of that country' for the purposes of the Refugee Convention also has some scholarly support. According to Storey, the argument that it would be contrary to international law to regard NSAs such as de facto authorities as 'protection of that country':

> is difficult to square with the prevailing—extremely minimalist—international law criteria for statehood and appears to depend on the highly

[50] *R v Secretary of State for the Home Department, Immigration Appeals Tribunal, Ex parte Anthonypillai Francis Robinson* [1998] QB 929 [16]; James Hathaway, *The Law of Refugee Status* (Butterworths 1991) 135; *Randhawa v Minister for Immigration, Local Government and Ethnic Affairs* (1994) 52 FCR 437, 124 ALR 265, 441.

[51] Kneebone, 'Refugees, Accountability and Protection' (n 49).

[52] *Elmi v Minister of Citizenship and Immigration* IMM-580-98; UK AIT, *DM (Majority Clan Entities Can Protect) Somalia v Secretary of State for the Home Department* [2005] UKAIT 00150.

[53] *Salah Sheekh v the Netherlands*, App no 1948/04, 23 May 2007.

[54] Ingo Winkelmann, *Responsibility to Protect* (Max Planck Encyclopedia of Public International Law 2012).

> dubious notion that protection can only be afforded to citizens by liberal democratic states, or at least those that have agreed to be bound by major international human rights treaties.[55]

Similarly, Nykänen argues that although the situations in which NSAs could offer truly effective protection would, in practice, be very rare:

> there are no legal obstacles for recognising the state of affairs [as] this approach would take the process of fragmentation of power seriously; relevant power to persecute and to protect from persecution is not held only by state authorities, but potentially also by other actors.[56]

The following sections will examine to what extent such an interpretation is compatible with the Refugee Convention. A discussion on NSAs in general is beyond the scope of this chapter, and thus the focus will be on the UNHCR owing to its significant role in the protection of IDPs. The analysis will commence with section 5.4, which will examine whether and to what extent the term 'protection of that country' can include protection provided by an NSA such as the UNHCR.

5.4 Interpreting 'Protection of that Country': Article 31(1) of the 1969 Vienna Convention on the Law of Treaties

According to the Refugee Convention, a refugee is a person who:

> owing to well-founded fear of being persecuted for reasons of race, religion, nationality, membership of a particular social group or political opinion, is outside the country of his nationality and is unable or, owing to such fear, is unwilling to avail himself of the protection of that country.[57]

[55] Hugo Storey, 'EU Refugee Qualification Directive: a Brave New World?' (2008) 20(1) International Journal of Refugee Law 1, 25. See also O'Sullivan, who states that 'it is arguable that certain international organizations, such as the UN, may provide such protection, if they are acting as a stable, state-like authority, are supported by an international mandate and are acting in an agency relationship, that is, in place of a "failed state" or with the consent of the government in question'. O'Sullivan, 'Acting the Part' (n 49) 107.

[56] Eeva Nykänen, *Fragmented State Power and Forced Migration: A Study on Non-State Actors in Refugee Law* (Martinus Nijhoff Publishers 2012) 201.

[57] Convention Relating to the Status of Refugees (adopted 28 July 1951, entered into force 22 April 1954) 189 UNTS 137 (hereafter Refugee Convention) art 1A.

Neither the refugee definition nor its *travaux préparatoires* make any reference to the possibility of 'protection of that country' being provided by an international organization.[58] This is not surprising, considering that at the time of drafting of the Refugee Convention, the general understanding was that states had exclusive control over their territories and NSAs had little or no role to play in international law and international relations. Nonetheless, a contemporary reading of the Refugee Convention may lead to a different result. The starting point for any exercise in treaty interpretation is Article 31(1) of the 1969 Vienna Convention on the Law of Treaties (VCLT):

> A treaty shall be interpreted in good faith in accordance with the ordinary meaning to be given to the terms of the treaty in their context and in the light of its object and purpose.[59]

This rule contains separate principles which must be applied together in order to close in on the true meaning of a phrase in a treaty.[60] By applying this rule, the following paragraphs will examine to what extent 'protection of that country' may be interpreted as protection provided by the UNHCR to IDPs.

5.4.1 The Meaning of 'Protection'

The ordinary meaning of the term 'protection' is not elaborated upon in the Refugee Convention and therefore it is unclear what exactly will satisfy the protection element of the refugee definition. The reasons for the lack of definition of this term become clear if we turn to its overall context: protection is inextricably linked to the content and form of persecution, and thus the method of protection required for an individual depends on the persecution feared.[61] Thus it is not possible to definitively state whether an international organization may provide protection which would satisfy that envisaged by the Refugee

[58] However, art 1D of the Refugee Convention refers to the provision of protection by international organizations other than the UNHCR. This provision is directed at the provision of protection by UNRWA to Palestinian refugees, rather than being of general applicability. For further discussion, see chapter 6.

[59] Vienna Convention on the Law of Treaties (adopted 23 May 1969, entered into force 27 January 1980) 1155 UNTS 331 (hereafter VCLT).

[60] Richard K Gardiner, *Treaty Interpretation* (OUP 2010) 142 (hereafter Gardiner, *Treaty Interpretation*).

[61] *Horvath (A.P.) v Secretary of State for the Home Department* [2000] 1 AC 489 (hereafter *Horvath*).

Convention, as the level of protection required will vary in each individual case according to the nature of the persecution feared.[62]

However the objective of treaty interpretation is to produce an outcome which advances the aim of the treaty.[63] As such, the content of the term 'protection' must be effective in practice and it should provide an 'antidote'[64] from the persecution feared. In the case of *Horvath v Secretary of State for the Home Department* (2001),[65] the House of Lords held that it was not possible to devise any complete or comprehensive exposition which would exhaustively define the relevant level of protection required by the Refugee Convention. However, there must have been laws in force in the country which made violent attacks by perpetrators punishable by sentences commensurate with the gravity of the offences. Furthermore, there must have been a reasonable willingness by law enforcement agencies to prosecute and punish offenders and the victim must not have been exempt from the protection of the law. A similar standard of protection is found in the EC Qualification Directive,[66] which will be elaborated upon in more detail below.[67]

The UNHCR has also set out 'critical factors' for the existence of 'effective protection'.[68] Although these factors were set out in the context of returning to third states, the same document stipulates that, in this respect, the distinction between the so-called 'safe' third country and the country of first asylum concepts is not relevant.[69] Consequently, the notion of 'effective protection' as described by the UNHCR is synonymous with its perception of 'protection' in the refugee definition.

[62] Hugo Storey has offered a working definition of persecution, based on art 9 of the EC qualification directive. See Storey, 'What Constitutes Persecution?' (n 49).

[63] Gardiner, *Treaty Interpretation* (n 60) 190.

[64] James C Hathaway and Michelle Foster, *The Law of Refugee Status* (2nd edn, OUP 2014).

[65] *Horvath* (n 61); *SA (political activist-internal relocation) Pakistan* [2011] UKUT 30 (IAC); *AB (Protection-criminal gangs-internal relocation) Jamaica CG* [2007] UKAIT 00018; *Bagdanavicius & Anor, R (On the Application of) v Secretary of State for the Home Department* [2005] EWCA Civ 1605.

[66] Council Directive 2011/95/EU of the European Parliament and of the Council of 13 December 2011 on standards for the qualification of third-country nationals or stateless persons as beneficiaries of international protection, for a uniform status for refugees or for persons eligible for subsidiary protection, and for the content of the protection granted (recast) [2011] OJ L337/9 (hereafter Council Directive (EC) 2011/95/EU).

[67] It is important to note that many legal theorists take a broader view of what constitutes a legal system, which consists of mechanisms and practices of legal rules and their enforcement. See Brian Tamanaha, *A General Jurisprudence of Law and Society* (OUP 2001); William Twining, *General Jurisprudence: Understanding Law from a Global Perspective* (CUP 2009); Denis J Galligan, *Law in Modern Society* (OUP 2006).

[68] UNHCR 'Summary Conclusions on the Concept of "Effective Protection" in the Context of Secondary Movements of Refugees and Asylum-Seekers', Lisbon Expert Roundtable (9–10 December 2002) <http://www.unhcr.org/3e5f323d7.html> accessed 11 June 2014, 3–4.

[69] ibid 3–4.

The elements of 'effective protection' according to the UNHCR are as follows: (a) no well-founded fear of persecution exists; (b) fundamental human rights are respected, including but not limited to the prohibition of torture or cruel, inhuman, or degrading treatment and the protection of the right to life and liberty of the person; (c) there is no real risk of being sent to another state where effective protection would not be available; ... (e) the third state has acceded to and is in compliance with the 1951 Refugee Convention and/or its 1967 Protocol or the third state has developed a practice akin to the aforementioned instruments; ... (f) the person has access to means of subsistence sufficient to maintain an adequate standard of living; (g) account is taken of any special vulnerabilities of the person concerned, and the privacy interests of the person and their family are respected.[70]

As was discussed in more detail in the previous chapter relating to the internal protection alternative inquiry, the UNHCR's concept of 'effective protection' may go beyond that which was intended by the drafters of the Refugee Convention. In no place in the Refugee Convention is there any mention of criteria (b), (f), or (g), which seem to have their roots in human rights considerations. Although the Refugee Convention as a whole is influenced by human rights considerations, regard must be had to the textual limits of the Refugee Convention. Human rights considerations are therefore relevant to the concept of 'effective protection' in two respects; first, insofar as a state is prohibited from engaging in indirect *refoulement*; and secondly, to determine whether effective protection from persecution exists in the country of nationality or habitual residence. As was set out in *Horvath*, such effective protection may take the form of a legal system to prevent and prosecute acts of persecution.

In sum, therefore, the meaning of protection will vary in each individual case and will depend on the nature of the persecution feared. The UNHCR is therefore not automatically excluded from being a provider of 'protection' within the meaning of the refugee definition. Yet the term 'protection' in the refugee definition has a qualifier because it refers to 'protection of that country'. The next section will examine whether the protection offered by NSAs can be equated with protection offered by 'that country'.

[70] ibid 3–4. Both Hathaway and Storey also argue that 'protection' should be understood to have positive content. See Hathaway and Storey, 'The Meaning of State Protection in Refugee Law' (n 7).

5.4.2 The Meaning of 'that Country'

Unlike the term 'protection', there are many hints in the 1951 Refugee Convention's text regarding the meaning of 'that country'. For the purposes of clarity, different aspects of the VCLT rules of interpretation will be applied to the term 'that country' in turn.

5.4.2.1 The Ordinary Meaning of 'that Country'

In order to determine the meaning of 'that country', primary recourse must be had to the ordinary meaning of the term. The difficulty with this approach is that the term 'that country' has various meanings. If 'country' is synonymous with the concept of 'state', then only the authorities of the state can provide protection within the meaning of the refugee definition. If, on the other hand, 'country' is to be understood in its geographical sense, protection provided by NSAs could potentially satisfy this requirement. One must therefore look to the other components of Article 31(1) of the VCLT to discover the true meaning of 'that country'.

5.4.2.2 The Context of 'that Country'

Numerous arguments based on the Refugee Convention's context have been put forward in support of a geographical interpretation of the term 'that country'. First, in the broader context of the treaty as a whole, various provisions explicitly refer to the 'authorities of the country' where the role of the state is concerned.[71] According to this argument, the employment of the term 'that country' in the refugee definition therefore implies that the actor of protection need not exclusively be the authorities of the state.

Second, Article 1D of the Refugee Convention supports the fact that protection may be provided by an international organization:

> This Convention shall not apply to persons who are at present receiving from organs or agencies of the United Nations other than the United Nations High Commissioner for Refugees protection or assistance.[72]

Article 1D's applicability to protection activities on behalf of IDPs will be returned to in chapter 6.

[71] See, for example, arts 1E, 19, 24, 25, 31, 35, 41.

[72] Refugee Convention (n 57), art 1D; Hathaway and Storey, 'The Meaning of State Protection in Refugee Law' (n 7) (Storey's argument).

Third, the wording of the Refugee Convention may be contrasted to that of the Convention against Torture and Other Cruel, Inhuman and Degrading Treatment 1984 ('CAT'), which specifies that the ill-treatment in question must be attributable to the state in order to engage the state's responsibility under the CAT.[73]

However, the arguments supporting the former interpretation of the term 'that country' (ie that it is synonymous with state authorities) are more convincing. Since 'that country' forms part of a phrase, that is, the refugee definition, that phrase is the obvious initial contextual assessment that must be made. In the context of the refugee definition, 'that country' refers to the earlier term 'country of nationality', which implies that protection can only be granted by an entity which is capable of granting nationality, that is, a state.[74]

An examination of the broader contextual picture leads to the same result, as evidence for interpreting 'that country' as the state may be found elsewhere in the Refugee Convention. First, the cessation clauses also speak of re-availment of the protection of the country of nationality.[75] Second, the Refugee Convention's accountability mechanisms and the obligations set out in Articles 2–33 are specifically addressed to 'states'.[76] According to Mathew, Hathaway, and Foster, this implies that the Refugee Convention arguably requires that protection will be provided by a government which may be held accountable under international law for its actions, and not by some legally unaccountable entity with de facto control.[77]

Third, the 'Article 1D' argument outlined above is quite weak. This argument maintains that because Article 1D refers to the possibility of protection being provided by an international organization, such a meaning may be inferred to the term 'that county' in the refugee definition. This argument may be turned on its head by stating that the reference to protection provided by an

[73] Convention Against Torture and Other Cruel, Inhuman or Degrading Treatment or Punishment (adopted 10 December 1984, entered into force 26 June 1987) 1465 UNTS 85 art 1(1).

[74] Penelope Mathew, James C Hathaway, and Michelle Foster, 'The Role of State Protection in Refugee Analysis: Discussion Paper No. 2 Advanced Refugee Law Workshop, International Association of Refugee Law Judges, Auckland, New Zealand, October 2002' (2003) 15(3) International Journal of Refugee Law 444, 457 (hereafter Mathew, Hathaway, and Foster, 'The Role of State Protection in Refugee Analysis'); Hathaway and Storey, 'The Meaning of State Protection in Refugee Law' (n 7) 485 (Hathaway's argument).

[75] Arts 1C(1), 1C(2), 1C(5); Maria O'Sullivan, *Refugee Law and Durability of Protection: Temporary Residence and Cessation of Status* (Routledge 2019) (hereafter O'Sullivan, *Refugee Law and Durability of Protection*).

[76] Mathew, Hathaway, and Foster, 'The Role of State Protection in Refugee Analysis' (n 74) 457.

[77] James Hathaway and Michelle Foster, 'Internal Protection/Relocation/Flight Alternative as an Aspect of Refugee Status Determination' (Global Consultation on International Protection, Expert Roundtable Discussion organised by the UNHCR, 2001) 46.

international organization in Article 1D excludes this possibility from other provisions of the Refugee Convention.

Fourth, the Refugee Convention uses the term 'territory' when referring to a geographic area. This terminology appears in 19 of the Convention's 46 articles,[78] and is thus strong evidence in favour of the argument that the terminology 'protection within the territory of that country' would have been used if the term 'that state' were to be interpreted in its geographic sense.[79]

Fifth, the meaning of the word 'protection' as used in the refugee definition informs the interpretation of the term 'that country'. At the time the Refugee Convention was concluded, the term 'protection' in the refugee definition referred to diplomatic protection rather than protection within the refugee's country of origin, in the sense that a refugee, being outside the country of their nationality, was unable to access their country's protection abroad.[80] Diplomatic protection can only be provided by a state, which further supports the fact that 'that country' refers to protection provided by a state. An argument stemming from this point which supports interpreting 'that country' as the territory of the state is that if the meaning of 'protection' has changed in light of modern-day practices of states, then surely the meaning of 'that country' could have changed in a similar fashion. This argument can be countered by the fact that although 'protection' no longer exclusively refers to diplomatic protection, the nature of the actor or provider of that protection has not changed.

In line with the arguments outlined above, this chapter strongly supports interpreting 'that country' as the state. Although NSAs may be a source of *persecution* where the state is unable or unwilling to provide protection, the same cannot be said for the source of *protection* from the persecution feared. The refugee definition does not refer to whom or what may qualify as an actor of persecution. In contrast, the refugee definition does make reference to the source of protection, that is, a 'country'. Accordingly, the range of possible actors of protection needs to be interpreted more strictly than possible actors of persecution.

5.4.2.3 The Refugee Convention's Object and Purpose

Further support for this position may be found by examining the meaning of 'that country' in light of the object and purpose of the Refugee Convention. The preamble makes reference to the 'widest possible exercise' of fundamental

[78] Arts 7, 10, 11, 14, 15, 17, 18, 19, 21, 23, 24, 25, 26, 27, 28, 30, 31, 32, 44.

[79] Hemme Battjes, *European Asylum Law and International Law* (Martinus Nijhoff 2006) 248.

[80] Antonio Fortin, 'The Meaning of "Protection" in the Refugee Definition' (2000) 12(4) International Journal of Refugee Law 548.

rights and freedoms for refugees, and the desire to extend the scope of protection afforded to refugees. It may be stated therefore that the primary aim of the Refugee Convention is to further the protection of refugees.[81]

The obligation to interpret a treaty in good faith is set out in Article 31 of the VCLT and has been said to be an extension of the obligation to interpret a treaty 'in light of its object and purpose'. The good faith requirement is also found in Article 26 of the VCLT and it forms a general principle of international law.[82] In the words of Villiger:

> Good faith requires the parties to a treaty to act honestly, fairly and reasonably, and to refrain from taking unfair advantage. The prohibition of the abuse of rights, flowing from good faith, prevents a party from evading its obligations . . .[83]

The good faith argument was raised in the House of Lords case of *R v Immigration Officer at Prague Airport*.[84] One of the issues before the Court was whether, in denying leave to enter the United Kingdom to asylum-seekers within their country of origin, the United Kingdom was seeking to avoid its obligations and thus was not implementing the Refugee Convention in good faith. The House of Lords accepted the argument that the principle of good faith requires the state to refrain from actions which are incompatible with the object and purpose of the treaty. However, it held that such an argument had to be treated with caution and it could not be used to override what the treaty itself provides.[85] As the Refugee Convention only applies to refugees, who are by definition outside of their country of nationality, the House of Lords held that no duty under the Refugee Convention was owed to the applicants as they had not crossed an international frontier. In the words of the Court, to argue that the United Kingdom's actions were:

[81] Hathaway makes an alternative argument, but one which nonetheless supports this chapter's position. He notes that the goal of the international refugee regime is also 'to restore relevantly at-risk persons to the protection of a State . . . It is completely at odds with the object and purpose of the Convention to require an individual to entrust his or her welfare to the efforts of some entity that, whatever its past record or de facto authority or power, bears no ongoing legal duty to protect anyone.' Hathaway and Storey, 'The Meaning of State Protection in Refugee Law' (n 7) 485–86.

[82] *Nuclear Tests (Australia v France)* (Judgment) [1974] ICJ Rep 243, 268.

[83] Mark Eugen Villiger, *Commentary on the 1969 Vienna Convention on the Law of Treaties* (Brill Nijhoff 2009) 425.

[84] *Regina v Immigration Officer at Prague Airport and another (Respondents) ex parte European Roma Rights Centre and others (Appellants)* [2004] UKHL 55.

[85] ibid [19].

> incompatible with the principle of good faith as they defeat[ed] the object and purpose of the treaty [would be] to argue for the enlargement of the obligations which are to be found in the Convention.[86]

Although the appellants were unsuccessful, this case supports the existence of an obligation to interpret the Refugee Convention in good faith, provided that this does not override the actual wording of the text. The Refugee Convention may be viewed 'as a general legal standard against which performance can be reviewed in the context of the regime of international protection as a whole',[87] and thus actions carried out which defeat the aim of refugee protection cannot be said to be performed in good faith. In the context of this chapter, there is a danger that states will use internal protection by international organizations, without inquiring as to its effectiveness, as a basis for turning away refugees. Such an interpretation would fall foul of the requirement to interpret the Refugee Convention in good faith and, as outlined above, would be incompatible with the meaning of the term 'that country'.

5.4.3 A 'Special Meaning' of 'Protection of that Country'?

This chapter has argued that 'protection of that country' in the refugee definition is to be interpreted as protection provided by the authorities of that country, rather than protection provided on the territory of that country. However, there is one final means by which the latter interpretation may be valid. Article 31(4) of the VCLT provides that 'a special meaning shall be given to a term if it is established that the parties so intended'. Did the parties to the Refugee Convention intend that a 'special meaning' be given to the term 'that country', so that it is to be interpreted in its broader geographical sense? In the *Conditions of Admission* Advisory Opinion, the International Court of Justice stated that 'a decisive reason would be required' to displace the natural meaning of the terms used.[88]

Beyond referring to a definition article in a treaty, there is little practice showing clearly what would amount to the necessary evidence to prove the

[86] ibid [64].

[87] Guy S Goodwin-Gill, 'State Responsibility and the "Good Faith" Obligation in International Law' in Malgosia Fitzmaurice and Dan Sarooshi (eds), *Issues of State Responsibility before International Judicial Institutions* (Hart 2004) 85.

[88] *Admission of a State to Membership in the United Nations (Charter, Art. 4)* (Advisory Opinion) [1948] ICJ Rep 57, 63.

existence of a special meaning of a term. If no definition is provided it is a matter of assessing the intent of the parties in light of the available evidence. Regarding the meaning of 'that country', the refugee definition's *travaux préparatoires* do not shed light on the relevance of NSAs. The practice of interpreting this term in its geographical sense has only emerged relatively recently, and thus the evidence supporting this interpretation is weak, at best. It is therefore submitted that there does not exist a 'decisive reason' to consider that the interpretation of 'that country' as the authorities of a state should be displaced by a special meaning of the term.

5.4.4 'Protection of that Country'—Conclusions

This chapter has argued that the term 'protection of that country' in the refugee definition refers to protection provided by state authorities. Although it is not clear whether the term 'protection', taken on its own, excludes the activities of international organizations such as the UNHCR, it is clear when analysed as part of the term 'protection of that country' that only the activities of the territorial state are intended by this term. However, the VCLT also provides that, 'subsequent practice' should be taken into account when determining the meaning of a treaty.[89] Both judgments of domestic courts and the practice of regional systems created by states (such as the EU) constitute subsequent practice for the purposes of interpreting the refugee definition, and hence the term 'protection of that country'.[90] In addition, the VCLT also directs us to take into account 'other relevant rules of international law' when interpreting the meaning of a treaty.[91] Understanding how protection provided by international organizations has been interpreted in other treaty regimes also helps us to understand how it should be interpreted in relation to the 1951 Refugee Convention.

There is both state and regional (specifically EU) law which supports an interpretation to the effect that 'protection' may be provided by international organizations. Thus while this chapter views the Refugee Convention as containing a more restricted meaning of the term 'that country', it is accepted that this presumption may be displaceable. Moreover, the line between state and NSA protection in reality is often blurred. Situations of internal displacement

[89] Art 31(3)(b).
[90] Oliver Dörr and Kirsten Schmalenbach (eds), *Vienna Convention on the Law of Treaties: A Commentary* (Springer 2012) 597 (hereafter Dörr and Schmalenbach, *Vienna Convention*).
[91] Art 31(3)(c).

are highly complex, and they 'demand collaborative, multilateral and multi-sectoral responses'.[92] Often it is not a question of protection being provided by *either* a state *or* an international organization, but rather that 'missions led by an international organisation or international forces operate within the territory of the state, with that state's consent and often in cooperation of that state'.[93] The UNHCR's operations with IDPs generally involve a 'multi-stake-holder, whole of society approach' and the UNHCR works with 'local and national authorities; local civil society, community-based organizations, local women's organizations, and faith-based groups; UN entities including political and peacekeeping missions; regional and international organizations; development actors and financial institutions; the private sector'.[94]

This chapter thus agrees with Hathaway, and argues that the term 'protection of that country' refers to protection provided by state authorities, but that this may include contracted-out mechanisms of protection which are genuinely accessible and for which the state remains fully accountable. Moreover, 'the efforts of an "international organization" (other than UNRWA: Article ID) are similarly relevant only to the extent that the organization is accountable to the State for its actions'.[95] The next section will outline the state practice that has dealt with this issue.

5.5 State Practice

Domestic and regional practice on international organizations as actors of protection is limited,[96] most of which stems from Europe and deals with protection provided by international organizations in Kosovo. Nonetheless, the following paragraphs will engage in an examination of the caselaw which sheds light on this issue, with particular reference to whether the jurisprudence may be applicable to the UNHCR's IDP operations. Caselaw from other jurisdictions (such as Australia and Canada) will be cited where relevant.

[92] UNHCR, 'UNHCR's Engagement in Situations of Internal Displacement: Provisional Guidance' <https://cms.emergency.unhcr.org/documents/11982/41779/UNHCR+Provisional+Guidance+on+Engagement+in+Situations+of+Internal+Displacement/e3879a40-cba3-4ec3-ba2e-40df1c0edef1> accessed 1 July 2021.

[93] Markos Karavias, 'Non-State Actors in Control of Territory as "Actors of Protection" in International Refugee Law' (2014) Revue Belge de Droit International 487.

[94] UNHCR, 'Policy on UNHCR's Engagement' (n 39).

[95] Hathaway and Storey, 'The Meaning of State Protection in Refugee Law' (n 7) 486 (Hathaway).

[96] European Commission, 'Evaluation of the Application of the Recast Qualification Directive (2011/95/EU)' (2019) available at https://www.statewatch.org/media/documents/news/2019/feb/eu-ceas-qualification-directive-application-evaluation-1-19.pdf (accessed 12 July 2021) (hereafter European Commission, 'Evaluation of the Application of the Recast Qualification Directive').

5.5.1 EU States

EU law is relevant in the interpretation of international law for various reasons. First, the Member States of the EU remain bound by their obligations under international law, and therefore EU asylum law must be 'in accordance' with the Refugee Convention.[97] According to Battjes, this establishes a clear hierarchical relationship between EU law and international refugee law, with the latter taking precedence insofar as states' (as opposed to the EU's) obligations under international law are concerned.[98] Secondly, the EU is formed of 27 Member States, all of which are States Parties to the Refugee Convention. Thus the practice of these states is relevant for the purposes of interpreting the Refugee Convention.[99]

5.5.1.1 The Qualification Directive

The term 'actors of protection' has woven its way into EU asylum law, purportedly in response to international developments in peacekeeping,[100] and to reject an influx of asylum-seekers from Kosovo,[101] which was being overseen by the UN Mission in Kosovo (UNMIK) and Kosovo Force (KFOR). Of relevance to this chapter are the measures adopted in the area of minimum standards

[97] Battjes, *European Asylum Law and International Law* (n 79) 1.

[98] ibid 1.

[99] VCLT (n 59) art 31(3)(b) provides that '[t]here shall be taken into account, together with the context … any subsequent practice in the application of the treaty which establishes the agreement of the parties regarding its interpretation'. Subsequent practice of the parties to a treaty may be 'reflected in, or initiated by, the pronouncements of other actors, such as the practice of … international organizations … [such practice] of the parties by international organizations … should not, however, be confounded with the … practice of the parties in question'. Georg Nolte, 'Report 3: Subsequent Agreements and Subsequent Practice of States Outside of Judicial or Quasi-Judicial Proceedings—Third Report for the ILC Study Group on Treaties over Time' in Georg Nolte (ed), *Treaties and Subsequent Practice* (OUP 2013) 317. However, the Qualification Directive cannot constitute a subsequent agreement as per art 31(3)(a) of the VCLT (n 59), because a 'subsequent agreement' in this sense must involve states acting in consensus and the agreement cannot be one 'regarding the interpretation of application' of the treaty in question (Dörr and Schmalenbach, *Vienna Convention* (n 90) [74]). Neither criterion is satisfied by the Qualification Directive.

[100] Select Committee on the European Union, 'Defining Refugee Status and those in Need of International Protection' HL (2001–02) [78] (hereafter Select Committee on the European Union, 'Defining Refugee Status'); Kay Hailbronner (ed), *EU Immigration and Asylum Law: Commentary on EU Regulations and Directives* (Beck, Hart, Nomos 2010) 1050; UNHCR, *Asylum in the European Union—A Study of the Implementation of the Qualification Directive* (2007) 47 (hereafter UNHCR, *Asylum in the European Union*); Council Directive (EC) 2011/95/EU (n 66).

[101] Madeline Garlick, 'UNHCR and the Implementation of Council Directive 2004/83/EC on Minimum Standards for the Qualification and Status of Third Country Nationals or Stateless Persons as Refugees or as Persons who Otherwise Need International Protection and the Content of the Protection Granted (The EC "Qualification Directive")' in Karin Zwaan (ed), *The Qualification Directive: Central Themes, Problem Issues, and Implementation in Selected Member States* (Wolf Legal Publishers 2007) 65; UNHCR, *Asylum in the European Union* (n 100) 47.

with respect to the qualification of nationals of third countries as refugees. Article 7 of the Recast Qualification Directive states that:

> 1. Protection against persecution or serious harm can only be provided by:
>   (a) the State; or
>   (b) parties or organisations, including international organisations, controlling the State or a substantial part of the territory of the State;
>
>   provided they are willing and able to offer protection in accordance with paragraph 2.
> 2. Protection against persecution or serious harm must be effective and of a non-temporary nature. Such protection is generally provided when the actors mentioned under points (a) and (b) of paragraph 1 take reasonable steps to prevent the persecution or suffering of serious harm, inter alia, by operating an effective legal system for the detection, prosecution and punishment of acts constituting persecution or serious harm, and when the applicant has access to such protection.
> 3. When assessing whether an international organisation controls a State or a substantial part of its territory and provides protection as described in paragraph 2, Member States shall take into account any guidance which may be provided in relevant Union acts.

Hailbronner and Alt see the approach in the Qualification Directive as 'flexible ... taking into account that increasingly international organisations have assumed state like functions'.[102] This provision of the Qualification Directive was interpreted by the ECJ in the *Abdulla* case, which was a reference for a preliminary ruling concerning the circumstances of cessation of refugee status. Germany asked the ECJ, inter alia, whether it was sufficient under Article 7 that protection could be provided only with the help of multinational troops. The ECJ held that Article 7(1) does not rule out protection from being guaranteed by international organizations, including protection ensured through the presence of a multinational force in the territory of the third country.[103]

[102] Kai Hailbronner and Simone Alt, 'Council Directive of 29 April 2004 on Minimum Standards for the Qualification and Status of Third Country Nationals or Stateless Persons as Refugees or as Persons who Otherwise Need International Protection and the Content of the Protection Granted. Arts 1–10' in Kai Hailbronner and Daniel Thym (eds), *EU Immigration and Asylum Law: Commentary on EU Regulations and Directives* (Hart 2010) 1024, 1029.

[103] Joined cases C-175/08, C-176/08, C-178/08 and C-179/08 *Aydin Salahadin Abdulla (C-175/08), Kamil Hasan (C-176/08), Ahmed Adem, Hamrin Mosa Rashi (C-178/08) and Dler Jamal (C-179/08) v Bundesrepublik Deutschland* [2010] All ER (D) 54 (Mar) ECLI:EU:C:2010:105 [75].

Some additional clarification on this issue was provided by Advocate General Hogan, in his 2020 Opinion on the *OA* case. He stated that:

> The protection envisaged by the 1951 Convention is fundamentally, in substance, the traditional protection offered by a State, namely, a functioning legal and policing system based on the rule of law. Non-State protection envisaged by Article 7(1)(b) of the Qualification Directive is not simply the protection which might be offered by purely private parties — such as, for example, that of a private security firm guarding a gated compound, but is rather that offered by non-State actors who control all or a substantial part of the territory of a state and who have also sought to replicate traditional State functions by providing or supporting a functioning legal and policing system based on the rule of law ... Mere financial and/or material support supplied by non-State actors falls below the threshold of protection envisaged by Article 7 of the Qualification Directive.[104]

This was also the approach taken by the CJEU to this issue in its decision of 20 January 2021.[105]

Although the aforementioned clarification on the meaning of Article 7(1) is helpful, a number of issues remain unclear. For example it is unclear whether the territory controlled by international organizations must be clearly defined and/or of a significant size or stability.[106] Concerning multinational troops, it is also unclear whether they must be present in the territory for a minimum time period,[107] what the role of the multinational troops should be (would forces undertaking peacekeeping or humanitarian missions suffice or would they have to be carrying out state-like functions relating to rule of law institutions),[108] and whether the forces need to be supported by a mandate from the international community.[109] The lack of clarity regarding when an international

[104] *Secretary of State for the Home Department v OA* [2020] ECLI:EU:C:2020:342, Opinion of AG Hogan, [78], [84] (hereafter *OA*, Opinion of AG Hogan).

[105] *Secretary of State for the Home Department v OA* [2021] ECLI:EU:C:2021:36.

[106] The draft of the original 2004 Directive included an additional qualification—that the territory controlled was clearly defined and of significant size and stability: Commission of the European Communities, Proposal for a Council Directive laying down minimum standards for the qualification and status of third country nationals and stateless persons as refugees, in accordance with the 1951 Convention relating to the status of refugees and the 1967 protocol, or as persons who otherwise need international protection, COM (2001) 510 final, 12 September 2001, art 9.

[107] Maria O'Sullivan, 'Territorial Protection: Cessation of Refugee Status and Internal Flight Alternative Compared' in Satvinder S Juss (ed), *The Ashgate Research Companion to Migration Law, Theory and Policy* (Routledge 2013).

[108] ibid.

[109] ibid; Roger Errera, 'Cessation and Assessment of New Circumstances: A Comment on *Abdulla*, CJEU, 2 March 2010' (2011) 23(3) International Journal of Refugee Law 521.

organization might constitute 'protection' for the purposes of Article 7 is concerning, as it is possible that states will take advantage of this lack of guidance to decrease the amount of individuals they recognize as refugees.

A further—more fundamental—problem with the inclusion of international organizations as actors of protection in the Qualification Directive is that it gives rise to an incompatibility with the Refugee Convention. Section 5.4 has illustrated that according to the rules of the VCLT, interpreting 'that country' as an international organization is not compatible with the wording of the Refugee Convention. Recital 3 of the Qualification Directive indicates that the Refugee Convention is the primary binding instrument on Member States, which would imply that there is an internal incompatibility in the text of the Qualification Directive, specifically between Article 7 and Recital 3. Indeed, Advocate General Hogan in his abovementioned Opinion noted that 'Article 7(1)(b) of the Qualification Directive departs from the actual text of the Geneva Convention'[110] although he did not clearly stipulate whether he perceived there to be an incompatibility with this article and the Refugee Convention.

As such, the inclusion of international organizations as actors of protection within the 2011 Recast Qualification Directive raises many concerns both in terms of its compatibility with the Refugee Convention and in its potential for wide interpretation by Member States. The latter issue will be the focus of the following section.

5.5.1.2 Domestic Implementation of EU Asylum Law

A 2019 European Commission survey on the implementation of the Qualification Directive in Member States found that despite the inclusion of 'actors of protection' in the Qualification Directive,[111] most Member States had little experience with the assessment of protection provided by NSAs. For example, Latvia, Malta, and Poland seemed to have never applied the concept of an NSA of protection.[112] However, a few common approaches can be distilled from those few Member States with experience of such cases. First, higher scrutiny is applied when protection is offered by an NSA rather than a state actor. For example in Austria, if an NSA is considered as an actor of protection, the actor must have had de facto the same power as a state. The threshold of

[110] *OA*, Opinion of AG Hogan (n 104) [77].

[111] Ireland is included in the state practice below. However, Ireland is not bound by the 2011 recast Directive and thus kept the transposing legislation of Directive 2004/83. The UK's practice is addressed in the following section.

[112] European Commission, 'Evaluation of the Application of the Recast Qualification Directive' (n 96).

having, de facto, the power of a state became even higher when a real state actor existed at the same time.[113]

Second, most Member States tend to assess the main elements of protection (ie effectiveness of protection, durability of protection, and access to protection) when examining the protection provided by NSAs.[114] On effectiveness of protection, the majority of Member States' laws provide that actors of protection must be willing and able to protect. Several Member States stated that protection does not need to be absolute, taking into account the United Kingdom's *Horvath* case.[115] This case—which is addressed in more detail in section 5.4.1—set the standard of protection to be applied 'not that which would eliminate all risk and would amount to a guarantee of protection in the home state', but rather 'a practical standard, which takes proper account of the duty which the state owes to all its own nationals'.[116] Like the approach in the *Horvath* case, the main criterion used by Member States for such assessment is the existence and operation of a legal system for the detection, prosecution, and protection of acts of persecution or serious harm.[117]

On durability of protection, although most national laws have transposed the requirement that protection should be of a non-temporary nature, only a few Member States have assessed the durability of such protection in practice.[118] Member States' jurisprudence gives little guidance on the question of control of 'a substantial part of the territory of the State', although German Ministry of Interior Guidelines stated that effective control over a certain region is considered sufficient.[119] In addition, the French *Cour nationale du droit d'asile* has found that:

> organisations controlling a substantial part of the territory of a State are those which have stable institutional structures allowing them to exercise exclusive and continuous civil and armed control on a delimitated territory within which the State no longer fulfils the obligations or exercises the authority of its sovereignty.[120]

113 ibid.
114 ibid.
115 ibid.
116 *Horvath* (n 61), 8.
117 European Commission, 'Evaluation of the Application of the Recast Qualification Directive' (n 96).
118 ibid.
119 As cited in Julian Lehmann, *'Protection' in European Union Asylum Law* (Brill 2020) 113 (hereafter Lehmann, *'Protection' in European Union Asylum Law*.)
120 Cour nationale du droit d'asile (CNDA) (National Court of Asylum) of 3 May 2016, No 15033525; *OA*, Opinion of AG Hogan (n 104) [4].

Third, some Member States have provided examples of which international organizations might constitute 'actors of protection'. For example the Office of the Refugee Applications Commissioner (ORAC) Guidance in Ireland stated that the protection afforded by NSAs would usually not constitute 'sufficient state protection' except where the NSAs would be constituted under international law as a body responsible for the protection of the citizens of a state, such as the KFOR and the United Nations Relief and Works Agency for Palestine Refugees in the Near East (UNRWA).[121] The Dutch Circular on Foreigners specifies that NATO and the UN are relevant for the provision of protection.[122] The French courts have held that missions established by the Security Council under Chapter VII of the UN Charter (Kosovo, Bosnia) may satisfy the protection requirement, whereas missions established under Chapter VI (Democratic Republic of the Congo, Haiti) cannot.[123] This is because missions established under Chapter VII have administrative and coercive powers. However, in order for such missions to constitute actors of protection, it must be shown that the protection provided is effective.[124] The French courts have also considered whether the UN Stabilization Mission in Haiti (MINUSTAH) and UNMIK were in control of territory and able to provide effective protection, but found this not to be the case.[125]

In sum therefore, many EU states seem to accept that NSAs (and specifically, international organizations) may be actors of protection in principle, but that this rarely—if ever—occurs in practice. In fact, none of the jurisprudence of EU Member States studied by this author found that, on the facts, an international organization was an actor of protection for the purposes of the Qualification Directive.[126] This high threshold seems to stem from the Qualification Directive's requirement that the relevant actor needs to control a substantial part of the territory of the state. According to Lehmann, this ensures that the relevant actors are vested with sufficient power to provide protection

[121] See also Canada, which has recognized KFOR and UNMIK as actors of protection: *Isufi v Canada (Minister of Citizenship and Immigration)* [2003] FCJ No 1208; 2003 FC 880, Canada Federal Court, 15 July 2003.

[122] Vreemdelingencirculaire 2000 (C) of 1 December 2017, section 3.4. As cited in Lehmann, *'Protection' in European Union Asylum Law* (n 119).

[123] European Council on Refugees and Exiles, *The Impact of the EU Qualification Directive on International Protection* (2008) 110.

[124] ibid 110.

[125] S, CRR, 28 June 2005, no 519680; CRR, 30 October 2006, 580781, V; *Mlle Y*, CNDA, 4 September 2009, no 645353/09004158, D; *Mlle Y*, CRR 30 November 2006, no 535001; *Mlle S*, CRR 15 March 2007, no 585846; *Mlle A*, CNDA, 3 April 2008, no 584799 (all cited in Lehmann, *'Protection' in European Union Asylum Law* (n 119)); Saint-Phart, 25 June 2005, 54; Valens, 6 July 2005, 67; Vil, 30 Oct. 2006, 45 (MINUSTAH in Haiti); Qerimi, 23 Sept. 2004, 51 (KFOR, Kosovo) (all cited in O'Sullivan, *Refugee Law and Durability of Protection* (n 75)).

[126] UNHCR, *Asylum in the European Union* (n 100) 48.

in practice,[127] a standard that will rarely—if ever—be met by NSAs, including international organizations. Similarly, it is unimaginable that the requirement of durable protection could ever be met by NSAs.

The following section will examine the jurisprudence of other states that have dealt with the question of international organizations as actors of protection. This section will focus on the UK specifically, because it has produced a significant amount of jurisprudence and hence needs to have its own section of analysis. Jurisprudence of other non-EU states will be cited where relevant. Further reasons for examining the UK's jurisprudence separately to the above section include: (i) many of the cases in the UK were decided prior to the conclusion of the Qualification Directive and hence do not relate to the implementation of EU law; (ii) although the UK was bound by the 2004 Qualification Directive, it was never bound by the 2011 Qualification Directive, which most of the above jurisprudence relates to; (iii) the UK is no longer a member of the EU.

5.5.2 The United Kingdom

5.5.2.1 Introduction

Most of the jurisprudence from England and Wales concerns UNMIK and KFOR. An understanding of the role and mandate of UNMIK and KFOR is therefore essential before engaging in an analysis of relevant jurisprudence. From 24 March to 9 June 1999, NATO conducted military operations against the government of the Federal Republic of Yugoslavia (FRY) in response to events in Kosovo, which was part of the FRY. These operations ceased on 10 June after the FRY government agreed to withdraw its forces from Kosovo in accordance with a set of principles which were subsequently attached to Annex 2 to the United Nations Security Council Resolution 1244 (1999).[128] The resolution provided for the establishment and deployment in Kosovo of international and security presences, known respectively as UNMIK and KFOR.[129] The resolution did not alter the status of Kosovo as part of the FRY.

The main function of UNMIK was:

> to provide an interim administration for Kosovo under which the people of Kosovo can enjoy substantial autonomy within the Federal Republic of Yugoslavia, and which will provide transitional administration while

[127] Lehmann, *'Protection' in European Union Asylum Law* (n 119).
[128] UNSC Res 1244 (10 June 1999) UN Doc S/RES/1244.
[129] ibid, operative paragraph 5.

establishing and overseeing the development of provisional democratic self-governing institutions to ensure conditions for a peaceful and normal life for all inhabitants of Kosovo.[130]

UNMIK's further responsibilities included (i) 'maintaining civil law and order, including establishing local police forces and meanwhile through the deployment of international police personnel to serve in Kosovo'; (ii) 'protection and promoting human rights'; and (iii) '[a]ssuring the safe and unimpeded return of all refugees and displaced persons to their homes in Kosovo'.[131] In essence, the effect of Security Council Resolution 1244 was that all legislative and executive powers, including the administration of the judiciary, were transferred to UNMIK.

The responsibilities of KFOR included 'establishing a secure environment in which refugees and displaced persons can return home in safety, the international civil presence can operate, a transitional administration can be established, and humanitarian aid can be delivered' and 'ensuring public safety and order until the international civil presence can take responsibility for this task'.[132]

As such, KFOR and UNMIK's mandate was far reaching and incorporated many state-like functions. The following section will illustrate to what extent the courts of England and Wales found that these entities were providing 'protection' in the sense of the Refugee Convention definition.

5.5.2.2 Principles Emerging from the Jurisprudence of the United Kingdom

The jurisprudence of the United Kingdom has developed a number of general principles relevant to the capacity of international organizations to provide protection in the sense of the refugee definition. The first principle is that 'protection of that country' can include protection provided by NSAs, including international organizations. This question was dealt with in the case of *Fadil Dyli v The Secretary of State for the Home Department* [2000] ('*Dyli*'), where the Asylum and Immigration Tribunal noted that the refugee definition did not employ the term 'authorities' and thus held that it should be interpreted in its geographical sense.[133] In *The Queen on the Application of Altin Vallaj v a Special Adjudicator* ('*Vallaj*'),[134] Dyson J accepted the submission that the agent of

130 ibid, operative paragraph 10.
131 ibid, operative paragraph 11.
132 ibid, operative paragraph 9.
133 *Fadil Dyli v Secretary of State for the Home Department* (n 5) [12].
134 *The Queen on the Application of Altin Vallaj v A Special Adjudicator* [2002] Imm AR 16 (hereafter *Vallaj*).

protection did not have to be the body which grants nationality, holding that 'the phrase "protection of that country" is capable of including protection by the authorities that have the duty to provide protection in that country'.[135]

In both of the above cases, it was held that the source of protection was irrelevant. The Court in *Vallaj* affirmed the opinion of Professor Christopher Greenwood:

> [I]f the protection which a person is entitled to expect is in fact being provided by a United Nations administration in the territory from which that person comes, it would be unduly formalistic and contrary to common sense to hold that, since the United Nations is not a country, that person is not able to obtain protection.[136]

The main argument behind this interpretation is that modern circumstances must be taken into account in the interpretation of the Refugee Convention. In *Vallaj*, Dyson J noted that because the Refugee Convention 'should be construed as a living instrument' it was necessary to take into account the fact that since 1990, the Security Council has shown 'an increased willingness to intervene in the affairs of states' and that these developments should inform the interpretation of 'protection of that country'.[137] This approach was affirmed in Advocate General Hogan's Opinion in the *OA* case above.[138]

A note of caution should be taken at this juncture. The 'living instrument' approach, also termed the 'dynamic' or 'evolutive' approach, is an interpretive technique common to many domestic systems and has featured significantly in the jurisprudence of the European Court of Human Rights.[139] However, this approach is not enshrined in the VCLT.[140] The 'living instrument' approach should therefore only be employed where its resulting interpretation does not conflict with the general rule of interpretation in the VCLT, namely the obligation set out in Article 31 to interpret a treaty 'in good faith in accordance with the ordinary meaning to be given to the terms of the treaty in their context and in the light of its object and purpose'.[141] As outlined in section 5.4 of this chapter, an application of Article 31 to the Refugee Convention leads to

135 ibid [31].
136 ibid [24].
137 ibid [25].
138 *OA*, Opinion of AG Hogan (n 104).
139 See, for example, *Tyrer v United Kingdom* App no 5856/72 (ECHR, 25 April 1979) [31]; *Loizidou v Turkey* App no 15318/89 (ECHR, 18 December 1996).
140 VCLT (n 59).
141 ibid, art 31.

the conclusion that the term 'that country' refers to the authorities of the state. The conclusion reached in *Vallaj* that UNMIK and KFOR were capable of constituting protection of that country therefore seems to be at odds with Article 31 of the VCLT and thus represents an incorrect interpretation of the Refugee Convention. Nonetheless, for the sake of argument, the conclusion reached in *Vallaj* will be applied in section 5.6 of this chapter to the UNHCR's activities with IDPs owing to the fact that, as discussed above, in the absence of an international monitoring body, it is inevitably a domestic court that will have the last word on questions of interpretation of the Refugee Convention and therefore the conclusion in *Vallaj* is highly relevant to this chapter.

The second principle to emerge from the jurisprudence of England and Wales is the relevance of the consent of the territorial state. In *Vallaj*, despite the argument of the appellant that there was no true consent in the case of Kosovo, since the FRY was forced to submit to the terms of the resolution,[142] Dyson J held that consent was given, citing operative paragraphs 2 and 5 of the resolution.[143] However, Dyson J did not stipulate whether such consent was a necessary condition for the protection of UNMIK to preclude the granting of refugee status, although this was later implied in the case of *Gardi v Secretary of State for the Home Department* ('*Gardi*') where it was held that the protection of the Kurdish Autonomous Region could not preclude application of the refugee definition because Iraq had not ceded its protection obligations to it.[144] Neither the EU Qualification Directive nor any of the jurisprudence from EU countries analysed above refers to the relevance of consent, although it is arguable that if 'protection of that country' can include protection provided by an international organization, the consent of the territorial state or authorization of the Security Council regarding the presence and activities of that international organization is required. This is because the international organization in question has otherwise breached international law. As aforementioned, the Refugee Convention must be interpreted in line with the general rules of international law and there is a duty on all states not to recognize as lawful a situation created by a serious breach of peremptory norms such as the prohibition of the use of force against the territorial integrity or political independence of any state.[145] Hence even if the term 'protection of that country' can include protection

[142] *Vallaj* (n 134) [32].
[143] ibid.
[144] *Gardi v Secretary of State for the Home Department* [2002] EWCA Civ 750, [2002] WLR 2755 (hereafter *Gardi*).
[145] Stefan Talmon, 'The Duty Not to "Recognise as Lawful" a Situation Created by the Illegal Use of Force or Other Serious Breaches of a Jus Cogens Obligation: an Obligation without Real Substance?' in Christian Tomuschat and Jean-Marc Thouvenin (eds), *The Fundamental Rules of the International Order: Jus Cogens and Obligations Erga Omnes* (Brill-Nijhoff 2005).

offered by an international organization, an international organization that is present illegally on a territorial state (ie without the consent of the host state or UN Security Council authorization) could not constitute 'protection of that country'. It is important to note, however, that the UNHCR always requires the consent of the state concerned before commencing operations on its territory. This issue will be analysed in more detail in section 5.6.

The third principle to emerge from this jurisprudence is that the relevant entity must have assumed the international obligation to protect. In *Vallaj* it was held that UNMIK had accepted the protection obligation as set out in the Refugee Convention, and that such obligations had been tasked to it because such protection was not available by the host state.[146] In the words of Dyson J:

> The surrogacy principle is engaged when there has been a failure in the basic duty of protection owed to the nationals of a state. The duty of protection is owed by the country of nationality, unless it is transferred, as a matter of international law, to another entity. In these circumstances, it seems to me that the better analysis is that 'protection of that country' refers to the protection by the entity that is charged with the duty of protection, and that, on the true construction of article 1A(2), a person may have a well-founded fear of persecution only if there has been a failure to protect *by that entity or its agent.*[147]

This third principle seems to overlap slightly with the second principle, in that an international organization which has a mandate to be present in the state (eg via a Security Council Chapter VII resolution or the consent of the territorial state) may have assumed an international obligation to protect under that mandate. However, principle 3 is somewhat different from principle 2 because according to principle 2 an organization could be present in the territorial state legally but be merely assisting the state. In such circumstances, the state retains the international duty to protect people within its territory and subject to its jurisdiction, whereas under principle 3 the international organization has taken on, as a matter of law, the state's duty to protect the individuals within the state. Although these principles are not contained explicitly in the Qualification Directive, it is important to note that, prior to the handing

[146] *Vallaj* (n 134) [29]; *Gardi* (n 144).
[147] *Vallaj* (n 134) [36] (emphasis in original).

down of the decision in *Abdulla*, Advocate General Mazák provided an advisory opinion, which stated:

> I consider however that in order to comply with the terms of Article 7 of Directive 2004/83, a State may only rely on the assistance of multinational troops provided such troops operate under the mandate of the international community, for example under the auspices of the United Nations.[148]

As aforementioned, the ECJ did not directly address this point. However, it nonetheless lends support to the contention that in order to be an actor of protection for the purposes of the refugee definition, the actor's presence in the state in question needs to be in accordance with international law.

5.5.3 Concluding Thoughts on State Practice

In sum, although this chapter has argued that the term 'protection of that country' refers to the authority of the state, there is some state practice that informs a geographical interpretation of this term. In deciding whether protection provided by an international organization is 'protection' for the purposes of the Refugee Convention, states have tended to take a two-pronged approach. First, can it be stated that an international organization is capable in law of providing such protection? In answering this question, states have taken into account: (i) whether the international organization in question is present on the territory legally—either by way of consent of the territorial state, or via a UN Security Council resolution; (ii) whether it has assumed the international obligation to protect nationals of the state (and, if the answer is in the affirmative, whether all the relevant powers and functions of the state have been transferred to the NSA); and finally, (iii) whether the NSA has control over a substantial part of the territory of the state.[149] Second, is the international organization capable in fact of providing such protection? The courts of various states have held that such protection need not be absolute, but there must be an accessible and effective legal system for the detection, prosecution, and punishment of persecutory acts.[150] In

[148] Cases C-175/08, C-176/08, C-178/08 and C-179/08 *Abdulla and others* [2009] ECLI:EU:C:2009:551, Opinion of AG Mazák [54].

[149] See also Australia: 1603711 (Refugee) [2016] AATA 3793 (28 April 2016) Decision Record Division: Migration & Refuge.

[150] ibid.

addition, the protection available must be of a non-temporary nature. The next section will apply these principles to the UNHCR's activities on behalf of IDPs.

5.6 'Protection of that Country' and the UN High Commissioner of Refugees' Activities with Internally Displaced Persons

As outlined in the introductory chapters to this book, the UNHCR has taken the lead role in the protection, camp management, and emergency shelter of IDPs since 2005 and the protection of IDPs is no longer solely a matter of internal affairs. Thus a 'living instrument' interpretation of the term 'protection of that country' may in fact allow for UNHCR in-country protection to constitute the same. The following sections will therefore assess to what extent the UNHCR's activities on behalf of IDPs might bring it within the definition of 'actor of protection' for the purposes of the refugee definition.

5.6.1 Is the UNHCR Capable in Law of Providing Such Protection?

5.6.1.1 Is the UNHCR Present on the Territory Legally—Either by Way of Consent of the Territorial State, or Via a UN Security Council Resolution?

The basis of the UNHCR's involvement with IDPs can be summarized in UN General Assembly Resolution 53/125 (1998), which reiterates 'support for the role of the Office of the High Commissioner in providing humanitarian assistance and protection to internally displaced persons, on the basis of specific requests from the Secretary-General or the competent organs of the United Nations and *with the consent of the State concerned . . .*'[151] In addition, the UNHCR has stated that before it will become involved with IDP protection efforts, there must be consent from the state concerned and, where applicable, other entities in a conflict.[152] If consent of the state concerned is a criterion in order to be considered an 'actor of protection' for the purposes of the refugee definition, it is satisfied by the UNHCR's activities on behalf of IDPs.

[151] UNGA Res 53/125 (9 December 1998) (n 24) (emphasis added).
[152] UNHCR, 'The Role of the High Commissioner for Refugees' (n 28), 2.

5.6.1.2 Has the UNHCR Assumed the International Obligation to Protect Nationals of the State? If the Answer is in the Affirmative, Have All the Relevant Powers and Functions of the State been Transferred to the UNHCR?

The UNHCR,[153] the Human Rights Council,[154] the General Assembly,[155] and the Guiding Principles on Internal Displacement have all emphasized that the primary protection responsibility lies with states for their nationals.[156] The UNHCR's protection activities on behalf of IDPs do not result in a delegation of responsibility from the state, and its purpose is 'not to substitute but to strengthen national efforts for protecting and assisting the internally displaced'.[157] Moreover, the 2016 Operational Guidelines for the UNHCR's Engagement in Situations of Internal Displacement, stated:

> Inherent in the notion of national sovereignty is the responsibility of States to ensure that the needs of all citizens, including those who are internally displaced, are met and that their rights are respected. Such responsibilities cannot be delegated to international agencies. Wherever possible, therefore, UNHCR must seek to complement, not substitute, for the State when it engages in situations of internal displacement.[158]

The UNCHR thus generally provides support to the state in addressing situations of internal displacement. For example, in 2020 the UNHCR played a significant role in supporting government responses to the Covid-19 pandemic. In Iraq, the UNHCR provided personal protective equipment and medical equipment support to public health facilities delivering services to IDP camps, sites, and urban areas. Building on its partnerships with the national and

[153] UNHCR, 'The Protection of Internally Displaced Persons and the Role of UNHCR' (27 February 2007) [25]; UNHCR EXCOM 'Support of an Enhanced Humanitarian Response to Situations of Internal Displacement: Policy Framework and Implementation Strategy' (4 June 2007) UN Doc EC/58/SC/CRP.18 [19] (hereafter UNHCR EXCOM, 'UNHCR's Role in Support'); UNHCR, 'Guidance Package for UNHCR's Engagement in Situations of Internal Displacement (September 2019) (hereafter UNHCR, 'Guidance Package'); UNHCR, 'Operational Guidelines' (n 33); UNHCR, 'The IDP-Initiative: Quarterly Update June 2020 (2020) (hereafter UNHCR, 'Quarterly Update').

[154] UN Human Rights Council Res 20 'Human Rights of Internally Displaced Persons' (29 June 2012) UN Doc A/HRC/20/L.14.

[155] UNGA Res 62/153 (6 March 2008) UN Doc A/RES/62/153.

[156] UNCHR, 'Report of the Representative of the Secretary-General, Mr. Francis M. Deng, submitted pursuant to Commission resolution 1197/39. Addendum: Guiding Principles on Internal Displacement' (11 February 1998) UN Doc E/CN.4/1998/53/Add.2, Principle 3.

[157] See Walter Kälin, 'Report of the Representative of the Secretary General on the Human Rights of Internally Displaced Persons, Walter Kälin. Addendum: Framework for National Responsibility' (23 December 2005) UN Doc E/CN.4/2006/71/Add.1 [49].

[158] UNHCR, 'Operational Guidelines' (n 33); See also UNHCR, 'The Protection of Internally Displaced Persons' (n 153) [26].

governorate health authorities, the UNHCR also advocated for the inclusion of IDPs in the Iraqi Covid-19 preparedness and response plan. The UNHCR was also involved in consultations with local authorities in South Sudan, supporting the Ministry of Health for the drafting of the country's Covid-19 preparedness and response plan and advocating for a critical assessment to establish the pandemic's impact. In Burkina Faso, the UNHCR provided local authorities with substantial and much needed support through the purchase of over one million dollars' worth of medicines and personal protective equipment including masks, housing units, handwashing stations, and water tanks.[159]

As such the UNHCR's role is to support the state, not to assume the state's obligation to protect individuals on its territory. It logically follows, therefore, that the relevant powers and functions of the state have not been transferred to the UNHCR where it is involved with IDPs. To contrast this with the jurisprudence above, UNMIK constituted an agent of protection because all the relevant powers and functions of the state had been transferred to an international body, and that body had assumed the international obligation to protect nationals of the state. In its protection activities on behalf of IDPs, the UNHCR does not exercise such powers and therefore does not satisfy this criterion.

5.6.1.3 Does the UNHCR Control the State or a Substantial Part of the Territory of the State?

This criterion stems from the Qualification Directive,[160] which was drafted at a time when UNMIK and KFOR were providing protection in Kosovo. Kosovo was under the effective control of UNMIK and KFOR, and this was most likely to be the type of scenario envisaged by the drafters of the Directive which would constitute 'protection'. Unlike UNMIK and KFOR, the UNHCR has not had any of the powers and functions of the state transferred to it, and nor does it control the state or a substantial part of the state. This is further underscored by the fact that often the UNHCR does not have access, let alone control, of the many areas where IDPs exist. The criterion of control of territory, or a significant part of territory, is therefore not satisfied by the UNHCR's activities on behalf of IDPs.

[159] UNHCR, 'Quarterly Update' (n 153).
[160] Council Directive (EC) 2011/95/EU (n 66) art 7(2).

5.6.2 Is the UNHCR in Fact Providing Such Protection?

As argued above, the standard of protection required is inextricably linked to the nature of persecution feared. Thus it is not possible to set out definitively the standard of protection necessary to preclude the granting of refugee status. Nonetheless, as the jurisprudence shows, the operation of an effective legal system for the detection, prosecution, and punishment of persecutory acts is a good indication of effective protection, and such protection must be non-temporary in nature. Is such protection being provided by the UNHCR?

5.6.2.1 Is the UNHCR Operating an Effective Legal System for the Detection, Prosecution, and Punishment of Persecutory Acts, and is Such Protection Accessible?

According to the UNHCR, the parameters of its involvement with IDPs will normally be aligned with its 'leadership and coordination responsibilities related to protection, camp coordination and camp management and shelter, with a particular emphasis on displacement owing to conflict and violence'.[161] 'Protection' in the sense of the UNHCR's activities has not been defined in its statute. Nonetheless, the UNHCR has articulated that 'the challenge of international protection is to secure admission, asylum, and respect by states for basic human rights, including the principle of non-*refoulement*'.[162] This also encompasses ensuring the 'physical safety and security' of refugees.[163]

This concept of protection does not encompass operating a legal system. The operation of a legal system, according to the abovementioned jurisprudence, requires the establishment of, inter alia, a legislative system, a police force, a court system, and detention facilities, all of which require powers and functions which are generally attributable to states. The UNHCR is not endowed with such powers and, as such, does not have the capacity to operate such a system.[164] The UNHCR's role in respect of the legal system only extends to assisting the authorities to develop national legislation and appropriate administrative support arrangements, so as to strengthen the IDP protection framework.[165] Its activities usually comprise of providing guidance and technical advice to state authorities; engaging civil society and IDP communities in the

[161] UNHCR, 'Policy on UNHCR's Engagement' (n 39).
[162] UNHCR, 'Note on International Protection' (7 July 2000) UN Doc A/AC.96/930 [9].
[163] ibid [2].
[164] Even if we take the broader conception of legal system as outlined in note 67, the UNHCR cannot be said to operate a legal system because it does not create and enforce legal rules concerning the detection, prosecution, and punishment of persecutory acts.
[165] UNHCR, 'The Protection of Internally Displaced Persons (n 153) [28].

process of law and policy development; providing cash grants to IDPs, carrying out studies, assessments, and analyses to identify gaps in existing law and policy frameworks for the protection of IDPs; promoting government-led laws on IDP protection; providing support and training for members of parliament, national human rights institutions, relevant authorities and partners; and/or supporting the ratification, domestication, and implementation of relevant regional and subregional legal instruments on internal displacement, consistent with the IASC Framework for Durable Solutions, the Guiding Principles on Internal Displacement, and other applicable international standards.[166]

In 2020, for example, the UNHCR supported the development of national frameworks for the protection of IDPs by providing legal and technical advice in 14 states, including Colombia, El Salvador, Ethiopia, Honduras, Mali, Mexico, Mozambique, the Philippines, South Sudan, and Ukraine.[167] Through its provision of legislative and technical support, the 'UNHCR seeks to support Governments' primary responsibility in providing protection and assistance to IDPs'.[168] This aim can be contrasted to UNMIK's mandate, which has the broader duty to provide an interim administration, to maintain civil law and order, and to protect and promote human rights. Thus the protection activities carried out by the UNHCR do not indicate a standard of protection which may, in certain circumstances, preclude the granting of refugee status.

5.6.2.2 Is the UNHCR's Protection Non-Temporary in Nature?

The UNHCR recognizes that '[it] can only play a limited role in addressing the issue of internal displacement'.[169] The UNHCR's role with IDPs in any given situation is of a transient nature, with the long-term aim being that states themselves will be able to effectively address displacement challenges. It aims to 'disengage responsibly when local and national actors can meaningfully take over operational delivery, coordination, and monitoring in relation to protection and solutions for IDPs'.[170] Consequently, the UNHCR's protection of IDPs is not of a 'non-temporary nature', and therefore would not come within the definition of 'actors of protection' as set out in the recast Qualification Directive.

166 UNHCR, 'Policy on UNHCR's Engagement' (n 39); UNHCR, 'Guidance Package' (n 153); UNHCR, 'Operational Guidelines' (n 33); UNHCR, 'Quarterly Update' (n 153).

167 UNHCR, *Global Trends 2020* (n 2); UNHCR, 'UNHCR's Initiative on Internal Displacement' (2020–2021) <https://reporting.unhcr.org/sites/default/files/UNHCR%20Initiative%20on%20Internal%20Displacement%202020-2021.pdf> accessed 12 July 2021.

168 UNHCR, *Global Trends 2020* (n 2).

169 UNHCR EXCOM, 'UNHCR's Role in Support' (n 153) [20].

170 UNHCR, 'Policy on UNHCR's Engagement' (n 39).

5.6.2.3 Even if Not the Body with the Legal Duty to Provide Protection, Can the UNHCR Be Considered an Actor of Protection if it is in Fact Providing Protection?

It is submitted that this third possibility, as raised in *Vallaj*, is inapplicable to the UNHCR's activities with IDPs as the discussion above indicates that the UNHCR is not in fact providing protection to an extent which would preclude the application of the refugee definition.

5.7 Conclusion

The question that this chapter set out to answer was whether, in providing protection to IDPs, the UNHCR's activities could be classified as 'protection of that country' and thus where UNHCR protection is available in the country of origin, refugee status could be denied to persons seeking asylum abroad.

An initial analysis of the wording of the Refugee Convention supports the contention that 'protection of that country' refers to protection provided by state authorities. However, this may include contracted-out mechanisms of protection which are genuinely accessible and for which the state remains fully accountable.[171] The efforts of an international organization such as the UNHCR might be relevant to the protection inquiry but only where the UNHCR remains accountable to the state for its activities.

State practice has provided some indication of when the activities of an international organization might constitute 'protection of that country'. The standard of protection required is very high, and the UNHCR is lacking certain traits that are essential for it to be considered an actor of protection in this respect. Where the UNHCR provides in-country protection, the obligation of a state to protect its nationals is not, as a matter of international law, transferred to the UNHCR and the UNHCR is not endowed with the powers and attributes of the state. In addition, the UNHCR is not in control of the state or a substantial part of the territory of the state. Put simply, the UNHCR is not capable in law as constituting an actor of protection which would preclude the application of the refugee definition.

Moreover, the UNHCR is not capable, in fact, of providing such protection. As outlined above, it is impossible to give a definitive exposition as to the standard of protection required by the refugee definition. This is because the standard of protection required is dependent on the nature of the persecution

[171] Hathaway and Storey, 'The Meaning of State Protection in Refugee Law' (n 7) 486 (Hathaway).

feared. Nonetheless, the operation of a legal system for the detection, prosecution, and punishment of persecutory acts is a good indication of whether protection is effective. The UNHCR does not have the capacity or legal authority to operate such a system. Furthermore, the UNHCR's protection efforts are of a transient nature, designed to capacitate states in finding a long-term solution to the IDP problem.

Put simply, therefore, although state practice supports the contention that 'protection of that country' may be provided by an international organization, it is highly unlikely that the activities of the UNHCR, ipso facto, would qualify as 'protection of that country'. Its activities may nonetheless be relevant when determining whether the state has provided protection from persecution. This approach strikes a middle ground between recognizing the significant power and influence of international organizations such as the UNHCR, but at the same time recognizing that there are limits to what they can provide in terms of protection. International organizations such as the UNHCR play a significant and highly valuable role in the protection and assistance of IDPs. They can provide shelter, food, sanitation, and cash grants to IDPs themselves, and they can support and advise governments in building state institutions and drafting laws on behalf of IDPs. Yet, there are limits to what they can do in terms of protection. In objecting to the inclusion of international organizations as actors of protection under EU law, NGOs have referred to numerous examples of the inadequacy of protection by international organizations, including Rwanda, Sierra Leone, and Kosovo.[172] According to Gilbert, 'actors of protection' cannot include a safe haven or a refugee camp under the auspices of the UNHCR, the UN, or another international organization, as such examples would not amount to adequate protection.[173] My own work on safe zones which are established in conflict areas by international organizations lends further support to this point.[174]

Moreover, international organizations do not have the attributes of states, cannot enforce the rule of law, and hence cannot be actors of protection in the sense of the refugee definition.[175] In addition, because international

[172] Select Committee on the European Union, 'Defining Refugee Status' (n 100) [73], [75].

[173] Geoff Gilbert, 'Is Europe Living Up to its Obligations to Refugees?' (2004) 15(5) European Journal of International Law 963, 976.

[174] Bríd Ní Ghráinne, 'Safe Zones and the Internal Protection Alternative' (2020) 69 International and Comparative Law Quarterly 335.

[175] ECRE, 'ECRE Information Note on the Council Directive 2004/83/EC of 29 April 2004 on Minimum Standards for the Qualification of Third Country Nationals and others in need of International Protection' (2004) 7 (hereafter ECRE, 'ECRE Information Note on the Council Directive 2004/83/EC'); Select Committee on the European Union, 'Defining Refugee Status' (n 100) [72], [74], [76].

organizations are not generally parties to human rights treaties, they cannot be held accountable as a matter of international law.[176] In addition, the absence of state authority is often an indication of political instability and thus it is unlikely that an international organization could be regarded as enjoying sufficient, durable stability and as having the political, military, and civil police capacity that would enable it to offer a level of protection required by the Refugee Convention.[177]

It is safe to say, therefore, that by protecting and assisting IDPs, the UNHCR is not, at least as a matter of law, undermining its primary mandate towards refugees.

[176] ECRE, 'ECRE Information Note on the Council Directive 2004/83/EC' (n 175) 7; Select Committee on the European Union, 'Defining Refugee Status' (n 100) [73], [79].

[177] Select Committee on the European Union, 'Defining Refugee Status' (n 100) [73].

6

Article 1D of the 1951 Refugee Convention and Internally Displaced Persons

6.1 Introduction

Article 1D of the Refugee Convention provides that:

> The Convention shall not apply to persons who are at present receiving from organs or agencies of the United Nations other than the United Nations High Commissioner for Refugees protection or assistance.
>
> When such protection or assistance has ceased for any reason, without the position of such persons being definitively settled in accordance with the relevant resolutions adopted by the General Assembly of the United Nations, these persons shall ipso facto be entitled to the benefits of this Convention.

A similar provision is found in paragraph 7 of the UNHCR statute, which provides that 'the competence of the High Commissioner ... shall not extend to a person ... who continues to receive from other organs or agencies of the United Nations protection or assistance'.[1]

Article 1D is drafted in vague terms,[2] and it has been accepted that, in theory, this provision could be applied to any group of refugees that satisfies its conditions, including those who have previously been IDPs within their country of origin.[3] Thus this chapter asks a pertinent question which has not

[1] United Nations General Assembly 'Statute of the Office of the United Nations High Commissioner for Refugees', Annex to Resolution 428/V (14 December 1950) UN Doc A/RES/428(V).

[2] James Hathaway and Michelle Foster, *The Law of Refugee Status* (2nd edn, CUP 2014) 509 (hereafter Hathaway and Foster, *The Law of Refugee Status*); Brenda Goddard, 'UNHCR and the International Protection of Palestinian Refugees' (2010) 28 Refugee Survey Quarterly 475, 476 (hereafter Goddard, 'Protection of Palestinian Refugees').

[3] Mutaz Qafisheh and Valentina Azarov, 'Article 1D, 1951 Convention' in Andreas Zimmerman (ed), *The 1951 Convention Relating to the Status of Refugees and its 1967 Protocol: A Commentary* (OUP 2011) 542 (hereafter Qafisheh and Azarov, 'Article 1D'); UNHCR Policy Development and Evaluation Service and Division of Operational Services, 'UNHCR's Expanded Role in Support of the Inter-Agency Response to Situations of Internal Displacement' (November 2006), UN Doc PDES/2006/06, 9 (hereafter UNHCR Policy Development and Evaluation Service and Division of Operational Services, 'Response to Situations of Internal Displacement'); Erika Feller, 'UNHCR's Role

Internally Displaced Persons and International Refugee Law. Bríd Ní Ghráinne, Oxford University Press. © Ní Ghráinne 2022.
DOI: 10.1093/oso/9780198868446.003.0006

yet been answered in the literature—could the availability of IDP protection within an asylum-seeker's country of nationality from UN agencies other than the UNHCR trigger the application of Article 1D, rendering the Refugee Convention inapplicable to those persons? For example, if an IDP receives assistance from the World Food Programme (WFP), would that assistance render them, ipso facto, ineligible for refugee status should they leave the state and seek asylum? Such an interpretation would appeal to states, because most (if not all) states perceive it in their interests to limit the number of persons they recognize as refugees. This question is important because if it is answered affirmatively, the availability of IDP protection would undermine the rights of IDPs to leave their country and to seek asylum in another country.

Article 1D may be relevant in the context of IDP protection because there are various agencies of the United Nations that are cluster leaders or co-leaders within the cluster approach of IDP protection. Such agencies include the WFP, WHO, UNICEF, OCHA, UNDP, OHCHR, and the Food and Agriculture Organization (FAO).[4] In addition, jurisprudence dealing with the role of international organizations offering internal protection has not excluded the possibility that Article 1D could be invoked in a broad manner.[5] States could invoke the application of Article 1D by relying on its 'ordinary meaning', arguing that it does not explicitly state that it only applies to Palestinians.[6] Secondly, states could explore the 'evolutionary approach' of interpretation or the concept of the Refugee Convention as a 'living instrument'—an interpretative approach that is common in many domestic legal systems and affirmed by the International Court of Justice and the European Court of Human Rights.[7] States could argue that the involvement of various UN agencies and bodies other than UNHCR in IDP interpretation should be taken into account in Article 1D's interpretation, and that it therefore applies in a broad manner.

in IDP Protection: Opportunities and Challenges' [2006] Forced Migration Review 11 (hereafter Feller, 'UNHCR's Role in IDP Protection').

[4] 'What is the Cluster Approach?' (OCHA Services) https://www.humanitarianresponse.info/en/coordination/clusters/what-cluster-approach accessed 7 July 2021 (hereafter 'What is the Cluster Approach?' (OCHA Services)).

[5] *Fadil Dyli v Secretary of State for the Home Department* [2000] Imm AR 652 (hereafter *Fadil Dyli v Secretary of State*).

[6] Art 31 of the 1969 Vienna Convention on the Law of Treaties (VCLT) provides that the 'ordinary meaning' of a treaty provision is a primary aid in its interpretation and the terms of Article 1D appear to be of broad application. Vienna Convention on the Law of Treaties (adopted 23 May 1969, entered into force 27 January 1980) 1155 UNTS 331 (hereafter 'VCLT').

[7] *Tyrer v United Kingdom* App no 5856/72 (ECHR, 25 April 1979) [31]; *Loizidou v Turkey* App no 15318/89 (ECHR, 18 December 1996); Dispute regarding Navigational and Related Rights *(Costa Rica v Nicaragua)* (Judgment) [2009] ICJ Rep 2009 [70]–[71].

This chapter argues that both the drafting history and practical application of Article 1D indicates that 1D is only applicable to Palestinian refugees receiving protection from the United Nations Relief and Works Agency (UNRWA). Article 1D therefore does not apply more generally to IDPs who receive protection from UN bodies other than UNHCR and go on to cross a border. In building this argument, this chapter will first set out a brief history of the Palestinian question within the UN and will illustrate why a special regime was felt to be necessary for Palestinian refugees. This chapter will then engage in an interpretative analysis of Article 1D, illustrating, line by line, its inapplicability to IDP protection activities outside of the Palestinian context. Finally, this chapter will argue that even when the historic context is disregarded in favour of a purely textual approach, it is illogical to apply Article 1D in the context of inter-agency IDP protection activities. This is because the issue of Article 1D's applicability only arises at the same time that the question of refugee status arises, namely after an individual has crossed a border. As an IDP, generally speaking, has not crossed a border,[8] the question of refugee status does not arise, and thus Article 1D cannot be applied where protection is made available to IDPs by UN agencies other than the UNHCR.

6.2 The Relevance of the *Travaux Préparatoires*

This chapter relies heavily on the drafting history, or *travaux préparatoires*, of Article 1D. Article 31 of the 1961 Vienna Convention on the Law of Treaties (VCLT) provides that the ordinary meaning of a treaty's terms is a primary aid in its interpretation, whereas the *travaux préparatoires* are assigned a supplementary role as per Article 32 VCLT.[9] However, as put by Klabbers, no serious lawyer would totally disregard the *travaux préparatoires*, and would consult them to confirm their understood meaning of a text.[10] In addition, Mortenson argues that to relegate *travaux* to an inferior position is simply wrong and cannot be reconciled with the agreement actually reached in 1969.[11]

[8] UNCHR 'Report of the Representative of the Secretary-General, Mr. Francis M. Deng, submitted pursuant to Commission resolution 1197/39. Addendum: Guiding Principles on Internal Displacement' (11 February 1998) UN Doc E/CN.4/1998/53/Add para 2 (hereafter UNCHR, 'Guiding Principles on Internal Displacement').

[9] VCLT (n 6).

[10] Jan Klabbers, 'Interpretation as the Continuation of Politics by Other Means' (*Opinio Juris*, 2 March 2009) <http://opiniojuris.org/2009/03/02/continuation/> accessed 3 June 2016.

[11] Julian D Mortenson, 'The *Travaux* of *Travaux:* Is the Vienna Convention Hostile to Drafting History?' (2013) 107 American Journal of International Law 780, 781.

There are various reasons why the *travaux* ought to be used to decipher the meaning of Article 1D. First, Article 31(4) of the VCLT requires an interpreter to apply the intended meaning of treaty terms if it is 'established' that they were intended to have a special meaning, that is, a meaning other than its ordinary one. This process often requires reference to the *travaux*. In the *Conditions of Admission* Advisory Opinion, the International Court of Justice stated that 'a decisive reason would be required' to displace the natural meaning of the terms used.[12] This chapter argues that this 'decisive reason' is provided by the *travaux*, which illustrate clearly the intention of the drafters to apply Article 1D to a narrow category of individuals.

Second, where a treaty provision proves ambiguous or obscure even after careful study of the text, Article 32(a) of the VCLT provides that interpreters should consult the *travaux* for further guidance in 'determining' its meaning. As Advocate General Sharpston noted in her Opinion on the *Bolbol* case before the CJEU, Article 1D gives little clue as to either the geographical boundaries or time-limit for persons receiving protection or assistance; the difference (if any) between receipt of protection and entitlement to protection, as well as the nature of UNRWA registration; the circumstances which amount to a cessation of protection or assistance; or the meaning of 'these persons shall *ipso facto* be entitled to' the benefits of the Refugee Convention.[13] Thus although they may seem clear at first glance, the terms of Article 1D are in fact ambiguous and recourse to the *travaux* is necessary to determine their meaning.

Third, Article 32(b) of the VCLT allows the *travaux* to be taken into account where the initial reading of the text in accordance with Article 31 renders a result that is 'manifestly absurd or unreasonable'. As will be argued below, a literal interpretation of Article 1D is unreasonable because it would allow an undefined category of individuals to automatically qualify for refugee status once protection from the particular UN organ or agency ceased. To create such an open category is at odds with the intention of the drafters to narrow the scope of those eligible for refugee protection under international law, which is evidenced by the narrow formulation of the refugee definition in Article 1A of the Refugee Convention.

[12] *Admission of a State to the United Nations* (Charter, Art 4) (Advisory Opinion) [1948] ICJ Rep 57, 63. See also the analysis of 'special meaning' in chapter 4.

[13] Opinion of Advocate General Sharpston, *Nawras Bolbol v Bevándorlási és Állampolgársági Hivatal* [2010] ECLI:EU:C:2010:351 (hereafter Opinion of Advocate General Sharpston, *Bolbol*), [46]–[47]. See also *Minister for Immigration and Multicultural Affairs v WABQ* [2002] FCAFC 329 [18], where the Federal Court of Australia described Article 1D as 'pregnant with ambiguity' (hereafter *Minister for Immigration and Multicultural Affairs v WABQ*).

Fourth, Article 32 of the VCLT allows the use of *travaux* to confirm the provisional understanding of a provision rendered by Article 31. As this chapter will argue, the examination of Article 1D's *travaux* illustrates that the drafters meant to convey something other than what initially appears. The examination of the *travaux* reveals that a special meaning was intended by the drafters, allowing recourse to the *travaux* as per Article 31(4); that there are ambiguities in the text, allowing recourse to the *travaux* as per Article 32(a) of the VCLT; and/or that the provisional interpretation would produce absurd results in the sense of Article 32(b) of the VCLT, again allowing recourse to the *travaux*. This chapter argues that the *travaux* are the most important interpretational aid for understanding the meaning of Article 1D, and they are therefore relied on heavily throughout this chapter.

6.3 A Special Regime for Palestinians—Article 1D and UNRWA

Section 6.3.1 will set out the history of UNRWA's establishment and the nature of its operations with Palestinians. Section 6.3.2 will go on to show that the drafters of the Refugee Convention did not want all Palestinian Arabs to be recognized as refugees, as to do so would pose a significant burden on states hosting such individuals. At the same time, the drafters wanted to make sure that Palestinian refugees would benefit from a protection regime. Article 1D was therefore inserted into the Refugee Convention to ensure that Palestinian refugees would be entitled to the benefits of the Refugee Convention should UNRWA's assistance cease.

6.3.1 The Establishment of UNRWA

On 29 November 1947, the General Assembly voted in favour of the partition of Palestine in two, forming separate Arab and Jewish states.[14] On 15 May 1948, the day after the British mandate over the territory ended, the Jewish community proclaimed the state of Israel. Between December 1947 and May 1948 civil and guerrilla warfare erupted, during which 750,000 Palestinians fled the territory. These Palestinian refugees were denied a right to return, and were retroactively effectively deprived of their citizenship by Israel.

[14] UNGA Res 181 (III) (29 November 1947) UN Doc A/RES/181 (11).

On 14 May 1948, Count Folke Bernadotte, President of the Swedish Red Cross, was appointed to the newly established position of United Nations Mediator for Palestine.[15] His suggestions to the Israeli government that a limited number of refugees should be given permission to return were not acted upon. He also indicated in his reports to the UN that the refugees' right to return should be affirmed.[16] However, his mediation attempts came to an abrupt halt when he was assassinated by terrorists on 17 November 1948.

Two days after his assassination, the General Assembly established the United Nations Relief for Palestine Refugees fund (UNRPR), a new $32m relief plan.[17] On 11 December of that same year, the General Assembly established the UN Conciliation Commission for Palestine (UNCCP), which was instructed to take steps to assist the governments and authorities concerned to achieve a final settlement and to facilitate the repatriation, compensation, resettlement, and economic and social rehabilitation of the refugees as set out in paragraph 11 of General Assembly Resolution 194 (III).[18] France, Turkey, and the United States were subsequently appointed to the UNCCP.

UNCCP made various failed efforts regarding the implementation of paragraph 11, such as an attempted repatriation scheme with Israel. Aside from progress in the recovery of property belonging to Palestinian refugees, UNCCP made no further substantial contribution to the implementation of paragraph 11. By the mid-1950s, it was clear that the UNCCP was unable to fulfil its dual mandate of international protection agency and mediator, mainly due to Israel's opposition to repatriation. Although the UNCCP was never formally terminated, its operations wound down due to political impasse, lack of support, and UN de-funding, and it has been inactive since the mid-1960s.[19] The UNCCP was never replaced by any international agency with an explicit mandate focusing on durable solutions for the Palestinian refugee population defined under Resolution 194 (III).[20]

[15] UNGA Res 186 (S-2) (14 May 1948) UN Doc A/RES/186 (S-2).

[16] UNGA, 'Progress Report of the United Nations Mediator on Palestine Submitted to the Secretary-General for Transmission to the Members of the United Nations' (16 September 1948) UN Doc A/648 [14].

[17] UNGA Res 212 (III) (19 November 1948) UN Doc A/RES/212 (III).

[18] UNGA Res 194 (III) (11 December 1948) UN Doc A/RES/194 (III) (hereafter UNGA Res 194 (III) (11 December 1948)); Francesca P Albanese and Lex Takkenberg, *Palestinian Refugees in International Law* (2nd edition, OUP 2020) 77 (hereafter Albanese and Takkenberg, *Palestinian Refugees in International Law*).

[19] Kate Ogg, 'New Directions in Article 1D Jurisprudence' in Satvinder Singh Juss (ed), *Research Handbook on International Refugee Law* (Elgar 2019) 360, 365 (hereafter Ogg, 'New Directions in Article 1D Jurisprudence').

[20] Susan Akram, 'UNRWA and Forced Migration' in Elena Fiddian-Qasmiyeh and others (eds), *The Oxford Handbook of Refugee and Forced Migration Studies* (OUP 2014) 228 (hereafter Akram, 'UNRWA and Forced Migration').

On 8 December 1949, UNRWA was established with the dual mission of providing direct relief and establishing a 'works programme' for Palestinian refugees.[21] UNRWA's present working definition of a Palestine refugee is any person 'whose normal place of residence was Palestine and during the period of 1 June 1946 to May 1948 and who lost both home and means of livelihood as a result of the 1948 conflict'.[22] It also applies to the children of all such persons and its territorial scope extends to Lebanon, Syria, Jordan, the West Bank, the Gaza Strip, and Egypt. The assistance function of UNRWA relates only to the Palestinian refugee's daily needs, such as primary and vocational education, primary health care, relief and social services, infrastructure and camp improvement, microfinance, and emergency response.[23] It therefore provides a special scheme of protection for those that fall within its mandate.

6.3.2 Drafting Article 1D

During the Refugee Convention's drafting, the general consensus was that the definition should be narrowed, such that the categories of refugee to which it applied should be clearly enumerated. The United States, for example, argued the extent of responsibility for refugees must be known in advance and that too vague a definition would amount to a 'blank cheque' and thus would not be satisfactory.[24] In addition, the United States and France did not consider that certain groups should be included within the framework of the Refugee Convention, such as the approximately 600,000 Arab refugees for whom the United Nations had made special arrangements.[25]

During this debate, Egypt, Lebanon, and Saudi Arabia issued a joint resolution on behalf of the Palestine refugees to whom the United States and France

[21] UNGA Res 302 (IV) (8 December 1949) UN Doc A/RES/302 (IV).

[22] 'Palestine Refugees' (*United Nations Relief and Works Agency for Palestine Refugees in the Near East*, UNRWA) <http://www.unrwa.org/palestine-refugees> accessed 7 April 2021.

[23] 'What We Do' (*United Nations Relief and Works Agency for Palestine Refugees in the Near East*, UNRWA) <http://www.unrwa.org/what-we-do> accessed 18 June 2019 (hereafter 'What We Do' (UNRWA)).

[24] UN Ad Hoc Committee on Refugees and Stateless Persons, 'Ad Hoc Committee on Statelessness and Related Problems, First Session: Summary Record of the Third Meeting Held at Lake Success, New York' (17 January 1950) UN Doc E/AC.32/SR.3 [37].

[25] ibid [38]; UNGA Conference of Plenipotentiaries on the Status of Refugees and Stateless Persons, 'Conference of Plenipotentiaries on the Status of Refugees and Stateless Persons: Summary Record of the Nineteenth Meeting' (26 November 1951) UN Doc A/CONF.2/SR.19 (hereafter UNGA Conference of Plenipotentiaries on the Status of Refugees and Stateless Persons, 'Summary Record of the Nineteenth Meeting'), statements of Mr Rochefort (France) and Mr Warren (USA).

referred.[26] They found the definition of 'refugee' adopted by ECOSOC to be unduly restrictive because it was limited in time and space and omitted certain categories of refugees. However, they were unsupportive of the United Kingdom resolution, which noted that the High Commissioner's competence 'should extend throughout the world and to all refugees',[27] because it would 'submerge in the general mass of refugees certain groups which were the particular concern of the General Assembly and the right of which to repatriation had been recognised by General Assembly resolution'.[28]

The Arab states' resolution demanded that the definition include a section stating that 'the mandate of the High Commissioner's office shall not extend to categories of refugees at present placed under the competence of other organs or agencies of the United Nations'.[29] The motivation behind this was alluded to by the French delegate, which referred to a conversation it had with a 'delegation of an Arab state', in which the Arab state had remarked that it would find it difficult, owing to financial reasons, to participate in a Convention that allocated refugee status to Arab refugees it had taken in.[30] The Iraqi delegation supported this point, by stating that the Arab states did not wish to impose on Contracting States the burden of the Arab refugees from Palestine so long as the United Nations was caring for them.[31] Similarly, the representative of the United States warned that the inclusion of Palestinian refugees in the general refugee regime 'would present Contracting States with an undefined problem, and so reduce the number of states in Europe that would find it possible to sign the Convention'.[32]

However, the other Arab delegations put forward more idealized reasons for the creation of a special regime for Palestinian Arab refugees. First, Egypt

[26] UNGA, Official Records of the Third Committee, 5th session, 328th meeting (27 November 1950) 358 as cited in Sarah E Davies, *Legitimising Rejection: International Refugee Law in Southeast Asia* (Martinus Nijhoff 2008) 49 (hereafter Davies, *Legitimising Rejection*).

[27] UNGA, Official Records of the Third Committee, 5th session, 324th meeting (22 November 1950) 330 as cited in Davies, *Legitimising Rejection* (n 26) 45.

[28] UNGA, Official Records of the Third Committee, 5th session, 328th meeting (27 November 1950) [52] as cited in Lex Takkenberg, *The Status of Palestinian Refugees in International Law* (Clarendon 1998) 62 (hereafter Takkenberg, *The Status of Palestinian Refugees*); Maja Janmyr, 'No Country of Asylum: "Legitimizing" Lebanon's Rejection of the 1951 Refugee Convention' (2017) 29(3) International Journal of Refugee Law 438, 443.

[29] UN Doc A/C.3/L.128 as cited in Takkenberg, *The Status of Palestinian Refugees* (n 28).

[30] UNGA Conference of Plenipotentiaries on the Status of Refugees and Stateless Persons 'Conference of Plenipotentiaries on the Status of Refugees and Stateless Persons: Summary Record of the Twenty-ninth Meeting' (28 November 1951) UN Doc A/CONF.2/SR.29 (hereafter UNGA Conference of Plenipotentiaries on the Status of Refugees and Stateless Persons, 'Summary Record of the Twenty-ninth Meeting'), statement of Mr Rochefort (France).

[31] UNGA Conference of Plenipotentiaries on the Status of Refugees and Stateless Persons, 'Summary Record of the Nineteenth Meeting' (n 25) statement of Mr Al Pachachi (Iraq).

[32] ibid, statement of Mr Warren (USA).

(with support from Iraq) argued that the problem of the Arab refugees from Palestine had arisen out of action taken by the United Nations, and it was therefore the duty of members of the Conference to find a solution to the problem of those refugees.[33] Egypt also highlighted that the Arab refugees from Palestine had been excluded from the mandate of the UNHCR as a result of the action taken by the delegations of the Arab States at the fifth session of the General Assembly.[34] Subsequent literature on this topic has argued that there was a general recognition that Palestinians as a group met the persecution requirement of the refugee definition. However their plight was unique because a member of the UN (Israel) was preventing their return.[35] In addition, it was envisaged that the plight of the displaced Palestinians would be resolved within a short timescale on the basis of UN General Assembly Resolution 194 (III), particularly through compensation and repatriation in accordance with paragraph 11.[36] Palestinian refugees were therefore regarded as meriting special protection than that afforded to other refugees and it was for that reason that Article 1D was included in the Refugee Convention's text.

It is thus argued by this work that Article 1D is limited in its applicability to those who its drafters intended—Palestinian refugees receiving protection from UNRWA.[37] The drafting history explicitly states that the object of the Egyptian amendment was to 'make sure that Arab refugees from Palestine who were still refugees when the organs or agencies of the United Nations at present providing them with protection or assistance ceased to function, would automatically come within the scope of the Convention'.[38] In addition, all the delegations that spoke during the drafting of Article 1D made reference

[33] ibid, statements of Mr Mostafa Bey (Egypt) and Mr Al Pachachi (Iraq). See also Guy S Goodwin-Gill and Susan M Akram, 'Foreword to Amicus Brief on the Status of Palestinian Refugees Under International Refugee Law' (2000) 11 The Palestine Yearbook of International Law Online 185, 219 (hereafter Goodwin-Gill and Akram, 'Foreword to Amicus Brief'); Guy S Goodwin-Gill and Jane McAdam, *The Refugee in International Law* (3rd edn, OUP 2011) 157 (hereafter Goodwin-Gill and McAdam, *The Refugee in International Law*); Susan M Akram, 'Palestinian Refugees and their Legal Status: Rights, Politics, and Implications for a Just Solution' (2002) 31(3) Journal of Palestine Studies 36, 40 (hereafter Akram, 'Palestinian Refugees and their Legal Status').

[34] UNGA Conference of Plenipotentiaries on the Status of Refugees and Stateless Persons, 'Summary Record of the Nineteenth Meeting' (n 25) statement of Mr Mostafa Bey (Egypt).

[35] Akram, 'Palestinian Refugees and their Legal Status' (n 33) 40.

[36] ibid 40; Goodwin-Gill and McAdam, *The Refugee in International Law* (n 33) 155; UNGA Conference of Plenipotentiaries on the Status of Refugees and Stateless Persons, 'Summary Record of the Nineteenth Meeting' (n 25) statement of Mr Mostafa Bey (Egypt).

[37] Hathaway and Foster, *The Law of Refugee Status* (n 2) 510; Ogg, 'New Directions in Article 1D Jurisprudence' (n 19) 359.

[38] UNGA Conference of Plenipotentiaries on the Status of Refugees and Stateless Persons, 'Summary Record of the Twenty-ninth Meeting' (n 30) statement of Mr Mostafa Bey (Egypt); Albanese and Takkenberg, *Palestinian Refugees in International Law* (n 18) 82.

to Palestinian refugees.[39] Although Israel and Norway also referred briefly to Korean refugees, for reasons elaborated on below in section 6.4.2.2, this reference was incorrect.[40] Furthermore, in light of the general consensus amongst drafters that the definition should be narrowed, there is no way that they would be willing to create an open category that would bring a group within the remit of the Refugee Convention upon the happening of a particular event (the cessation of UN assistance). However, for the sake of argument this chapter will be open to the possibility of it applying to other groups of persons, and that proposition will be examined in detail below.

6.4 Interpreting Article 1D of the Refugee Convention: The First Sentence

The first sentence of Article 1D provides that:

> This Convention shall not apply to persons who are at present receiving from organs or agencies of the United Nations other than the United Nations High Commissioner for Refugees protection or assistance.

The following subsections will analyse the various clauses in this sentence, applying the rules of treaty interpretation and setting out how the clauses might apply in the context of inter-agency IDP protection.

6.4.1 'The Convention shall not apply to persons'

The meaning of 'shall not apply' is relatively straightforward—the Refugee Convention will be inapplicable to those falling within the scope of Article 1D. The phrase 'to persons' in Article 1D refers to a category or group of persons, rather than to individuals.[41] This is supported by the general recognition at

[39] UNGA Conference of Plenipotentiaries on the Status of Refugees and Stateless Persons, 'Summary Record of the Nineteenth Meeting' (n 25) statements of Mr Rochefort (France), Mr Mostafa Bey (Egypt), Mr Al Pachachi (Iraq), Mr Hoare (United Kingdom), Mr Robinson (Israel), Mr Anker (Norway); UNGA Conference of Plenipotentiaries on the Status of Refugees and Stateless Persons, 'Summary Record of the Twenty-ninth Meeting' (n 30) statements of Mr Mostafa Bey (Egypt), Mr Rochefort (France).

[40] UNGA Conference of Plenipotentiaries on the Status of Refugees and Stateless Persons, 'Summary Record of the Nineteenth Meeting' (n 25) statements of Mr Robinson (Israel) and Mr Anker (Norway).

[41] Atle Grahl-Madsen, *The Status of Refugees in International Law* (AW Sijthoff 1966) 265 (hereafter Grahl-Madsen, *The Status of Refugees in International Law*); *Minister for Immigration and Multicultural Affairs v WABQ* (n 13) [69]; Susan Akram, 'Closing Protection Gaps: Handbook on Protection

the time of drafting that Palestinians as a group were presumed to fall within the refugee definition.[42] UNHCR identifies the following groups as falling within the personal scope of Article 1D:[43] (i) Palestine refugees;[44] (ii) displaced persons;[45] and (iii) descendants.[46] For the purposes of this chapter, the term 'Palestine refugees' is used to encompass 'Palestine refugees', 'displaced persons', and 'descendants'.[47]

However, as set out in chapter 2, it could be argued that the term IDPs also indicates a category or group of persons. This may be a somewhat obvious observation, given the fact that they are described in terms of internally displaced 'persons' rather than in terms of internally displaced 'individuals'. Thus, the interpretation of the term 'to persons' set forth in this section does not necessarily exclude IDPs from Article 1D's application.

6.4.2 'who are at present receiving from organs or agencies of the United Nations other than the United Nations High Commissioner for refugees'

6.4.2.1 Temporal Scope of Article 1D

According to Grahl-Madsen, the term 'at present' refers to the date the Refugee Convention was signed because if any other date was intended, it would have

of Palestinian Refugees in States Signatories to the 1951 Convention' (*BADIL Resource Center for Palestinian Residency and Refugee Rights*, 2015) https://reliefweb.int/report/world/closing-protection-gaps-handbook-protection-palestinian-refugees-states-signatories accessed 7 July 2021, 42 (hereafter Akram, 'Closing Protection Gaps').

[42] Akram, 'Palestinian Refugees and their Legal Status' (n 33) 40.

[43] UNHCR, 'Guidelines on International Protection no 13: Applicability of Article 1D of the 1951 Convention relating to the Status of Refugees to Palestinian Refugees' (December 2017) UN Doc HCR/GIP/17/13 (hereafter UNHCR, 'Guidelines on International Protection No. 13') [8].

[44] Persons who are 'Palestine refugees' within the sense of UN General Assembly Resolution 194 (III) of 11 December 1948 and subsequent UN General Assembly Resolutions and who, as a result of the 1948 Arab–Israeli conflict, were displaced from that part of Mandate Palestine which became Israel, and who have been unable to return there. See Albanese and Takkenberg, *Palestinian Refugees in International Law* (n 18).

[45] Persons who are 'displaced persons' within the sense of UN General Assembly Resolution 2252 (ES-V) of 4 July 1967 and subsequent UN General Assembly resolutions, and who, as a result of the 1967 conflict, have been displaced from the Palestinian territory occupied by Israel since 1967 and have been unable to return there. It also includes those persons displaced by 'subsequent hostilities'. See ibid.

[46] 'Descendants' refers to all persons born to Palestine refugees or displaced persons, as defined above. Based on principles of gender equality and non-discrimination on the basis of sex, as well as the principle of family unity, these descendants, whether they are descended through the male or female line, would be considered to fall within the purview of Article 1D. This includes descendants who were born outside of and who have never resided in UNRWA's areas of operation, where the criteria for the application of Article 1D are met. See ibid.

[47] This approach mirrors that of UNHCR, 'Guidelines on International Protection No. 13' (n 43) [9].

been stated in the Refugee Convention.[48] On this interpretation, only organs or agencies existing in 1951, and their possible successor bodies, come within the scope of the Refugee Convention.[49] Hathaway and Foster agree with this interpretation.[50] They refer to the statement of the United Kingdom's representative, which set out that '[paragraph 1D was intended] to exclude persons who ... at the time when the Convention came into force were receiving protection or assistance from United Nations organs or agencies'.[51] Takkenberg also supports this interpretation, opining that although the Refugee Convention was drafted in general terms, its intention was to provide for existing groups of refugees (those who had become refugees as a result of events occurring before 1951) and there is therefore no reason to believe that this was different in respect of Article 1D.[52]

Although the English Court of Appeal in *El-Ali* found that Article 1D was relevant only to persons who were receiving protection or assistance on or before 28 July 1951,[53] this temporal interpretation was overruled by the CJEU.[54] Thus the term 'at present receiving' means 'persons who were and/or are now receiving' protection or assistance from organs or agencies (and their successor bodies) of the UN other than the UNHCR that were in existence at the time the Refugee Convention was signed.[55] To adopt the temporal limitation in *El-Ali* would have the effect of limiting Article 1D's application to a relatively small number of Palestinians who were alive in 1951 and receiving assistance from UNRWA at that time.[56] It also ignores the motivation underlying the drafting of Article 1D, which was continuity of protection for Palestinian refugees,[57] or

[48] Grahl-Madsen, *The Status of Refugees in International Law* (n 41) 264.

[49] There are 3 organs/agencies that were in existence in 1951 that currently offer protection and/or assistance to IDPs—FAO, WHO, and UNICEF.

[50] Hathaway and Foster, *The Law of Refugee Status* (n 2) 514.

[51] UNGA Conference of Plenipotentiaries on the Status of Refugees and Stateless Persons, 'Summary Record of the Nineteenth Meeting' (n 25) [20], statement of Mr Warren (USA).

[52] Takkenberg, *The Status of Palestinian Refugees* (n 28) 97.

[53] *El-Ali v Secretary of State for the Home Department* [2002] EWCA Civ 1103 [28]–[39] (hereafter *El-Ali v Secretary of State*).

[54] *Nawras Bolbol v Bevándorlási és Állampolgársági Hivatal* [2010] ECLI:EU:C:2010:351 (hereafter *Bolbol*); *Said (Article 1D: interpretation)* [2012] UKUT 00413(IAC) (hereafter *Said (Article 1D)*) [23]. See also the New Zealand case of *AD (Palestine)* [2015] NZIPT 800693-695, 23 December 2015 [133], [148].

[55] UNHCR 'Guidelines on International Protection No. 13' (n 43) [13]; The Australian Federal Court in the case of *Minister for Immigration and Multicultural Affairs v WABQ* (n 13) [69] took the position that 'the word "receiving" should be read in its ordinary grammatical sense and not as meaning "entitled to receive"'.

[56] Goddard, 'Protection of Palestinian Refugees' (n 2) 498.

[57] UNHCR, 'Guidelines on International Protection No. 13' (n 43) [17].

if we take a more cynical approach, to shift the cost of protecting Palestinian refugees onto UNRWA for as long as UNRWA continued to operate.[58]

The extent of UNRWA's mandate also supports an expansive temporal interpretation of Article 1D.[59] General Assembly resolutions are evidence of 'subsequent practice' in the application of the treaty made by State Parties to the Refugee Convention as per Article 31(3)(b) of the VCLT and therefore indicate how the concept of a Palestinian refugee and the extent of UNRWA's mandate should be interpreted.[60] The fact that UNRWA's mandate has been repeatedly extended by the General Assembly supports the argument that Article 1D applies to those who are present recipients of UNRWA's protection or assistance.[61] This 'continuing effect' approach has been described by Goodwin-Gill and McAdam as reconciling any apparent discrepancy between the first and second paragraph of Article 1D, minimizing ambiguity, avoiding arbitrary distinctions, and is the interpretation most consistent with the original intentions of the states and with later General Assembly resolutions.[62]

The 'continuing effect' approach leaves open the possibility that Article 1D applies to IDPs in a modern-day context, as IDPs continue to receive protection from various organs and agencies other than the UNHCR that were in existence in 1951, such as the WHO, UNICEF, and FAO. It is therefore necessary to examine whether Article 1D can be interpreted to apply broadly to organs or agencies other than UNRWA.

6.4.2.2 Actors of Protection Referred to by Article 1D

Article 1D does not explicitly refer to any particular organ or agency by name. In addition, the use of the plural and the term 'or' in 'organs or agencies' implies that this clause does not refer to just one organ and/or agency.[63] It is therefore necessary to establish which actor(s) of protection falls within the scope of Article 1D.

The UNHCR is of the view that:

[58] UNGA Conference of Plenipotentiaries on the Status of Refugees and Stateless Persons, 'Summary Record of the Twenty-ninth Meeting' (n 30) statement of Mr Rochefort (France).

[59] Goodwin-Gill and McAdam, *The Refugee in International Law* (n 33) 157.

[60] ibid 172.

[61] The current mandate runs until 2023. See 'Immense Support for the Renewal of the UNRWA Mandate at the UN General Assembly' (*United Nations Relief and Works Agency for Palestine Refugees in the Near East*, UNRWA) <https://www.unrwa.org/newsroom/press-releases/immense-support-renewal-unrwa-mandate-un-general-assembly> accessed 7 April 2021 (hereafter 'Immense Support for the Renewal of the UNRWA Mandate at the UN General Assembly' (UNRWA)).

[62] Goodwin-Gill and McAdam, *The Refugee in International Law* (n 33) 157–58.

[63] Hugo Storey, 'The Meaning of "Protection" within the Refugee Definition' (2016) 35(3) Refugee Survey Quarterly 1, 23.

> Exclusion under this clause applies to any person who is in receipt of protection or assistance from organs or agencies of the United Nations, other than the United Nations High Commissioner for Refugees. Such protection or assistance was previously given by the former United Nations Korean Reconstruction Agency (UNKRA) and is currently given by the United Nations Relief and Works Agency for Palestine Refugees In the Near East (UNRWA). There could be other similar situations in the future.[64]

This final sentence clearly leaves open the possibility that Article 1D is applicable outside of its historical context. However, this interpretation is 'almost certainly incorrect'.[65] First, the *travaux préparatoires* clearly illustrate that the drafters intended to make arrangements for existing groups of refugees. In fact, the drafting history of the Refugee Convention illustrates that the only situation discussed in detail in reference to Article 1D was that of the Palestinian refugees.[66] Arguably, this rules out future groups of refugees, and hence rules out actors other than UNRWA. This is supported by the reference in the second sentence to 'the settlement of those persons', as it reinforces the contention that Article 1D referred to one category of refugees concerning which the UN had adopted resolutions—that is, Palestinian refugees.

Second, although the ordinary meaning of the phrase 'organs or agencies' need not be restricted to one particular entity, Article 31(4) of the VCLT provides that 'a special meaning shall be given to a term if it is established that the parties so intended'. As set out above in section 6.4.2.1, it is clear that the drafters intended for Article 1D to be limited in its applicability to Palestinian refugees and therefore the term 'organs or agencies of the United Nations' refers solely to those agencies that were providing such protection or assistance at the time—UNRWA and UNCCP.[67] UNCCP's operations shrank during the 1950s,[68] therefore nowadays the reference to 'organs or agencies' should be interpreted as referring to UNRWA. Third, the argument that Article 1D refers to protection provided by UNRWA to Palestinian refugees is supported by case law.[69]

64 UNHCR 'Handbook on Procedures and Criteria for Determining Refugee Status under the 1951 Convention and the 1967 Protocol relating to the Status of Refugees' (Re-edited January 1992) UN Doc HCR/IP/4/Eng/REV.1 [142].

65 Goodwin-Gill and Akram, 'Foreword to Amicus Brief' (n 33) 219, 233.

66 The Israeli and Norwegian delegations also referred to Korean refugees. UNGA Conference of Plenipotentiaries on the Status of Refugees and Stateless Persons, 'Summary Record of the Nineteenth Meeting' (n 25) statements of Mr Robinson (Israel) and Mr Anker (Norway).

67 Albanese and Takkenberg, *Palestinian Refugees in International Law* (n 18) 80.

68 Akram, 'UNRWA and Forced Migration' (n 20) 228.

69 *Refugee Appeal No. 1/92 Re SA*: Refugee Status Appeals Authority (New Zealand), 30 April 1992; Eleanor Drywood, 'Who's In and Who's Out? The Court's Emerging Case Law on the Definition of a

The historical context of the term 'organs or agencies of the United Nations other than the UNHCR' therefore clearly refers to protection or assistance given by UNRWA alone, and this meaning has been confirmed by the CJEU.[70] However, setting the historical context aside, could the ordinary meaning of the words apply to agencies that are involved in IDP protection? In the case of *R (on the application of Vallaj) v Special Adjudicator*, the Court of Appeal of England and Wales did not rule out that protection activities by organs or agencies aside from UNRWA could trigger the application of Article 1D.[71] It must therefore be ascertained which, if any, organs or agencies of the UN which were in existence in 1951 are still in existence at present and providing protection or assistance to IDPs. Within the cluster approach of IDP protection, the FAO, established in 1945, is the co-lead for food security; the WHO, established in 1948, is the cluster lead on health; UNICEF, established in 1946, is the cluster co-lead for education and cluster lead for nutrition.[72] Therefore, an interpretation of Article 1D which ignores its historical context leads to the conclusion that protection efforts provided by the FAO, WHO, and/or UNICEF for IDPs could possibly trigger the application of Article 1D as they were in existence in 1951 and are still providing protection to IDPs at present.

6.4.3 'protection or assistance'

The *travaux préparatoires* of the Refugee Convention illustrate that the terms 'care for' and 'aid' were employed when describing the meaning of 'protection or assistance'. This implies that 'protection' and 'assistance' had not been intended to imply a technical or legal meaning. The plain meaning of the word 'or' indicates that those de facto refugees who are not receiving either protection or assistance require the alternate protection scheme of the Refugee Convention triggered by Article 1D, second sentence. The CJEU case of *Alheto* has clarified that an assessment of whether an individual is receiving protection or assistance from UNRWA must take into account whether the protection and/or assistance is effective.[73]

Refugee' (2014) 51 Common Market Law Review 1903, 1109; Opinion of Advocate General Sharpston, *Bolbol* (n 13) [44]; *MA v Refugee Appeal Tribunal and Ors* [2013] IEHC 36 [21] (Ireland); *Said (Article 1D)* (n 54) [11].

[70] *Abed El Karem El Kott and Others v Bevándorlási és Állampolgársági* [2012] ECLI:EU:C:2012:826 [48], [44] (hereafter *Abed El Karem El Kott and Others*).

[71] *R (on the application of Vallaj) v Special Adjudicator* [2001] EWCA Civ 782, [2001] INLR 342.

[72] International Organisation for Migration, 'The Cluster Approach' (2019), available at: <https://emergencymanual.iom.int/entry/21212/the-cluster-approach> 01 July 2021.

[73] *Serin Alheto v Zamestnik-predsedatel na Darzhavna agentsia za bezhantsite* [2018] ECLI:EU:C:2018:584 [90] (hereafter *Serin Alheto*).

It is evident that the activities of the various agencies involved in IDP protection which were in existence in 1951 satisfy the criteria of providing 'protection or assistance' to IDP populations. UNICEF is responsible for education, nutrition, and water, sanitation, and hygiene (with OHCHR, UNHCR, and Save the Children);[74] WHO is responsible for health;[75] and the FAO is responsible for food security (with WFP).[76] Thus if we take a textual view of Article 1D, the first criterion for its application is satisfied by the provision of 'protection or assistance' to various agencies involved in IDP protection.

6.4.4 Concluding Thoughts: The Meaning of the First Sentence of Article 1D

This chapter argues that an application of the rules of treaty interpretation to the first sentence of Article 1D leads to the conclusion that it solely refers to Palestinian Arabs who are currently receiving protection or assistance from UNRWA. However, this section has also found that a purely textual reading of the first sentence of Article 1D could lead to the conclusion that it also applies to IDPs who are receiving protection from organs or agencies of the UN other than the UNHCR which were in existence in 1951 and are still in existence today, such as UNICEF, the WHO, or the FAO. The following sections will examine the second sentence of Article 1D, and illustrate that it clearly rules out Article 1D's application as a whole to IDPs who receive protection in an inter-agency context.

6.5 Interpreting Article 1D of the Refugee Convention: The Second Sentence

The second sentence of Article 1D provides that:

> When such protection or assistance has ceased for any reason, without the position of such persons being definitively settled in accordance with the relevant resolutions adopted by the General Assembly of the United Nations, these persons shall ipso facto be entitled to the benefits of the Convention.

[74] 'What is the Cluster Approach?' (OCHA Services) (n 4).

[75] Inter-Agency Standing Committee 'Reference Module for Cluster Coordination at Country Level' (July 2009) <https://www.who.int/health-cluster/about/cluster-system/cluster-coordination-reference-module-2015.pdf?ua=1> accessed 14 June 2019.

[76] 'What is the Cluster Approach' (OCHA Services) (n 4).

The following subsections will analyse the various clauses in this sentence, applying the rules of treaty interpretation and setting out how the clauses might apply in the context of IDP protection.

6.5.1 'when such protection or assistance has ceased for any reason'

The term 'when such protection or assistance has ceased' has been interpreted by the CJEU to mean that mere voluntary departure from UNRWA's area of operations will not qualify as cessation of protection or assistance for the purposes of Article 1D.[77] Cessation can occur in three circumstances: where the agency ceases to exist;[78] where the agency is unable to fulfil its mandate;[79] or where the person had to leave the zone of operation for reasons beyond their control, for example, where their personal safety is at risk and it is impossible for UNRWA to guarantee living conditions in the respective area commensurate to their mission.[80]

It is argued here that the limited interpretation of the term 'ceased' by the CJEU was incorrect, because the courts ignored the words 'for any reason', which indicates the cessation of UNRWA assistance under any circumstances.[81] This reading accords with the historical context of the Refugee Convention's drafting, during which the Palestinian problem was treated as a short-term issue. This interpretation was supported by the UNHCR, which has stated that if a person is outside UNRWA's area of operations, that person no longer enjoys the protection or assistance of UNRWA and therefore falls within the scope of Article 1D.[82] This is further supported by the broader purpose of Article 1D, which was intended to ensure continued protection and assistance to Palestinian refugees at all times, either through the distinct framework combining the UNCCP and UNRWA or an alternative regime comprised of the

[77] *Abed El Karem El Kott and Others* (n 70) [49], [159].

[78] ibid [56]; UNHCR, 'Guidelines on International Protection No. 13' (n 43) [22].

[79] *Abed El Karem El Kott and Others* (n 70) [56]; UNHCR, 'Guidelines on International Protection No. 13' (n 43) [22].

[80] *Abed El Karem El Kott and Others* (n 70) [63]; *Serin Alheto* (n 73) [86]; UNHCR, 'Guidelines on International Protection No. 13' (n 43) [22].

[81] Goodwin-Gill and McAdam, *The Refugee in International Law* (n 33) 158–59; Qafisheh and Azarov, 'Article 1D' (n 3) 561–63.

[82] UNHCR, 'Revised Note on the Applicability of Article 1D of the 1951 Convention relating to the Status of Refugees to Palestinian Refugees' (October 2009) [8]. See also the jurisprudence analysed in Goddard, 'Protection of Palestinian Refugees' (n 2) 499.

UNHCR and the Refugee Convention.[83] As stated by the Egyptian delegation during the drafting process, it was clear that so long as United Nations institutions and organs cared for such refugees their protection would be a matter for the United Nations alone. However, when that aid came to an end the question would arise of how their continued protection was to be ensured. It would only be natural to extend the benefits of the Refugee Convention to them.[84]

What is the significance of this analysis for IDPs? Once an international border is crossed, generally speaking, an individual would no longer be an IDP and hence no longer in receipt of protection directed for IDPs. The individual would thus satisfy one of the textual criteria for the application of Article 1D ('when such protection or assistance has ceased for any reason'). However, the term 'at present receiving' implies that in order for Article 1D to apply, an individual would have to be within the area of protection (ie would have to be an IDP) *at the same time* that the question of refugee status arises. Logically, these two conditions cannot co-exist—a person cannot be a refugee and an IDP at the same time.[85] Being outside of one's country of nationality is a precondition for satisfying the refugee definition, and according to the Guiding Principles on Internal Displacement, a person generally does not fall within the IDP description once a state border has been crossed.[86] An analogous situation arose before the Immigration Appeal Tribunal of England and Wales in the case of *Dyli v Secretary of State for the Home Department*. The question of the applicability of Article 1D arose in the context of an asylum-seeker who had available to him protection from UNMIK in his place of origin, Kosovo. The Tribunal held:

> UNMIK operates only within Kosovo, itself part of the Federal Republic of Yugoslavia. Insofar as UNMIK offers assistance to citizens of the Federal Republic of Yugoslavia, it follows that that assistance is not being offered to persons who might otherwise be refugees: they cannot be, because they are not outside their country of nationality. In our view, as they could not in any event be entitled to the protection of the Convention, Article ID does not apply to them.[87]

[83] The roles of these bodies are set out in section 6.3.

[84] 'The provisions of [paragraph D] would cease to be applicable the moment the aid at present being given by the United Nations to Arab refugees ceased; the latter would then be eligible for the benefits of the Convention'. See UNGA Conference of Plenipotentiaries on the Status of Refugees and Stateless Persons, 'Summary Record of the Nineteenth Meeting' (n 25) statement of Mr Mostafa Bey (Egypt).

[85] Unless they have crossed a border and have been subsequently displaced in the host country. See below.

[86] UNCHR, 'Guiding Principles on Internal Displacement' (n 8).

[87] *Fadil Dyli v Secretary of State* (n 5).

Generally speaking therefore, and even disregarding its historical context, Article 1D cannot be triggered by the availability of agencies offering protection and/or assistance to IDPs within a refugee's country of origin. Article 1D's application is precluded by the fact that the recipients of IDP protection measures will have not crossed an international frontier and thus the question of refugee status does not arise.

However, one question which remains open is the legal status of an individual who is outside of their country of nationality, but who has been internally displaced in the receiving country and is 'at present receiving' protection or assistance from an organ or agency of the UN other than the UNHCR (ie someone who is a displaced refugee within the host state). Although such persons would generally not, strictly speaking, fall within the description of an IDP within the Guiding Principles,[88] the Guiding Principles do not provide a legal definition of an IDP and, furthermore, many such persons would fall within the remit of IDP protection activities provided by international actors. UNRWA, for example, has provided protection to Palestinian refugees in Syria, Jordan, and Lebanon, who are in situations of internal displacement.[89] Thus it is clear that UNRWA extends 'protection or assistance' to IDPs who are technically outside of their country of nationality. Could such 'protection or assistance' be relied upon by a receiving state to trigger the applicability of Article 1D, and thus preclude the granting of refugee status?

Put simply, the answer is 'yes'.[90] However such an interpretation is in line with Article 1D's object and purpose, namely that it should be applied to Palestinian refugees receiving protection from UNRWA. In addition, Article 1D would only be applicable for the duration of which such protection or assistance is being provided.

If a refugee who is not Palestinian becomes displaced in the host state, and receives protection from a UN agency other than the UNHCR, there may be an argument (albeit a weak one) that Article 1D has been triggered. However, this would be based on a total disregard of Article 1D's drafting history and thus it is argued that it would fly in the face of Article 31 of the VCLT, which sets out that the object and purpose of a treaty has to be taken into account when interpreting a treaty provision. Furthermore, in light of the fact that Article 1D was designed to provide a separate protection regime for a specific category of refugees,[91] it would be contrary to the principle of good faith to interpret this

[88] Guiding Principles on Internal Displacement (n 8). See analysis in chapter 2.
[89] 'What We Do' (UNRWA) (n 23).
[90] *Serin Alheto* (n 73) [143].
[91] Albanese and Takkenberg, *Palestinian Refugees in International Law* (n 18) 83.

Article in a manner that contravenes its original purpose and further narrows the category of those eligible for international protection.[92]

A second issue that is often raised with regard to the meaning of the phrase 'when such protection or assistance has ceased for any reason' is whether it is necessary to have actually used UNRWA's assistance or protection activities to fall within the remit of Article 1D, or whether it is sufficient to be eligible to receive protection or assistance. This question came before the CJEU in the form of a preliminary ruling in the *Bolbol* case, where the Court was asked to interpret Article 1D in its context of forming part of EU law by virtue of Article 12(1)(a) of the Qualification Directive 2004.[93] The Court, referring to the 'clear wording of Article 1D' supported this former interpretation.[94] However, it is argued here that this interpretation was incorrect.[95] This interpretation provides that similarly situated persons who were displaced as a result of the same conflict would be subject to different treatment depending on whether they availed themselves of assistance or not and depending on when they fled. Some would be examined under Article 1D and some under Article 1A(2).[96] This can be criticised on the grounds that the drafters did not intend such distinctions to be made.[97] The aim of Article 1D was to provide for a particular refugee population, not create a protection gap for the most vulnerable members of that population; namely those not receiving assistance from the UN.[98] Moreover, interpreting Article 1D in a way that would not include those Palestinians who are eligible for UNRWA's protection but have not availed themselves of it would lead to the duplication of mandates in respect of the same refugee population between UNHCR and UNRWA inside UNRWA's area of operation.[99] In

[92] VCLT art 31.

[93] Council Directive (EC) 2004/83/EC of 29 April 2004 on minimum standards for the qualification and status of third country nationals or stateless persons as refugees or as persons who otherwise need international protection and the content of the protection granted [2004] OJ L304/12. Article 12(1)(1) states 'A third-country national or a stateless person is excluded from being a refugee if: he or she falls within the scope of Article 1(D) of the Geneva Convention, relating to protection or assistance from organs or agencies of the United Nations other than the United Nations High Commissioner for Refugees. When such protection or assistance has ceased for any reason, without the position of such persons being definitely settled in accordance with the relevant resolutions adopted by the General Assembly of the United Nations, those persons shall *ipso facto* be entitled to the benefits of this Directive.'

[94] *Bolbol* (n 54) [51]. See also Paul J Cardwell, 'Determining Refugee Status Under Directive 2004/83: Comment on Bolbol (C-31/09)' (2011) 36(1) European Law Review 135.

[95] UNHCR, 'Guidelines on International Protection No. 13' (n 43) [14].

[96] ibid [15].

[97] Marguerite Perin, 'European and International Law and Palestinian Refugees: Bolbol, El Kott and the Application of Article 1D of the Geneva Convention' (2014) 3 UCL Journal of Law and Jurisprudence 87, 99 (hereafter Perin, 'European and International Law and Palestinian Refugees').

[98] ibid 99.

[99] UNHCR, 'Guidelines on International Protection No. 13' (n 43) [16].

addition, the fact that Article 1D applies to a class or category of persons as a whole implies that the words 'receiving protection or assistance' do not require that a person or their family would receive actual support from the organization in question. That said, the above criticism of the *Bolbol* decision is likely to have little practical effect, given that many states have not applied Article 1D to those who are eligible for but have not actually accessed UNRWA's assistance.[100] Such subsequent practice of States Parties in the application of a treaty is authoritative when ascertaining its meaning.[101] Thus it seems that for Article 1D to be applied in the IDP context, the individual concerned must have actually accessed the protection available to them.

6.5.2 'without the position of such persons being definitively settled in accordance with the relevant resolutions adopted by the General Assembly of the United Nations'

'Such persons' are the persons referred to by the first sentence of Article 1D, which, as this chapter has illustrated, is Palestinian refugees receiving protection or assistance from UNRWA. The reference to 'the relevant resolutions adopted by the General Assembly' was a reference to Resolution 194 (III), which states that refugees have the right to be repatriated and compensated for their losses.[102] No Palestinian refugee can be described as 'definitively settled' for the purpose of Article 1D until as a group they are repatriated and compensated for their losses.[103] This is reflected by the fact that UNRWA's current mandate towards Palestinian refugees has been extended until 2023.[104] This further supports the interpretation that Article 1D was intended to apply solely to Palestinian refugees receiving protection or assistance from UNRWA and does not apply in the broader context of IDP protection activities.

100 Akram, 'Closing Protection Gaps' (n 41) 335.
101 VCLT art 31(2)(b).
102 UNGA Res 194 (III) (11 December 1948) (n 18); Qafisheh and Azarov, 'Article 1D' (n 3) 564.
103 Goodwin-Gill and Akram, 'Foreword to Amicus Brief' (n 33) 219, 243.
104 See 'Immense Support for the Renewal of the UNRWA Mandate at the UN General Assembly' (UNRWA) (n 61).

6.5.3 'these persons shall ipso facto be entitled to the benefits of this convention'

Once outside UNRWA's area of operations, or when protection or assistance has ceased within UNRWA's area of operations, the second sentence of Article 1D will apply. This sentence is open to two interpretations: first, that the individual will automatically be entitled to refugee status, or second, that the individual will be eligible to be considered for refugee status.

In order to determine the correct interpretation of this provision, we must look at the object and purpose of Article 1D. Although its first sentence excludes from refugee status those who are in receipt of protection and assistance from UNRWA, and it is placed in the Refugee Convention directly before the provisions which regulate inapplicability of, and exclusion from, refugee status (Article 1E and 1F, respectively); its purpose is not to exclude. Rather, the basic premise of its second sentence is to set out those Palestinian refugees who will be entitled to the benefits of the Refugee Convention should certain events occur and as such it has been referred to as a 'contingent inclusion',[105] 'deferred inclusion',[106] or a 'suspensive' clause.[107] Its intention was thus not exclusion from protection, but rather to provide a heightened protection regime to a category of persons who fit the refugee definition and it functions as a type of exception to an exclusion clause. As the Egyptian delegate stated at the time of drafting, the effect of Article 1D would be merely to postpone the inclusion of the Palestinian refugees within the refugee definition.[108]

Thus, Article 1D does not exclude one from refugee status rather, it pro vides that refugee status will be automatically granted to Palestinian refugees should certain events occur. This is supported by the comments made by the Iraqi and Egyptian delegates at the time of drafting, who clarified that when the assistance at present being given by the United Nations came to an end,

[105] Goodwin-Gill and McAdam, *The Refugee in International Law* (n 33) 153; Akram, 'Palestinian Refugees and their Legal Status (n 33) 39; Michael Kagan, 'Is There Really a Protection Gap? UNRWA's Role vis-á-vis Palestinian Refugees' (2009) 28 Refugee Survey Quarterly 511, 526; Akram, 'UNRWA and Forced Migration' (n 20) 233; Ogg, 'New Directions in Article 1D Jurisprudence' (n 19) 360; Kate Ogg, 'International Solidarity and Palestinian Refugees: Lessons for the Future Directions of Refugee Law' [2020] Human Rights Review.

[106] Maja Zarkovic 'Palestinian Refugees and the (Mis-)Interpretation of Article 1D of the 1951 Refugee Convention' (2017) City Research Online https://openaccess.city.ac.uk/id/eprint/24197/ accessed 7 July 2021.

[107] Grahl-Madsen, *The Status of Refugees in International Law* (n 41) 263; Takkenberg, *The Status of Palestinian Refugees* (n 28) 93.

[108] UNGA Conference of Plenipotentiaries on the Status of Refugees and Stateless Persons, 'Summary Record of the Nineteenth Meeting' (n 25).

the Refugee Convention automatically became applicable to those refugees.[109] This interpretation is further supported by scholars,[110] the UNHCR,[111] domestic jurisprudence,[112] and by the CJEU.[113]

This interpretation puts weight behind the argument that Article 1D cannot possibly apply to IDPs. Article 1D is clearly designed to provide a separate regime under international law for whomever falls within its scope of application. In the case of Palestinian refugees, there are numerous reasons, as outlined above in section 6.3, why the international community decided to provide a separate regime for them. IDPs are different from Palestinian refugees in the sense that the international community has traditionally been reluctant to create a special international regime for their protection. Owing predominantly to sovereignty concerns, the IDP issue has been left to the protection of national governments, which may, but by no means necessarily will, be the very entity that has caused a particular group of IDPs to flee in the first place.[114] In fact, the latest efforts of the international community to protect migrants—the Global Compacts on Refugees and for Safe, Orderly, and Regular Migration—have been criticised for 'virtually' ignoring IDPs.[115] To suggest that IDPs, in a general sense, fall within the scope of Article 1D of the Refugee Convention would give those persons a range of rights far beyond that which was envisaged by the drafters of the Refugee Convention, or indeed what is intended nowadays by the international community.

In addition, the fact that refugee status is conferred automatically on those falling within the scope of Article 1D when protection or assistance has ceased

[109] UNGA Conference of Plenipotentiaries on the Status of Refugees and Stateless Persons, 'Summary Record of the Twenty-ninth Meeting' (n 30) statements of Mr Mostafa Bey (Egypt) and Mr Al Pachachi (Iraq). See also Albanese and Takkenberg, *Palestinian Refugees in International Law* (n 19) 122.

[110] Akram, 'Closing Protection Gaps' (n 41) 335; Perin, 'European and International Law and Palestinian Refugees' (n 97) 94; Hathaway and Foster, *The Law of Refugee Status* (n 2) 518.

[111] UNHCR, 'Guidelines on International Protection No. 13' (n 43) [3].

[112] *El-Ali v Secretary of State* (n 53); *Daraz v Secretary of State for the Home Department* [2002] EWCA Civ 1103 [49].

[113] *Abed El Karem El Kott and Others* (n 70) [81].

[114] Bríd Ní Ghráinne, *Internally Displaced Persons* (Max Planck Encyclopedia of Public International Law 2015).

[115] UNHCR, 'The Global Compact on Refugees' (New York 2018) available at: <https://www.unhcr.org/en-ie/the-global-compact-on-refugees.html> accessed 28 July 2020; IOM, 'The Global Compact for Safe, Orderly, and Regular Migration' (2018) available at: <https://www.iom.int/global-compact-migration> accessed 8 April 2021; Elizabeth E Ferris and Susan F Martin, 'The Global Compacts on Refugees and for Safe, Orderly and Regular Migration: Introduction to the Special Issue' (2019) 57(6) International Migration 5. See also Thomas Alexander Aleinikoff, 'The Unfinished Work of the Global Compact on Refugees' (2018) 30(4) International Journal of Refugee Law 611; Alfredo dos Santos Soares, 'The (Un)Protection of Internally Displaced Persons under the Global Compact on Refugees' in Christopher Lazarski, Jesús García Cívico, and Alexander Sungurov (eds), *Current Issues on Human Rights* (Dykinson 2020) 289; Ben Hudson and Bríd Ní Ghráinne, 'Enhancing State-to-State Dialogue on Internal Displacement: Current Global Fora and Future Prospects?' (2020) 39 Refugee Survey Quarterly 425.

is a reflection of the fact that Palestinian refugees were regarded as a group as falling within the refugee definition. As outlined in chapter 2, IDPs, as a group, do not have many of the necessary criteria for qualification as a refugee, including: (i) IDPs, generally speaking, have not crossed an international frontier; and, (ii) IDPs need not necessarily have fled their place of origin owing to fear of persecution based on race, religion, nationality, membership of a particular social group, or political opinion. In addition, the *travaux préparatoires* of the Refugee Convention make it clear that the drafters were not concerned with protecting people within their countries of origin.[116] The Refugee Convention was clearly intended to apply to a narrow category of individuals, and thus Article 1D cannot be interpreted in a broader sense to apply to those who could receive protection as IDPs within their countries of origin from agencies other than the UNHCR.

6.5.4 Concluding Thoughts: The Meaning of the Second Sentence of Article 1D

Although section 6.4 found that a purely textual reading of the first sentence of Article 1D could lead to the conclusion that it applies to IDPs who are receiving protection from organs or agencies of the UN other than the UNHCR, the second sentence of Article 1D clearly rules out the Article's application as a whole to IDPs at a general level. This is primarily because Article 1D's applicability only arises at the same time as the question of refugee status arises, and logically, an IDP cannot be termed as such once outside their country of nationality and eligible to be considered as a refugee.

6.6 Conclusion

Article 1D is one of the most vaguely drafted provisions of the Refugee Convention, and this chapter has explored the issue of whether it could be applied to IDPs who receive protection from organs or agencies other than the UNHCR and go on to cross a border and claim asylum. Article 1D is applicable to persons who were and/or are now receiving protection or assistance

[116] The *travaux préparatoires* indicate that a proposal to include IDPs in the refugee definition was rejected on the basis that the delegates viewed the existence of sufficient national protection as inconsistent with the concept of a refugee. See Hathaway and Foster, *The Law of Refugee Status* (n 2) 29–31; *SZATV v Minister for Immigration and Citizenship* [2007] HCA 40 [49] (Australia).

from organs or agencies (and their successor bodies) of the UN other than the UNHCR that were in existence at the time the Refugee Convention was signed. This interpretation leaves open the possibility that Article 1D applies in a broader IDP protection context.

Nonetheless, the historic context of the Refugee Convention indicates strongly that the only group of persons to which Article 1D was directed was Palestinian refugees receiving protection or assistance from UNRWA. The drafting history of Article 1D therefore rules out its broader application in IDP protection activities. The *Bolbol* decision establishing that it is necessary to have actually availed oneself of UNRWA protection for Article 1D to apply, although helpful in explaining the meaning of Article 1D, does not impact significantly on the question dealt with by this chapter. If Article 1D applies only to those receiving protection from UNRWA, it cannot apply in a broader IDP protection context and the technicalities of its application are therefore irrelevant for our purposes. Moreover, the confirmation in *El Kott* that the cessation of protection leads to automatic qualification as a refugee further supports the argument that Article 1D cannot apply in a broader IDP protection context. This is because IDPs have not been given legal status and have not been singled out in international law terms as deserving a special legal regime. This can be contrasted to refugees generally, and Palestinian refugees specifically, the latter of which were presumed to qualify as a group as refugees.

Notwithstanding the interpretation put forward by this chapter, there has been a fear voiced by the UNHCR that a textual interpretation of Article 1D could trigger the application in the context of IDP protection by agencies other than the UNHCR.[117] In addition, there is some jurisprudence in England and Wales that has left open the possibility of such an interpretation.[118] However, this chapter has argued that such an interpretation would be incorrect because the issue of Article 1D's applicability only arises at the same time as the question of refugee status, and logically, an IDP cannot be termed as such once outside their country of nationality and eligible to be considered as a refugee. For those who become internally displaced outside of their country of nationality, it is possible that Article 1D could be applied. If the persons in question are Palestinian refugees receiving protection from UNRWA, such an interpretation is in line with the object and purpose of Article 1D. To interpret Article 1D in this sense as applying to all IDPs receiving protection or assistance from

[117] UNHCR Policy Development and Evaluation Service and Division of Operational Services, 'Response to Situations of Internal Displacement' (n 3); Feller, 'UNHCR's Role in IDP Protection' (n 3).

[118] *Fadil Dyli v Secretary of State* (n 5). See also the arguments raised by Max Gabriel Cherem, 'Inclusion in Exclusion' (2021) (on file with author).

agencies other than the UNRWA would be setting aside entirely the relevance of the drafting history of Article 1D and, as argued by this chapter, it would be contrary to the obligation to interpret a treaty in good faith in line with its object and purpose.

It is therefore safe to say that on the basis of the rules of treaty interpretation, and on the basis of the practical scope of Article 1D, the cluster approach to IDP protection will not, or at least should not, allow states to apply Article 1D except in the context of UNRWA's assistance to Palestinian refugees. Where an asylum-seeker could access protection in their country of nationality from a UN agency other than the UNHCR, the appropriate approach in such circumstances is to assess refugee status by reference to the availability of 'protection of that country' as per Article 1A of the Refugee Convention.[119] Article 1D would not be applicable in such circumstances.

[119] Hathaway and Foster, *The Law of Refugee Status* (n 2) 522.

7
Conclusion

IDPs and refugees are similar in many ways. As noted in chapter 2, their movement is involuntary and/or coerced and often both categories of persons may have fled their places of habitual residence for similar reasons. Many IDPs become refugees, and many refugees become IDPs. Both IDPs and refugees often experience violence, trauma, are isolated from their families back home, and may live for years or even decades in protracted displacement. IDPs and refugees can live in a variety of settings, but most of them live in urban areas in the Global South. IDPs and refugees often face the same practical problems such as lack of documentation (which may be necessary to enjoy certain rights or access services), adequate shelter, food, water, sanitation, healthcare, and access to justice and/or financial resources. Being an IDP or refugee also compounds existing vulnerabilities, such as for people with disabilities, elderly people, and children, and displacement exacerbates vulnerability to exploitation and gender-based violence.

At the same time, there are significant differences between IDPs and refugees. The most fundamental distinction is that the refugee has crossed an international frontier while the IDP remains within their country of origin. Moreover, the global refugee population is only roughly half that of IDPs, yet the legal and institutional IDP protection framework is significantly underdeveloped when compared to that of refugees. Refugees have a legal status, are protected by the 1951 Refugee Convention, and have a specific organization dedicated to their protection—the UN High Commissioner for Refugees. IDPs, on the other hand, have no global (as opposed to regional) treaty and they have no international organization specifically focused on their protection.

This aim of this book was to explore in detail the relationship between the protection of IDPs and international refugee law. Specifically, it aimed to examine to what extent the development of IDP protection undermines or complements international refugee law. Four key challenges in the relationship between these two frameworks were identified.

The first challenge identified was the overshadowing of the issue of IDP protection by that of refugee protection. As the *travaux préparatoires* of the

Internally Displaced Persons and International Refugee Law. Bríd Ní Ghráinne, Oxford University Press. © Ní Ghráinne 2022.
DOI: 10.1093/oso/9780198868446.003.0007

Refugee Convention illustrate, its drafters were not concerned with the provision of protection to individuals displaced within countries of origin. Refugees have crossed a border and are entitled to international protection whereas IDPs remain within their states and are primarily the responsibility of their own governments. As explained in chapter 3, the IDP issue gained significant momentum in the post-Cold War era when the recognition of refugees was no longer seen as a strategic political act, which would highlight the failure of the country of origin to protect its nationals. The 1990s and the 2000s heralded the development of legal and institutional protection of IDPs but many of these developments were part and parcel of the international community's broader agenda of limiting refugee flows. Even today, the issue of refugee protection continues to dominate the international agenda, to the detriment of IDP protection. This is exemplified by the fact that IDPs were excluded by the Global Compacts on Refugees and Migrants. Yet, the support of 57 states for the establishment of the UN Secretary-General's High-Level Panel on Internal Displacement offers some indication that momentum is slowly gathering behind IDP-specific initiatives. The Panel's final report, containing its recommendations for the UN and IDP stakeholder community, is due to be published in 2021.

A second, related key challenge in the relationship between IDPs and refugees is the development of an appropriate legal protection framework as regards the former. As chapter 3 has illustrated, IDPs benefit from protection under international human rights law, international humanitarian law, and international criminal law. However, this protection is based on their status as human beings, rather than being specific to their needs as IDPs. In recent years, soft law instruments have been concluded which are of relevance to IDPs, the most notable example being the Guiding Principles on Internal Displacement. The Guiding Principles have been referenced in various resolutions of the General Assembly and several states have adopted laws and policies that have been influenced by the Guiding Principles. In addition, IDPs in certain African states can benefit from protection under the 2006 Pact on Security, Stability and Development in the Great Lakes Region and the 2009 African Union Convention for the Protection and Assistance of Internally Displaced Persons in Africa. The conclusion of treaties specific to the needs of IDPs is a remarkable step forward, considering that at the time the Guiding Principles were drafted in the mid-1990s, the prevailing opinion was that states would be unwilling or would entirely reject committing to binding obligations vis-à-vis IDPs.

Although this shift in focus to the protection of IDPs is a welcome development, it is not without its drawbacks. As explained in chapter 3, examples such as the closing of the Turkey–Iraq border in 1991, the establishment of so-called 'safe havens' in Bosnia in 1992, 'Operation Turquoise' in Rwanda in 1994, and Turkey's 2019 establishment of a safe zone in Syria illustrate that the increased support for IDP assistance was to do in large part with a desire to curb refugee flows. Indeed, the curbing of refugee flows inevitably worsens an IDP situation, as such IDPs have no choice but to remain displaced within their states. Thus, the third challenge in the relationship between IDP protection and international refugee law is ensuring that the development of an IDP protection framework is not used as a substitute for asylum.

This challenge is more pertinent considering the practice by states of declining refugee status on the basis that an 'internal protection alternative' (IPA) is available in the country of origin. Chapter 4 examined whether and to what extent a real risk of becoming an IDP on return and/or the availability of IDP protection measures on return is relevant to the IPA inquiry in refugee status determination proceedings. It argued that the IDP label does not carry significant weight when determining whether a location qualifies as an IPA. Even though return to a situation of internal displacement might give rise to human rights violations, the fact that an individual will become an IDP on return does not rule a place out of being a valid IPA. This is the case even where that individual might have to live in an IDP camp or in a critical shelter arrangement, such as an unfinished or abandoned makeshift shelter, tent, mosque, or church, or squat in a government building. The chapter also argued that a situation of internal displacement and/or the availability of IDP protection measures are of even less relevance when assessing whether the Refugee Convention's cessation clauses are applicable. This is because the threshold of protection required for finding that refugee status has ceased is even higher than that required to determine the existence of an IPA.

The challenge of ensuring that internal protection is not seen as a substitute for asylum has an additional aspect, namely whether the UNHCR's activities on behalf of IDPs could undermine its primary mandate, which focuses on refugees. In this sense, the UNHCR could be perceived by states as an 'actor of protection' where it assists IDPs in a country of origin, and thus refugee status could be denied to persons seeking asylum abroad. In considering the refugee definition in its context, and in line with the obligation to interpret a treaty in good faith to achieve its object and purpose, chapter 5 argued that a textual interpretation of the Refugee Convention supports the contention that 'protection of that country' may in principle include contracted-out mechanisms of protection provided by international organizations such as the UNHCR which are genuinely accessible and for which the State remains fully accountable. However, the UNHCR is not capable of satisfying the high standard required to constitute 'protection of that country'. As such, the UNHCR's activities with IDPs do not—at least in a legal sense—undermine its primary mandate towards refugees.

The fourth and final challenge explored by this work is whether protection activities on behalf of IDPs from agencies other than the UNHCR could trigger the application of Article 1D of the Refugee Convention, which would render the Refugee Convention inapplicable to those persons. Chapter 6 argued that Article 1D cannot be triggered by activities of organs or agencies of the UN apart from the UNHCR in the context of the cluster approach to IDP protection. The historic context of the treaty leads to the conclusion that Article 1D is only applicable in the context of UNRWA protection or assistance to Palestinian refugees. Further, even when the historic context is disregarded, it is illogical to apply Article 1D in the context of inter-agency IDP protection activities as an IDP will not be outside his or her country of origin and thus the question of refugee status should not arise. It is therefore safe to say that the cluster approach to IDP protection will not—at least in terms of law—allow states to apply Article 1D outside of its historical context.

This book has therefore shown that IDP protection cannot—at least in legal terms—be a substitute for granting refugee status unless it constitutes effective protection from persecution and there is no danger of *refoulement*. However, some challenges remain. In particular, this book is not the final say on the relevance of internal protection in refugee status determination proceedings. The ultimate determination of whether an individual is recognized as a refugee lies with a domestic court, which may not necessarily align with the arguments presented in this book. Future case law may very well affect the conclusions of this book, especially in light of the fact that forced displacement, in terms of numbers, is rapidly growing and states regularly employ a wide array of restrictive border control measures to limit those who can reach their territories to claim asylum. Contemporary challenges such as the rise of populism and the Covid-19 pandemic have made states even more hostile to refugees. As mentioned in chapter 5, there is domestic jurisprudence to the effect that protection from international organizations can preclude the granting of refugee status and thus there remains the possibility that this (highly questionable) line of jurisprudence will be followed in future.

In addition, states are increasingly invoking the IPA concept in refugee status determination proceedings and the IPA may even become a mandatory part of refugee status determinations in the EU as part of the legislation proposed by the 2020 Pact on Asylum and Migration.[1] Moving forward, the arguments presented in this book will be of valuable assistance to those who wish to contest the invocation of IDP protection measures as an alternative to asylum, such as refugee advocates, NGOs, and the UNHCR. In addition, the much-anticipated recommendations of the High-Level Panel, if implemented, may introduce changes to the current IDP legal and institutional framework, which may in turn impact the relationship between the IDP framework and international refugee law.

This book has also provoked some questions which are outside of the work's scope but are nonetheless pertinent topics for future research. Such questions include whether the right to freedom of movement under international law entails that internal displacement is a human rights violation, the compatibility of the creation of safe zones with international refugee law, when IDP status begins and ends, the bindingness (or not) of the Guiding Principles on Internal Displacement, and the issue of a new global treaty and/or specific international organization for IDP protection. Moreover, this work is primarily of a legal nature and did not discuss in detail the logistics and empirical implications involved in the relationship between the protection of IDPs and international refugee law. Such research would make an extremely important contribution to knowledge and would be significantly complementary to the legal analysis in this work.

We are now witnessing the highest displacement figures on record—numbering 55 million at the end of 2020—and these figures are predicted to rise.[2] The relationship between IDP protection and refugee law is therefore more important than ever. This book has provided the first in-depth analysis of the IDP–refugee relationship but, at the same time, it has only scratched the surface of this research field. It is hoped that this book has laid the foundation for further debate on this topic, and that the relationship between IDP and refugee protection will be the subject of many more scholarly studies in future.

[1] European Union, 'Factsheet: New Pact on Asylum and Migration' (2020) available at www.ec.europa.eu accessed 14 July 2021.

[2] Internal Displacement Monitoring Centre, *Global Report on Internal Displacement 2021* (2021).

Bibliography

Books

Abebe A, *The Emerging Law of Forced Displacement in Africa: Development and Implementation of the Kampala Convention on Internally Displaced Persons* (Routledge 2017)

Adeola R, *The Internally Displaced Person in International Law* (Edward Elgar Publishing 2020)

Adeola R, *Development-Induced Displacement and Human Rights in Africa: The Kampala Convention* (Routledge Contemporary Africa 2021)

Albanese FP and Takkenberg L, *Palestinian Refugees in International Law* (2nd edn, OUP 2020)

Battjes H, *European Asylum Law and International Law* (Martinus Nijhoff 2006)

Boyle AE and Chinkin CM, *The Making of International Law* (OUP 2007)

Bradley M, *Protecting Civilians in War: The ICRC, UNHCR, and Their Limitations in Internal Armed Conflicts* (OUP 2016)

Bradley M, *The International Organization for Migration: Challenges, Commitments, Complexities* (Routledge 2020)

Burson B and Cantor DJ, *Human Rights and the Refugee Definition* (Brill 2016)

Cantor DJ, *Returns of Internally Displaced Persons During Armed Conflict: International Law and its Application of Colombia* (Brill 2018)

Chesterman S, *Just War or Just Peace?* (OUP 2009)

Costello C, *The Human Rights of Migrants and Refugees in European Law* (OUP 2015)

Costello C, Foster M, and McAdam J (eds), *The Oxford Handbook of International Refugee Law* (OUP 2021)

Crawford JR, *The Creation of States in International Law* (OUP 2007)

Davies SE, *Legitimising Rejection: International Refugee Law in Southeast Asia* (Martinus Nijhoff 2008)

Dörr O and Schmalenbach K, *Vienna Convention on the Law of Treaties: A Commentary* (Springer 2012)

Gardiner RK, *Treaty Interpretation* (OUP 2008)

Goodwin-Gill GS and McAdam J, *The Refugee in International Law* (3rd edn, OUP 2011)

Grahl-Madsen A, *The Status of Refugees in International Law* (AW Sijthoff 1966)

Haddad E, *The Refugee in International Society: Between Sovereigns* (CUP 2008)

Hailbronner K, *EU Immigration and Asylum Law: Commentary on EU Regulations and Directives* (Beck, Hart, Nomos 2010)

Hailbronner K and Thym D (eds), *EU Immigration and Asylum Law* (Hart 2016)

Hathaway JC, *The Law of Refugee Status* (Butterworths 1991)

Hathaway JC (ed), *Human Rights and Refugee Law*, vols I and II (Edward Elgar 2015)

Hathaway JC and Foster M, *The Law of Refugee Status* (2nd edn, CUP 2014)

Henderson C, *The Use of Force in International Law* (CUP 2018)

Hyndman J, *Managing Displacement: Refugees and the Politics of Humanitarianism* (University of Minnesota Press 2000)
Ineli-Cigur M, *Temporary Protection in Law and Practice* (Brill 2017)
Koh HH, *The Trump Administration and International Law* (OUP 2018)
Lehmann J, 'Protection' in *European Union Asylum Law* (Brill 2020)
Maru MT, *The Kampala Convention and its Contribution to International Law: Legal Analyses and Interpretations of the African Union Convention for the Protection and Assistance of Internally Displaced Persons* (Eleven International Publishing 2014)
McAdam J, *Complementary Protection in International Refugee Law* (OUP 2007)
McQueen C, *Humanitarian Intervention and Safety Zones* (Palgrave 2005)
Meron T, *Human Rights in Internal Strife: Their International Protection* (Grotius Publications 1987)
Moraru M, Cornelisse G, and De Bruycker P (eds), *Law and Judicial Dialogue on the Return of Irregular Migrants from the European Union* (Hart 2020)
Morel M, *The Right not to be Displaced in International Law* (Intersentia 2014)
Moreno-Lax V, *Accessing Asylum in Europe* (OUP 2017)
Nykänen E, *Fragmented State Power and Forced Migration: A Study on Non-State Actors in Refugee Law* (Martinus Nijhoff Publishers 2012)
Orchard P, *Protecting the Internally Displaced, Rhetoric and Reality* (Routledge 2019)
O'Sullivan M, *Refugee Law and Durability of Protection: Temporary Residence and Cessation of Status* (Routledge 2019)
Peers S, *EU Immigration and Asylum Law, Text and Commentary* (2nd edn, Martinus Nijhoff 2012)
Phuong C, *The International Protection of Internally Displaced Persons* (CUP 2004)
Pobjoy JM, The Child in International Refugee Law (Cambridge University Press 2017)
Roberts A, *Is International Law International?* (OUP 2017)
Roland Portmann, *Legal Personality in International Law* (CUP 2010)
Satiroglu I and Choi N (eds), *Development-Induced Displacement and Resettlement: New Perspectives on Persisting Problems* (Routledge 2015)
Schultz J, *The Internal Protection Alternative in Refugee Law* (Brill Nijhoff 2018)
Sharpe M, *The Regional Law of Refugee Protection in Africa* (OUP 2018)
Shelton D (ed), *The Oxford Handbook of International Human Rights Law* (OUP 2013)
Smith RKM, *International Human Rights Law* (9th edn, OUP 2020)
Takkenberg L, *The Status of Palestinian Refugees in International Law* (Clarendon 1998)
Tamanaha B, *A General Jurisprudence of Law and Society* (OUP 2001)
TMC Asser Instituut, *Yearbook of International Humanitarian Law* (TMC Asser Press 1998)
Twining W, *General Jurisprudence: Understanding Law from a Global Perspective* (CUP 2009)
Villiger ME, *Commentary on the 1969 Vienna Convention on the Law of Treaties* (Martinus Nijhoff 2009)
Wheeler NJ, *Saving Strangers: Humanitarian Intervention in International Society* (OUP 2000)
Yamashita H, *Humanitarian Spaces and International Politics: The Creation of Safe Areas* (Ashgate 2004)
Ziegler R, *Voting Rights of Refugees* (CUP 2017)
Zimmermann A, *The 1951 Convention Relating to the Status of Refugees and its 1967 Protocol: A Commentary* (OUP 2010)

Sections of Books

Akram S, 'UNRWA and Forced Migration' in Fiddian-Qasmiyeh E and others (eds), *The Oxford Handbook of Refugee and Forced Migration Studies* (OUP 2014)

Anastasiou T, 'Public International Law's Applicability to Migration as Adaptation: Fit for Purpose?' in Behrman S and Kent A (eds), *Climate Refugees: Beyond the Legal Impasse?* (Routledge Taylor and Francis 2018)

Bradley M, 'UNHCR and Accountablity of IDP Protection in Colombia' in Sandvik KB and Jacobsen KL (eds), *UNHCR and the Struggle for Accountability: Technology, Law, and Results-Based Management* (Routledge 2016)

Cantor DJ, 'Gang Violence as a Cause of Forced Migration in the Northern Triangle of Central America' in Cantor DJ and Rodríguez Serna N (eds), *The New Refugees: Crime and Forced Displacement in Latin America* (University of London, 2016)

Chimni BS, 'Incarceration of Victims: Deconstruction Safety Zones' in Al-Nauimi N and Meese R, *International Legal Issues Arising under the United Nations Decade of International Law: Proceedings of the Qatar International Law Conference '94* (Martinus Nijhoff 1995)

Cole G, 'The End of Refugee Status: Cessation and Durable Solutions' in Costello C, Foster M, and McAdam J (eds), *The Oxford Handbook of International Refugee Law* (OUP 2021)

Corten O, 'Human Rights and Collective Security: Is There an Emerging Right of Humanitarian Intervention?' in Alston P and Macdonald E (eds), *Human Rights, Intervention and the Use of Force* (OUP 2008)

Dos Santos Soares A, 'The (Un)Protection of Internally Displaced Persons under the Global Compact on Refugees' in Lazarski C, García Cívico J, and Sungurov A (eds), *Current Issues on Human Rights* (Dykinson 2020)

Fisher D, 'Epilogue: International Law on the Internally Displaced Persons' in Banerjee P and others (eds), *Internal Displacement in South Asia: The Relevance of the UN's Guiding Principles* (SAGE 2005)

Fitzpatrick J, 'Human Rights and Forced Displacement: Converging Standards' in Bayefsky AF and Fitzpatrick J (eds), *Human Rights and Forced Displacement* (Martinus Nijhoff 2000)

Foster M, 'Economic Migrant or Person in Need of Protection? Socio-Economic Rights and Persecution in International Refugee Law' in Burson B and Cantor DJ (eds), *Human Rights and the Refugee Definition* (Brill Nijhoff 2016)

Franco L, 'An Examination of Safety Zones for Internally Displaced Persons as a Contribution toward Prevention and Solution of Refugee Problems' in Al-Nauimi N and Meese R, *International Legal Issues Arising under the United Nations Decade of International Law: Proceedings of the Qatar International Law Conference '94* (Martinus Nijhoff 1995)

Frelick B, 'Preventing Refugee Flows: Protection or Peril' in *World Refugee Survey 1993* (US Committee for Refugees 1993)

Garlick M, 'UNHCR and the Implementation of Council Directive 2004/83/EC on Minimum Standards for the Qualification and Status of Third Country Nationals or Stateless Persons as Refugees or as Persons who Otherwise Need International Protection and the Content of the Protection Granted (The EC 'Qualification Directive')' in Zwaan K (ed), *The Qualification Directive: Central Themes, Problem Issues, and Implementation in Selected Member States* (Wolf Legal Publishers 2007)

Giuffré M, 'Access to Asylum at Sea? Non-refoulement and a Comprehensive Approach to Extraterritorial Human Rights Obligations' in Moreno-Lax V and Papastavridis E (eds), *'Boat Refugees' and Migrants at Sea: A Comprehensive Approach* (Brill 2016)

Goodwin-Gill GS, 'State Responsibility and the "Good Faith" Obligation in International Law' in Fitzmaurice M and Sarooshi D (eds), *Issues of State Responsibility before International Judicial Institutions* (Hart 2004)

Greenwood C, 'The Law of War (International Humanitarian Law)' in Evans MD (ed), *International Law* (2nd edn, OUP 2006)

Hailbronner K and Alt S, 'Council Directive of 29 April 2004 on Minimum Standards for the Qualification and Status of Third Country Nationals or Stateless Persons as Refugees or as Persons who Otherwise Need International Protection and the Content of the Protection Granted. Arts 1-10' in Hailbronner K and Thym D (eds), *EU Immigration and Asylum Law: Commentary on EU Regulations and Directives* (Hart 2010)

Hathaway J and Foster M, 'Internal Protection/Relocation/Flight Alternative as an Aspect of Refugee Status Determination' in Feller E and others (eds), *Refugee Protection in International Law: UNHCR's Global Consultations on International Protection* (CUP 2003)

Khan T, 'Sexual Orientation and Refugee Law: How Do Legal Sanctions Criminalizing Homosexuality Engage the Definition of Persecution?' in Juss SS (ed), *Research Handbook on International Refugee Law* (Edward Elgar 2019)

Kirk LJ, 'Island Nation: The Impact of International Human Rights Law on Australian Refugee Law' in Burson B and Cantor DJ (eds), *Human Rights and the Refugee Definition* (Brill Nijhoff 2016)

Kneebone S, 'Moving Beyond the State: Refugees, Accountability and Protection' in Kneebone S (ed), *The Refugees Convention 50 Years on: Globalisation and International Law* (Ashgate 2003)

Koskenniemi M, 'What is International Law For?' in Evans M (ed), *International Law* (OUP 2014)

Long K, 'Rethinking "Durable Solutions"' in Fiddian-Qasmiyeh E and others (eds), *The Oxford Handbook of Refugee and Forced Migration Studies* (OUP 2014)

Mooney M, 'In-Country Protection: Out of Bounds for UNHCR?' in Nicholson F and Twomey PM (eds), *Refugee Rights and Realities: Evolving International Concepts and Regimes* (CUP 1999) 200–19.

Ní Ghráinne B, 'Internally Displaced Persons in International Refugee Law' in Juss SS (ed), *Research Handbook on International Refugee Law* (Elgar 2019)

Ní Ghráinne B, 'Internal Protection Alternative' in Costello C, Foster M, and McAdam J (eds), *Oxford Handbook on International Refugee Law* (OUP 2021)

Ní Ghráinne B and Hudson B, 'The International Organization for Migration's Engagement with the Guiding Principles on Internal Displacement' in Costello C, Bradley M, and Sherwood A (eds), *IOM Unbound? Obligations and Accountability of the International Organization for Migration in an Era of Expansion* (CUP forthcoming 2022)

Nolte G, 'Report 3: Subsequent Agreements and Subsequent Practice of States Outside of Judicial or Quasi-Judicial Proceedings—Third Report for the ILC Study Group on Treaties over Time' in Nolte G (ed), *Treaties and Subsequent Practice* (OUP 2013)

Ogg K, 'New Directions in Article 1D Jurisprudence' in Juss SS (ed), *Research Handbook on International Refugee Law* (Elgar 2019)

O'Sullivan M, 'Territorial Protection: Cessation of Refugee Status and Internal Flight Alternative Compared' in Juss SS (ed), *The Ashgate Research Companion to Migration Law, Theory, and Policy* (Routledge 2013)

Qafisheh M and Azarov V, 'Article 1D 1951 Convention' in Zimmerman A (ed), *The 1951 Convention Relating to the Status of Refugees and its 1967 Protocol: A Commentary* (OUP 2011)

Roberts A, 'Legality v Legitimacy: Can uses of force be illegal but justified'? in Alston P and Macdonald E (eds), *Human Rights, Intervention and the Use of Force* (OUP 2008)

Rodley N, 'Humanitarian Intervention' in Weller M (ed), *The Oxford Handbook of the Use of Force in International Law* (OUP 2015)

Sandoz Y, 'Safety Zones for Internally Displaced Persons,' in Al-Nauimi N and Meese R (eds), *International Legal Issues Arising under the United Nations Decade of International Law: Proceedings of the Qatar International Law Conference '94* (Martinus Nijhoff 1995)

Scheinin M, Forced Displacement and the Covenant on Civil and Political Rights in Bayefsky A and Fitzpatrick J (eds), *Human Rights and Forced Displacement* (Brill 2001)

Schuppert GF, 'The Changing Role of the State Reflected in the Growing Importance of Non-State Actors' in Schuppert GF (ed), *Global Governance and the Role of Non-State Actors* (Nomos 2006)

Talmon S, 'The Duty Not to "Recognise as Lawful" a Situation Created by the Illegal Use of Force or Other Serious Breaches of a Jus Cogens Obligation: An Obligation without Real Substance?' in Tomuschat C and Thouvenin J (eds), *The Fundamental Rules of the International Order: Jus Cogens and Obligations Erga Omnes* (Brill-Nijhoff 2005)

Turk V, 'Non-State Actors of Persecution' in Chetail V and others (eds), *Switzerland and the International Protection of Refugees: A Colloquium of the Graduate Institute of International Studies, Geneva, in collaboration with the Office of the United Nations High Commissioner for Refugees = La Suisse et la Protection Internationale des Réfugiés: Colloque de l'Institut Universitaire de Hautes Études Internationales, Géneve, en Collaboration avec le Haut Commissariat des Nations Unies pour les Réfugiés* (Kluwer Law International 2002)

Journal Articles

Adeola R, 'The Kampala Convention and the Right not to be Arbitrarily Displaced' (2018) 59 Forced Migration Review 15

Adeola R, 'The Impact of the African Union Convention on the Protection and Assistance of Internally Displaced Persons in Africa' (2019) 19 African Human Rights Law Journal 591

Adeola R, 'Xenophobia and Internal Displacement in Africa: Defining Protection and Assistance through the Kampala Convention' (2020) 27 South African Journal of International Affairs 49

Adeola R and Viljoen F, 'The Right Not to Be Arbitrarily Displaced in Africa' (2017) 25 African Journal of International and Comparative Law 459

Adeola R and Viljoen F, 'Climate Change, Development Projects and Internal Displacement In Africa' (2018) 62(3) Journal of African Law 335

Akesson B, Basso AR, and Denov M, 'The Right to Home: Domicide as a Violation of Child and Family Rights in the Context of Political Violence' (2016) 30 Children and Society 369

Akram S, 'Palestinian Refugees and their Legal Status: Rights, Politics, and Implications for a Just Solution' (2002) 31(3) Journal of Palestine Studies 36

Aleinikoff TA, 'The Unfinished Work of the Global Compact on Refugees' (2018) 30(4) International Journal of Refugee Law 611

Al-Mahaidi A, 'Financing Opportunities for Durable Solutions to Internal Displacement: Building on Current Thinking and Practice' (2020) 39(4) Refugee Survey Quarterly 481

Anderson A and others, 'Imminence in Refugee and Human Rights Law: A Misplaced Notion for International Protection' (2019) 68 International and Comparative Law Quarterly 111

Arulanatham AT, 'Restructured Safe Havens: A Proposal for Reform of the Refugee Protection System' (2000) 22(1) Human Rights Quarterly 1

Asplet M and Bradley M, 'Introductory Note to the African Union Convention for the Protection of Internally Displaced Persons in Africa "Kampala Convention"' (2013) 52 International Legal Materials 397

Barutciski M, 'The Reinforcement of Non-Admission Policies and the Subversion of UNHCR: Displacement and Internal Assistance in Bosnia-Herzegovina (1992–94)' (1996) 8 International Journal of Refugee Law 49

Barutciski M, 'Tensions Between the Refugee Concept and the IDP Debate' (1998) 4(3) Forced Migration Review 11

Bednar NR and Penland M, 'Asylum's Interpretative Impasse: Interpreting Persecution and Particular Social Group Using International Human Rights Law' (2017) 26 Minnesota Journal of International Law 145

Bennett J, 'Forced Migration within National Borders: The IDP Agenda' (1998) 1 Forced Migration Review 4

Beyani C, 'The Elaboration of a Legal Framework for the Protection of Internally Displaced Persons in Africa' (2006) 50(2) Journal of African Law 187

Beyani C, 'Recent Developments in the African Human Rights System 2004-2004' (2007) 7(3) Human Rights Review 582

Boed R, 'The State of the Right of Asylum in International Law' (1994) 5 Duke Journal of Comparative & International Law 1

Boom CD, 'Beyond Persecution: A Moral Defence of Expanding Refugee Status' (2018) 30 International Journal of Refugee Law 512

Bradley M, 'Unintended Consequences of Adjacency Claims: The Function and Dysfunction of Analogies between Refugee Protection and IDP Protection in the Work of UNHCR' (2019) 25(4) Global Governance 620

Buck KG, 'Displacement and Dispossession: Redefining Forced Displacement and Identifying When Forced Displacement Becomes Pillage under International Humanitarian Law' (2017) 2 Journal of International Humanitarian Action 5

Cantor DJ, 'As Deadly as Armed Conflict? Gang Violence and Forced Displacement in the Northern Triangle of Central America' (2016) 23(34) Agenda Internacional 77

Cantor DJ, 'The IDP in International Law? Developments, Debates, Prospects' (2018) 30 International Journal of Refugee Law 191

Cantor DJ and Apollo JO, 'Internal Displacement, Internal Migration, and Refugee Flows: Connecting the Dots' (2021) 39(4) Refugee Survey Quarterly 647

Cardona-Fox G, 'The Politics of IDP Data' (2020) 39(4) Refugee Survey Quarterly 620

Cardwell PJ, 'Determining Refugee Status Under Directive 2004/83: Comment on Bolbol (C-31/09)' (2011) 36(1) European Law Review 135

Caterina M and Rodríguez AL, 'The Question of Data in Internal Displacement Law- and Policy-Making' (2021) 39(4) Refugee Survey Quarterly 634

Charney JI, 'Anticipatory Humanitarian Intervention in Kosovo' (1999) 93 American Journal of International Law 837

Clarance WD, 'Open Relief Centres: A Pragmatic Approach to Emergency Relief and Monitoring during Conflict in a Country of Origin' (1991) 3 International Journal of Refugee Law 320

Cohen R, 'The Guiding Principles on Internal Displacement: An Innovation in International Standard Setting' (2010) 10 Global Governance: A Review of Multilateralism and International Organizations 459

Coleman N, 'Non-Refoulement Revised Renewed Review of the Status of the Principle of Non-Refoulement as Customary International Law' (2003) 5(1) European Journal of Migration and Law 23

Davies A and Jenner A, 'A Tale of Two Cities—IDPs Plan for their Durable Solutions in Darfur' (2020) 39(4) Refugee Survey Quarterly 507

Dieng A, 'Protecting Internally Displaced Persons: The Value of the Kampala Convention as a Regional Example' (2017) 99 International Review of the Red Cross 263

dos Santos Soares A, 'Protecting Environmentally Displaced Persons under the Kampala Convention: A Brief Assessment' (2018) 9(1) Revista Catalana de Dret Ambiental 1

Drywood E, 'Who's In and Who's Out? The Court's Emerging Case Law on the Definition of a Refugee' (2014) 51 Common Market Law Review 1903

Eaton J, 'The Internal Protection Alternative Under European Union Law: Examining the Recast Qualification Directive' (2012) 24 International Journal of Refugee Law 765

Edwards A, 'Human Rights, Refugees and the Right "To Enjoy" Asylum' (2005) 17 International Journal of Refugee Law 293

Errera R, 'Cessation and Assessment of New Circumstances: A Comment on *Abdulla,* CJEU, 2 March 2010' (2011) 23(3) International Journal of Refugee Law 521

Feller E, 'International Refugee Protection 50 Years On: The Protection Challenges of the Past, Present and Future' (2001) 83 International Review of the Red Cross 581

Feller E, 'UNHCR's Role in IDP Protection: Opportunities and Challenges' [2006] Forced Migration Review 11

Ferris E, 'Internal Displacement and the Right to Seek Asylum' (2008) 27 Refugee Survey Quarterly 76

Ferris E and Martin SF, 'The Global Compacts on Refugees and for Safe, Orderly and Regular Migration: Introduction to the Special Issue' (2019) 57(6) International Migration 5

Fitzpatrick J, 'The End of Protection: Legal Standards for Cessation of Refugee Status and Withdrawal of Temporary Protection' (1998–1999) 13 Georgetown Immigration Law Journal 343

Fortin A, 'The Meaning of "Protection" in the Refugee Definition' (2000) 12 International Journal of Refugee Law 548–76

Fripp E, 'International Humanitarian Law and the Interpretation of Persecution in Article 1A(2) CSR51' (2014) 26 International Journal of Refugee Law 382

Gil-Bazo M-T, 'Asylum as a General Principle of International Law' (2015) 27(1) International Journal of Refugee Law 3

Gilbert G, 'Is Europe Living up to its Obligations to Refugees?' (2005) 15 European Journal of International Law 963

Goddard B, 'UNHCR and the International Protection of Palestinian Refugees' (2010) 28 Refugee Survey Quarterly 475

Goodwin-Gill GS, 'UNHCR and Internal Displacement: Stepping into a Legal and Political Minefield' [2000] US Committee for Refugees, World Refugee Survey 26

Goodwin-Gill GS and Akram SM, 'Foreword to Amicus Brief on the Status of Palestinian Refugees Under International Refugee Law' (2000) 11 The Palestine Yearbook of International Law Online 185

Hannum H, 'The Status of the Universal Declaration of Human Rights in National and International Law' 25 Georgia Journal of International and Comparative Law 287

Hathaway JC, 'International Refugee Law: The Michigan Guidelines on the Internal Protection Alternative' (1999) 21 Michigan Journal of International Law 131
Hathaway JC, 'Forced Migration Studies: Could We Agree Just to 'Date'?' (2007) 20 Journal of Refugee Studies 349
Hathaway JC and Neve RA, 'Making International Refugee Law Relevant Again: A Proposal for Collectivized and Solution-Oriented Protection' (1997) 10 Harvard Human Rights Journal 115
Hathaway JC and Storey H, 'What is the Meaning of State Protection in Refugee Law? A Debate' (2016) 28(3) International Journal of Refugee Law 480
Hilpold P, 'Humanitarian Intervention: Is there a Need for a Legal Reappraisal?' (2001) 12 European Journal of International Law 437
Hilpold P, The Kosovo Case and International Law: Looking for Applicable Theories' (2009) 8(1) Chinese Journal of International Law 47
Holmes J, 'Ten Years of the Guiding Principles' [2008] Forced Migration Review 3
Hudson B and Ní Ghráinne B, 'Enhancing State-to-State Dialogue on Internal Displacement: Current Global Fora and Future Prospects?' (2020) 39(4) Refugee Survey Quarterly 425
Hyndman J, 'Preventive, Palliative, or Punitive? Safe Spaces in Bosnia-Herzegovina, Somalia, and Sri Lanka' (2003) 16 Journal of Refugee Studies 167
International Committee of the Red Cross, 'The ICRC and Internally Displaced Persons' (1995) 305 International Review of the Red Cross 182
Jakasa B and Smith J, 'Africa: From Voluntary Principles to Binding Standards' [2008] Forced Migration Review 18
Janmyr M, 'No Country of Asylum: "Legitimizing" Lebanon's Rejection of the 1951 Refugee Convention' (2017) 29(3) International Journal of Refugee Law 438
Jovanović MA, 'Responsibility to Protect and the International Rule of Law' (2015) 14 Chinese Journal of International Law 757
Kagan M, 'Is There Really a Protection Gap? UNRWA's Role vis-á-vis Palestinian Refugees' (2009) 28 Refugee Survey Quarterly 511
Kälin W, 'The Guiding Principles on Internal Displacement—Introduction' (1998) 10 International Journal of Refugee Law 557
Kälin W, 'The Role of the Guiding Principles on Internal Displacement' [2005] Forced Migration Review 8
Kälin W, 'The Future of the Guiding Principles on Internal Displacement' [2006] Forced Migration Review 5
Kälin W, 'Guiding Principles on Internal Displacement Annotations' (2008) 38 Studies in Transnational Legal Policy 69
Kälin W, 'Consolidating the Normative Framework for IDPs' (2018) 30(2) International Journal of Refugee Law 314
Kälin W, 'Non-State Agents of Persecution and the Inability of the State to Protect' (2000–2001) 15 Georgetown Immigration Law Journal 415
Kelley N, 'Internal Flight/Relocation/Protection Alternative: Is it Reasonable?' (2002) 14 International Journal of Refugee Law 4
Kritsiotis D, 'The Kosovo Crisis and NATO's Application of Armed Force against the Federal Republic of Yugoslavia' (2000) 49 International and Comparative Law Quarterly 330
Kritsiotis D, 'The Arab Spring, Massive Violations of Human Rights and the Use of Force' (2013) 5(1) Amsterdam Law Forum 80–94
Kuosmanen J, 'What's So Special About Persecution?' (2014) 17 Ethical Theory and Moral Practice 129

Landgren K, 'Safety Zones and International Protection: A Dark Grey Area' (1995) 7 International Journal of Refugee Law 436
Langenkamp D, 'The Victory of Expediency: Afghan Refugees and Pakistan in the 1990s' (2003) 27 The Fletcher Forum of World Affairs 229
Lavoyer JP, 'Refugees and IDPs: International Humanitarian Law and the Role of the ICRC' (1995) 305 International Review of the Red Cross 162
Lee L, 'Internally Displaced Persons and Refugees: Toward a Legal Synthesis?' (1996) 9 Journal of Refugee Studies 27
Long K, 'In Search of Sanctuary: Border Closures, "Safe Zones" and Refugee Protection' (2013) 26 Journal of Refugee Studies 458
Marx R, 'The Criteria of Applying the "Internal Flight Alternative" Test in National Refugee Status Determination Procedures' (2002) 14 International Journal of Refugee Law 179
Mathew P, Hathaway JC, and Foster M, 'The Role of State Protection in Refugee Analysis: Discussion Paper No.2: Advanced Refugee Law Workshop, International Association of Refugee Law Judges, Auckland, New Zealand, October 2002' (2003) 15 International Journal of Refugee Law 444
Mortenson JD, 'The *Travaux* of *Travaux:* Is the Vienna Convention Hostile to Drafting History?' (2013) 107 American Journal of International Law 780
Muggah R, 'A Tale of Two Solitudes: Comparing Conflict and Development-induced Internal Displacement and Involuntary Resettlement' (2003) 41(5) International Migration 16
Nguya G and Siddiqui N, 'Triple Nexus Implementation and Implications for Durable Solutions for Internal Displacement: On Paper and in Practice' (2020) 39(4) Refugee Survey Quarterly 466
Ní Ghráinne B, 'The Internal Protection Alternative Inquiry and Human Rights Considerations—Irrelevant or Indispensable?' (2015) 27(1) International Journal of Refugee Law 29
Ní Ghráinne B, 'UNHCR's Involvement with IDPs—"Protection of that Country" for the Purposes of Precluding Application of the Refugee Convention?' (2015) 27(1) International Journal of Refugee Law 536
Ní Ghráinne B, 'Left to Die at Sea: State Responsibility for the May 2015 Thai, Indonesian, and Malaysian Pushback Operations' (2017) 10 Irish Yearbook of International Law 109
Ní Ghráinne B, 'Safe Zones and the Internal Protection Alternative' (2020) 69(2) International and Comparative Law Quarterly 335
Ní Ghráinne B, 'Complementary Protection and Encampment' (2021) 21 Human Rights Law Review 54
Ogg K, 'Protection from "Refuge": On What Legal Grounds Will a Refugee Be Saved from Camp Life?' (2016) 28(3) International Journal of Refugee Law 384
Ogg K, 'International Solidarity and Palestinian Refugees: Lessons for the Future Directions of Refugee Law' (forthcoming) Human Rights Review
O'Meara C, 'Should International Law Recognize a Right of Humanitarian Intervention?' (2017) 66 International and Comparative Law Quarterly 441
Orchard P, 'Protection of Internally Displaced Persons: Soft Law as a Norm-Generating Mechanism' (2010) 36 Review of International Studies 281
O'Sullivan M, 'Acting the Part: Can Non-State Entities Provide Protection Under International Refugee Law?' (2012) 24 International Journal of Refugee Law 85
Pandiaraj S, 'Sovereignty as Responsibility: Reflections on the Legal Status of the Doctrine of Responsibility to Protect' (2006) 15 Chinese Journal of International Law 795
Penz P, 'Development, Displacement, and Ethics' (2002) 12 Forced Migration Review 4

Perin M, 'European and International Law and Palestinian Refugees: Bolbol, El Kott and the Application of Article 1D of the Geneva Convention' (2014) 3 UCL Journal of Law and Jurisprudence 87

Pettersson B, 'Development-induced Displacement: Internal Affair or International Human Rights Issue?' (2002) 12 Forced Migration Review 16

Peukert A and others, 'To Allow or Refuse Entry: What Does the Law Demand in the Refugee Crisis at Europe's Internal State Borders?' (2017) 18(3) German Law Journal 618

Phuong C, 'The Office of the United Nations High Commissioner for Refugees and Internally Displaced Persons' (2005) 24(3) Refugee Survey Quarterly 71

Plender R, 'The Legal Basis of International Jurisdiction to Act with Regard to the Internally Displaced' (1994) 6(3) International Journal of Refugee Law 345

Posen BR, 'Military Responses to Refugee Disasters' (1996) 21 (1) International Security 72

Reisman WM, 'Unilateral Action and the Transformations of the World Constitutive Process: The Special Problem of Humanitarian Intervention' (2000) 11(1) European Journal of International Law 3

Scott M, 'Natural Disasters, Climate Change and Non-Refoulement: What Scope for Resisting Expulsion under Articles 3 and 8 of the European Convention on Human Rights?' (2014) 26 International Journal of Refugee Law 404

Scott M, 'Finding Agency in Adversity: Applying the Refugee Convention in the Context of Disasters and Climate Change' (2016) 35(4) Refugee Survey Quarterly 26

Scott M and Salamanca A, 'A Human Rights-Based Approach to Internal Displacement in the Context of Disasters and Climate Change' (2020) 39(4) Refugee Survey Quarterly 564

Shacknove A, 'Who is a Refugee?' (1985) 95 Ethics 274

Simma B, 'NATO, the UN and the Use of Force: Legal Aspects' (1999) 10 European Journal of International Law 1

Storey H, 'The Internal Flight Alternative Test: The Jurisprudence Re-examined' (1998) 10 International Journal of Refugee Law 499

Storey H, 'EU Refugee Qualification Directive: A Brave New World?' (2008) 20 International Journal of Refugee Law 1

Storey H, 'What Constitutes Protection? Towards a Working Definition' (2014) 26 International Journal of Refugee Law 272

Storey H, 'The Meaning of "Protection" within the Refugee Definition' (2016) 35(3) Refugee Survey Quarterly 1

Tiso, 'Safe Haven Refugee Programs: A Method of Combating International Refugee Crises' (1994) 8 Georgetown Immigration Law Journal 575

Williams RC, 'Guiding Principle 29 and the Right to Restitution' [2008] Forced Migration Review 23

Zambelli P, 'Knowing Persecution When We See It: Non-State Actors and the Measure of State Protection' (2020) 32 International Journal of Refugee Law 28

Zaragoza-Cristiani J, 'Containing the Refugee Crisis: How the EU Turned the Balkans and Turkey into an EU Borderland' (2017) 52(4) Italian Journal of International Affairs 59

Working Papers

Al-Mahaidi A, Gross L, and Cantor DJ, 'Revitalising IDP Research: A "State of the Art" Review' (2018) Refugee Law Initiative, University of London https://rli.sas.ac.uk/sites/default/files/files/Revitalising%20IDP%20Research_RLI%20Review.pdf accessed 6 July 2021

Beyani B, 'A View from Inside the Kitchen of the Kampala Convention: The Modernization of the International Legal Regime for the Protection of Internally Displaced Persons' (2020) LSE Working Papers http://eprints.lse.ac.uk/103693/4/SSRN_id3736788.pdf accessed 7 July 2021

Cherem MG, 'Inclusion in Exclusion' (2021) (on file with author)

Crisp J, 'Forced Displacement in Africa: Dimensions, Difficulties and Policy Considerations' (2006) New Issues in Refugee Research http://www.unhcr.org/refworld/pdfid/4ff15cc42.pdf accessed 6 July 2021

Gilbert G and Rüsch AM, 'Creating Safe Zones and Safe Corridors in Conflict Situations: Providing Protection at Home or Preventing the Search for Asylum?' (2017) Kaldor Centre for International Refugee Law Policy Brief https://www.kaldorcentre.unsw.edu.au/sites/kaldorcentre.unsw.edu.au/files/Policy_brief_Creating_safe_zones_and_safe_corridors.pdf accessed 24 June 2021

Koh H, 'The War Powers and Humanitarian Intervention' (2016) Yale Faculty Scholarship Series https://digitalcommons.law.yale.edu/cgi/viewcontent.cgi?article=6221&context=fss_papers accessed 7 July 2021

Long K, 'No Entry! A Review of UNHCR's Response to Border Closures in Situations of Mass Refugee Influx' (2010) UNHCR Policy Development and Evaluation Service and Division of Operational Services, UN Doc PDES/2010/07 https://www.unhcr.org/research/evalreports/4c207bd59/entry-review-unhcrs-response-border-closures-situations-mass-refugee-influx.html accessed 24 June 2021

Matter V and White P, 'Consistent and Predictable Responses to IDPs: A Review of UNHCR's Decision-Making Processes' (2005) UNHCR Evaluation and Policy Analysis Unit, UN Doc EPAU/2005/2 https://www.unhcr.org/423551522.html accessed 6 July 2021

Ní Ghráinne B, 'Covid-19, Border Closures and International Law' (2020) Reflection Paper, Institute of International Relations Prague <ttps://www.dokumenty-iir.cz/Publikace/Reflections/reflection_Br%C3%ADd%20N%C3%AD_04_2020_covid-19_DEF.pdf> accessed 8 July 2021

Ní Ghráinne B, 'The Syrian Safe Zone and International Law' (2021) Policy Brief, Institute of International Relations Prague <https://www.dokumenty-iir.cz/PolicyPapers/2020/SYRIAN_SAFE_ZONE_AND_INTERNATIONAL_LAW.pdf (ed) (ed)

Reed-Hurtado M, 'The Cartagena Declaration on Refugees and the Protection of People Fleeing Armed Conflict and Other Situations of Violence in Latin America' (2013) UNHCR Legal Protection and Policy Research Series PPLA/2013/03 https://www.refworld.org/docid/51c801934.html accessed 15 July 2021

Steets J and others, 'Cluster Approach Evaluation II Synthesis Report' (2010) Global Public Policy Institute https://www.gppi.net/2010/04/01/cluster-approach-evaluation-ii-synthesis-report accessed 6 July 2021

Stoddard A and others, 'Cluster Approach Evaluation' (2007) https://www.humanitarianresponse.info/sites/www.humanitarianresponse.info/files/documents/files/Cluster%20Approach%20Evaluation%201.pdf accessed 7 July 2021

Zarkovic M, 'Palestinian Refugees and the (Mis-) Interpretation of Article 1D of the 1951 Refugee Convention' (2017) City Research Online https://openaccess.city.ac.uk/id/eprint/24197/ accessed 7 July 2021.

Encyclopedia Articles

Editors of Encyclopedia Britannica, *25th Anniversary of Operation Desert Storm* (Encyclopedia Britannica) https://www.britannica.com/story/25th-anniversary-of-operation-desert-storm

Lampe JR, *Bosnian War* (Encyclopedia Britannica) https://www.britannica.com/event/Bosnian-War

Lowe V and Tzanakopoulos A, *Humanitarian Intervention* (Max Planck Encyclopedia of Public International Law 2012)

Ní Ghráinne B, *Internally Displaced Persons* (Max Planck Encyclopedia of Public International Law 2015)

Smith J, *Srebrenica Massacre* (Encyclopedia Britannica 2014)

Winkelmann I, *Responsibility to Protect* (Max Planck Encyclopedia of Public International Law 2012)

Theses

Clary DE, 'Operation Provide Comfort: A Strategic Analysis' (Thesis, Air War College, Air University 1994)

Gayibova L, 'The Evolutive Interpretation of the Term "Protection of that Country" in Article 1(2)A of the Convention Relating to the Status of Refugees' (Thesis, University of Sheffield 2017).

Hudson B, 'Challenges in the Law of IDP Returns' (Thesis, University of Bristol 2019)

Blog Posts

Bethlehem D, 'Stepping Back a Moment—The Legal Basis in Favour of a Principle of Humanitarian Intervention' (*EJIL Talk!*, 12 September 2013) http://www.ejiltalk.org/stepping-back-a-moment-the-legal-basis-in-favour-of-a-principle-of-humanitarian-intervention/#more-9297 accessed 6 July 2021

Ferris E, 'Order from Chaos: Unpacking the Numbers on Global Refugees' (*Brookings*, 20 June 2017) <https://www.brookings.edu/blog/order-from-chaos/2017/06/20/unpacking-the-numbers-on-global-refugees/> accessed 13 July 2021

Klabbers J, 'Interpretation as the Continuation of Politics by Other Means' (*Opinio Juris*, 2 March 2009) <http://opiniojuris.org/2009/03/02/continuation/> accessed 3 June 2016

Veridrame G, 'The Law and Strategy of Humanitarian Intervention' (*EJIL Talk!*, 30 August 2013) https://www.ejiltalk.org/the-law-and-strategy-of-humanitarian-intervention/ accessed 6 July 2021

Newspaper and Magazine Articles

Abi-Habib M and ur-Rehman Z, 'Poor and Desperate, Pakistani Hindus Accept Islam to Get By' *The New York Times* (4 August 2020) <https://www.nytimes.com/2020/08/04/world/asia/pakistan-hindu-conversion.html> accessed 8 July 2021

Ackerman S and others, 'Syria Missile Strikes: US Launches First Direct Military Action against Assad' *The Guardian* (7 April 2017) https://www.theguardian.com/world/2017/apr/06/trump-syria-missiles-assad-chemical-weapons accessed 7 July 2021

Barber T, 'The Bosnia Crisis: Serbs, Croats and Muslims: Who Hates Who and Why: Tony Barber in Zagreb Traces the Ancient Roots of a Culture Clash that has Shattered what was Yugoslavia into Warring Pieces' *The Independent* (9 August 1992) https://www.independent.co.uk/news/world/the-bosnia-crisis-serbs-croats-and-muslims-who-hates-who-and-why-tony-barber-in-zagreb-traces-the-1539305.html accessed 6 July 2021.

BBC News, 'Syrians Entering Lebanon Face New Restrictions' *BBC News* (Lebanon, 5 January 2015) https://www.bbc.com/news/world-middle-east-30657003 accessed 24 June 2021

BBC News, 'Rwanda Genocide: 100 Days of Slaughter' *BBC News* (4 January 2019) https://www.bbc.com/news/world-africa-26875506 accessed 6 July 2021

BBC News, 'Syria War: Turkey Ready to Create 'Safe Zone' for Kurds—Erdogan' *BBC News* (15 January 2019) < https://www.bbc.com/news/world-middle-east-46877308> accessed 8 July 2021

BBC News, 'Denmark Asylum: Law Passed to Allow Offshore Asylum Centres' *BBC News* (3 June 2021) https://www.bbc.com/news/world-europe-57343572 accessed 5 July 2021

Bendix A, 'Safe Zones in Syria' *The Atlantic* (4 May 2017) <https://www.theatlantic.com/news/archive/2017/05/russia-iran-and-turkey-agree-on-safe-zones-in-syria/525486/> accessed 8 July 2021

Cunningham E, 'U.S., Turkey Aim to Create Buffer Zone on Syrian Border. Nobody Knows How' *The Washington Post* (13 August 2015) <https://www.washingtonpost.com/world/middle_east/us-said-it-will-create-a-safe-zone-on-syrian-border-but-nobody-knows-how/2015/08/12/4c7d0baa-37e4-11e5-ab7b-6416d97c73c2 story.html> accessed 24 June 2021

Gessen M, 'Fleeing Anti-Gay Persecution in Chechnya, Three Young Women Are Now Stuck in Place' *The New Yorker* (1 October 2018) <https://www.newyorker.com/news/our-columnists/fleeing-anti-gay-persecution-in-chechnya-three-young-women-are-now-stuck-in-place> accessed 8 July 2021

Kingsley P, 'Migrants on Hungary's Border Fence: "This Wall, We Will Not Accept It" ' *The Guardian* (22 June 2015) <https://www.theguardian.com/world/2015/jun/22/migrants-hungary-border-fence-wall-serbia> accessed 8 July 2021

McKernan B, 'Greece Extends Wall on Turkish Border as Refugee Row Deepens' *The Guardian* (20 October 2020) https://www.theguardian.com/world/2020/oct/20/greece-extends-wall-on-turkish-border-as-refugee-row-deepens accessed 24 June 2021

Ochab EU, 'The Religious War In The Central African Republic Continues' *Forbes* (9 May 2018) <https://www.forbes.com/sites/ewelinaochab/2018/05/09/the-religious-war-in-central-african-republic-continues/?sh=1280e1f73c0d> accessed 8 July 2021

Ricks TE, 'Operation Provide Comfort: A Forgotten Mission with Possible Lessons for Syria' *Foreign Policy* (6 February 2017) https://foreignpolicy.com/2017/02/06/operation-provide-comfort-a-forgotten-mission-with-possible-lessons-for-syria/ accessed 6 July 2021.

Smyth P, 'EU Endorses Attacks on Syria by US, UK and France' *Irish Times* (14 April 2018) https://www.irishtimes.com/news/world/europe/eu-endorses-attacks-on-syria-by-us-uk-and-france-1.3462219; accessed 7 July 2021

The Guardian, 'Denmark Passes Law to Relocate Asylum Seekers Outside Europe' *The Guardian* (Copenhagen, 3 June 2021) <https://www.theguardian.com/world/2021/jun/03/denmark-passes-law-to-let-it-relocate-asylum-seekers-outside-europe> accessed 8 July 2021

Thorpe N, 'Hungary Deploys Army to Push Migrants Back to Syria' *BBC News* (Hungary, 14 July 2016) https://www.bbc.com/news/world-europe-36786438 accessed 29 June 2021\
Walker S, 'No Entry: Hungary's Crackdown on Helping Refugees' *The Guardian* (4 June 2018) <https://www.theguardian.com/world/2018/jun/04/no-entry-hungarys-crackdown-on-helping-refugees> accessed 8 July 2021

Index

For the benefit of digital users, indexed terms that span two pages (e.g., 52–53) may, on occasion, appear on only one of those pages.